# Chasing the Title

# Chasing the Title

## MEMORABLE MOMENTS FROM FIFTY YEARS OF FORMULA 1

## NIGEL ROEBUCK

Foreword by Frank Williams

**Haynes Publishing**

First published in October 1999

A catalogue record for this book is
available from the British Library

ISBN 1 85960 604 0

Library of Congress catalog card no. 99-73380

Haynes North America, Inc.,
861 Lawrence Drive, Newbury Park,
California 91320, USA.

Published by Haynes Publishing, Sparkford,
Nr Yeovil, Somerset BA22 7JJ, UK.

Tel: 01963 440635 Fax: 01963 440001
Int. tel: +44 1963 440635 Fax: +44 1963 440001
E-mail: sales@haynes-manuals.co.uk
Web site: www.haynes.co.uk

*Jacket illustrations*
*Front: Ayrton Senna, with (from top left, clockwise): Michael Schumacher*
*and Mika Hakkinen, contemporary superstars; Jimmy Clark en route to*
*victory at Zandvoort in 1967; Damon Hill, 1996 World Champion; Juan*
*Manuel Fangio winning at Silverstone in 1956.*

*Back: Fangio, with (from top left, clockwise): Phil Hill, America's first*
*World Champion, in 1961; Mario Andretti, 1978 World Champion,*
*leading Ronnie Peterson; Stirling Moss's first Grand Prix victory, at*
*Aintree in 1955; James Hunt wins at Zandvoort in 1975.*

*All jacket photographs courtesy of Sutton Motorsport Images.*

Designed and typeset by G&M, Raunds, Northamptonshire
Printed and bound in Great Britain by J. H. Haynes & Co. Ltd, Sparkford

# Contents

# Foreword

*by Frank Williams*

I HAVE DIRECTLY PARTICIPATED in Formula 1 Grand Prix racing for 30 years, and in that time seen a lot of things change, many people come and go. Looking back on it all, I can review the most marvellous kaleidoscope of human activity, sporting endeavour – and the occasional piece of skullduggery.

Tragedy, in my early days, was a frequent occurrence, but since the early eighties, happily, it's been a most rare event.

During my time in the Formula 1 pit lane, I've seen endless and significant technical change, a new set of commercial rules and attitudes, and a huge growth in global exposure and support for the sport.

In any era, the dynamo for change in all human activity comes from a few outstanding people. Of all the great, great, drivers – many of whom I never met – my personal favourites were, above all, Jochen Rindt, Ayrton Senna and Stirling Moss.

However, the driver I perhaps knew best, and with whom I certainly had the closest personal relationship, was Piers Courage. We were of similar age, if from very different backgrounds, and a pair of complete nuts when it came to motor racing.

We came into Formula 1 together, with Piers driving my car, and his loss caused me, and everyone around him, enormous

7

personal pain. In the society of today, people like him are no longer to be found. His style and approach to life were truly from a different time; he was the last of that dynasty of drivers. I'm delighted that he is remembered in a chapter of this book.

At the beginning of my time in Formula 1, there was certainly much more fun at each Grand Prix than you will find today. Far more adventure, too; one of those adventures was how you drove your hire car – and where you parked it! As far as the races themselves were concerned, simply getting your car to the finish was a great challenge. Thanks to the enormous technological changes which have come about in Formula 1, far more cars finish the races these days, and that's a great improvement.

Today it is arguable that Formula 1 is at its most competitive level ever. In the early nineties, you could say that only one or two teams made the best Grand Prix cars at any one time, but now that hegemony is over, and there are at least four more teams very close to being on terms with the leaders.

This remark may raise a few eyebrows, because we have had our well-publicised differences of opinion over the years, but I hope that Bernie and Max continue to lead Formula 1 for many more years, and I believe that most insiders feel the same way.

Nothing in life stays the same. In a man's lifespan, he has the privilege of living through a number of eras, each one special in itself – unforgettable, but also unrepeatable. I've had this privilege, and I've enjoyed it immensely.

I have known Nigel Roebuck for a long time; we met at Monaco in 1971, when my team was called 'Frank Williams Racing Cars', running a March for Henri Pescarolo. We got along famously from the beginning, and I identified him almost instantly as one of that small group of people who live and die for motor racing, and particularly for Formula 1.

This group, whether they be team principals, engineers, drivers or journalists, are the fundamental core of Formula 1 – the engine house that has driven the sport from success to further success. Nigel occupies a special place in this core, not least because of his defiant approach to the sport he loves. He writes exactly what he thinks, and that I have always much admired. Of his desire to recount events as he sees them, and to reproduce them accurately, there has never been any doubt. When I was asked to write the foreword for this book, I said I would be honoured to do so.

Frank Williams
Hockenheim, August 1999

# Introduction

WHEN I ASKED MIKA HAKKINEN what he thought of Michael Schumacher's attempt to push Jacques Villeneuve off the road, at Jerez in 1997, as always he paused before answering.

'It's easy for me to say, "Of course I wouldn't have done what Schumacher did", and actually I really don't believe I would. But in that situation it's easy to lose control of yourself. All the emphasis is on the World Championship these days, isn't it?'

Indeed so, and it occurs to me that the title of this book is somewhat misleading, for it puts rather more stress on the importance of the World Championship than its author feels.

Having followed Formula 1 from childhood, I remember being affronted in October 1958, when Stirling Moss, with four Grand Prix victories, and Tony Brooks, with three, were beaten to the World Championship by Mike Hawthorn, who won only once.

Even to a 12-year-old, that seemed to make not a lot of sense, and the fact that Moss was somehow never to win it diminished the worth of the title, rather than the man. That impression has remained.

In my perfect world, the man crowned 'World Champion' at the end of each season would be the one who had won the most races. A dozen times, though, this has not been the case, and on one occasion the title went to a driver with fewer *points* than another. In 1988, Alain Prost scored 105 to Ayrton Senna's 94, but at that time a driver counted only his 11 best results, and thus Senna became World Champion, by 90 points to 87. Since 1990, every point has counted.

As a rule, I have always been drawn to *racers* in Formula 1, those for whom 'driving for points' was anathema. Moss was a classic example, and so also was Gilles Villeneuve. 'If the World Championship comes along, I'm certainly not going to turn it away,' he would say, 'but for me what matters more is the record for the most wins'.

Therefore, if you are looking for a history of the World Championship, this is not your book. When first I discussed it with my publisher, he allowed me what amounted to *carte blanche*: the bookends were to be 1950, when the World Championship began, and the present day, but, within those five decades, I could write about whatever took my fancy. An enviable brief, for which I am grateful.

The result is perhaps a little quirky, a mix of times, places and people, some familiar, others less so. I have gone into a couple of seasons, 1967 and 1982, in some detail, and additionally picked out half-a-dozen or so races that were especially memorable; the remaining chapters are given over to characters who have touched my world in the course of nearly 30 years of working in the paddock.

Undeniably, my primary interest in motor racing has always lain with its people. In school days I leaned very much towards 'languages', rather than 'science', and my original requirement of a racing car – that it look fearsomely beautiful and go fast – has never much changed.

Nor, for that matter, has a disinterest in statistics, which can be made to say whatever you wish. Very well, certain of them can take your breath away – between the visits to Spa in June 1952 and June 1953, for example, no one but Alberto Ascari won a World Championship Grand Prix – but they are of little use when comparing different eras. Fangio's 24 victories may put him only eighth on the all-time winners' list, but then the great Juan Manuel competed in only 51 Grands Prix, fewer than, say, Giancarlo Fisichella.

It is Fangio's *strike rate* that so impresses, the fact that he won 47 per cent of his World Championship races. But even that is beaten by a man born the same year, in Schenectady, New York. By a curious anomaly, the Indianapolis 500 counted for the World Championship between 1950 and 1960; thus, Lee Wallard, whose two outings netted a sixth and a first, won precisely 50 per cent of the races he entered, a record unlikely to be surpassed. If anyone cares.

No, if you love motor racing, it is surely an emotional thing, rather than a matter of records and points. For me, the manner of winning has always been more important than the fact of it; I have seen exhibitions of genius, yes, but also defeats more triumphant than many a victory. And even now, after close to 400 Grands Prix, I still reach for my cigarettes as the cars come up to the grid.

Nigel Roebuck
Dorking, Surrey, 1999

# The day everything changed

MORE THAN ANYTHING, it's the doorstep in Fontanelice that brings it back, and it's the same every year. In the Imola paddock there is a resonance of that weekend, of course, but you're ready for that. The place is so cloaked in memories that their very rawness has faded with time.

That doorstep, though, acts like a trigger. I began staying at the little *pensione* 20 years ago, and Rosa, the owner, is a friend. In light of the events that Sunday in May 1994, who knew what time we would back, so we called, asked her to leave a key under the mat.

At two or thereabouts in the morning, we stumbled up the iron steps, felt around in the darkness for the key. Next morning, outside each bedroom door, was a bottle of red wine, Rosa's best. At breakfast not much was said. She was red-eyed, inconsolable.

That weekend, when the traumas seemed without end, I very nearly missed, having felt ill for days before. There was an extravagant Porsche dinner on the Thursday night, complete with fire-eating gypsy girl, and a raffle for a white 968. By late evening, I felt so out of it as to be past caring. After a night without sleep, my first thought on getting to the track next morning was to find 'The Prof'.

Professor Sidney Watkins is Formula 1's medical chief, and the most respected man in the paddock. 'I've got a circuit inspection to do,' he said, 'so I can't do anything for you just now. But I'll find you a man who can.' At the medical centre, he explained the situation to a local surgeon, who gave me an ECG and so on, said my problem was nothing to worry about, and handed me some pills.

Cheered by the instant diagnosis, I went to the press room, and took my seat in front of a bank of TV sets. And it was on one of those screens, the following afternoon, that I saw my Italian doctor again, at the scene of Roland Ratzenberger's accident. He and his colleagues were going through the motions, but their expressions said everything. Any worries I might have had about my own well-being fell sharply into perspective.

The press room went into a sort of frenzy in the aftermath of Ratzenberger's accident. A long time had passed since there had been a fatality at a Grand Prix, and for many journalists the presence of death at a race track was a new and devastating experience.

What amplified it further was that the previous day Rubens Barrichello had flipped his Jordan at high speed, and initially that accident, too, had given us cause to fear. When his car was righted, Barrichello's head flopped to one side, and it was a relief to learn he had merely been knocked out. Following treatment for cuts and bruises, he was back at the track later in the day.

After nearly 200 races without a death in the family, the thin veneer of safety in Formula 1 had gathered many coats, and Barrichello's escape served briefly to confirm us in our comfortable belief that these days a driver could walk away from anything.

By Saturday afternoon, though, the complacency was gone, not least among the drivers. At the scene of Ratzenberger's tragedy, Ayrton Senna talked with Watkins; the Professor has always rightly declined to go into detail about what was said, but allows that he attempted to give Senna some advice.

'It was the first fatality at a Grand Prix for a very long time, and for most of the drivers, it was the first time they had had to confront the situation. But, even allowing for that, I judged Ayrton's reaction abnormal. I told him I didn't think he should race the next day – and that he should think very seriously about racing again ever.

'He thought a great deal before he answered. A minute or more. If you asked a difficult question, there was always a long silence – he'd never come up with a rapid response, which he might regret. Eventually he said that ... he couldn't not race, in effect. There was no particular explanation, but I believe he felt trapped by every aspect of his life at that time. I honestly think he would have liked to step back; that was the impression I'd been getting for a while.

'His first two races with Williams had gone badly, and he was very upset about that. I think there's no doubt that he felt very much pressured that he *had* to win at Imola.'

On race morning the mood in the paddock was understandably sombre. Just before noon there was an accident in the Porsche Cup race, and while shunts in these events are normally ten a penny, on this occasion one of the drivers was seriously hurt, this serving to heighten the impression that normality had been somehow suspended.

Thus, there was intense relief when no driver was hurt in the startline accident at the beginning of the Grand Prix. JJ Lehto, fifth on the grid, stalled immediately before the green light, which left no time for the start to be aborted. Raising both arms to warn those behind, Lehto could only sit there, and hope, like an animal cowering in headlights.

For all the strength of contemporary Formula 1 cars, still we momentarily feared for Pedro Lamy, for when his Lotus hit the Benetton, it was as if a bomb had gone off. And although both drivers were unhurt, several spectators were injured by accident shrapnel.

Lehto was making his return to racing, having broken his neck in a pre-season testing shunt at Silverstone. As he went off to the motorhome to change, he felt gratified that at least his neck had suffered no further damage, but for JJ this was already a nightmare of a weekend, for he had driven to Imola with

Ratzenberger, his close friend. Returning to the pit to watch the race on the TV monitor, he arrived just as Senna hit the wall at Tamburello.

Somehow the real enormity of that moment was lost at first, in the sense that yet another accident was almost too much to take in. As the red flag was waved, indeed, everything fell curiously quiet.

It was that tiny movement of the yellow helmet that caused the gasp in the press room. We stared at the TV screens, mesmerised by the set of Senna's head. It was upright, not slumped, as one would expect of an unconscious man – but if he were not unconscious, then why was he not moving? We willed him to wave an arm, do something, *anything*, to indicate that all was essentially well with him.

Then his head moved. It was almost imperceptible, but enough for some to keep hoping that Ayrton was stunned, and nothing more. For others, though, there was something almost ghostly about the moment. 'He's dying, isn't he?' someone murmured.

He was. And what made this racing tragedy different from those gone before was that his life was ending on television. During the minutes after the accident, a TV helicopter lingered pitilessly over the scene, and if the BBC had the decency to cut to something else, some other companies did not.

This I thought unconscionable, and there can be no doubt that it contributed significantly to the revulsion for motor racing expressed by much of the outside world in the days that followed.

Eventually, after Watkins and his team had done what they could at the trackside, Senna was flown by helicopter to the Maggiore Hospital in Bologna, and there put on a life-support machine. His death was formally announced at 6.40 that evening, a little more than four hours after the accident.

Given the breadth of Ayrton's fame and popularity, it was no surprise that his death – even in the face of Nelson Mandela's impending victory in the South African elections – commandeered front-page leads the world over. By 1994 the top Grand Prix drivers were publicised like movie stars, and the name of Senna had a resonance everywhere. He was *the* racing driver of his time, recognised even by folk who had never seen a race, nor wished to.

By 1994, too, a dozen years had gone by since a driver had been killed at a Grand Prix, and in that time there had been profound sociological changes in the world. When Gilles Villeneuve and Riccardo Paletti died, in 1982, there was enormous media coverage, but the tone of it was much the same as it had always been: grief at the loss of these men, but also a sense that such accidents were in the very nature of the sport.

After the deaths of Ratzenberger and Senna, though, there was something new in the way newspapers handled their stories. I was working then for *The Sunday Times*, and within an hour of returning to England was required to write an exhaustive memo to the editor, detailing what might have caused Senna to go off.

'I want this newspaper,' the editor boomed, 'to be the first in the world to say why Senna crashed.' Very excited, he was, and in that moment I came to understand why I would always prefer to work for specialist magazines. It was enough just then to cope with the fact that Ayrton was gone; why could come later.

In point of fact, my editor differed little from any other. From the very start, journals everywhere were preoccupied with *why* Senna had crashed. Who was accountable? Whose *fault* was it?

We live in an age fixated with investigations, inquiries, culpability. A high moral tone was taken everywhere. 'In the name of sport,' trumpeted the *Daily Star*, sandwiching the headline between photographs of Senna and Ratzenberger, slumped in their cockpits. And at the bottom of the page: 'These young men were killed giving us thrills.'

In truth, young men like Roland and Ayrton had been 'killed giving us thrills' since the dawn of motor racing, and it had been traditionally accepted as an inevitable, if regrettable, occurrence in what was a dangerous sport. Niki Lauda, that fount of common sense, pointed out that more astonishing had been the absence of fatalities for so long. 'For 12 years,' he said, 'God had his hand over Formula 1. This weekend he took it away.'

By the mid-1990s, however, we were becoming daily accustomed to death on our TV screens and in our newspapers, to constant images of wars and bomb outrages and the like. And at the same time sports of every kind were being dragged ever more from their roots, increasingly blurred into showbiz.

That being so, it was not just a racing driver who lay dying on our TV screens; it was a *star*. And a star who had left this life in an apparently frivolous pursuit: proving he could drive a car faster than anyone else.

The matter of Senna's death transcended sport, like that of Clark's at Hockenheim in 1968, but although Jimmy, too, crashed in circumstances where driver error was inconceivable, there was no great public investigation into his accident. Ultimately, it was concluded that a tyre had failed on the Lotus, probably after running over debris, but no formal announcement was ever made – or, for that matter, demanded.

Different days, though. The reason for Senna's accident became a *cause célèbre*, and no one was more shocked by the media response than Max Mosley.

'I confess I was stunned,' the FIA President said, 'because, to me, being an F1 driver is like being a fighter pilot – there's a small but finite risk that you will come unstuck. It doesn't alter the fact that it's very sad, particularly if you know the person, but it can happen. However, the public doesn't seem to react like that these days.'

Like anyone else in racing, Mosley well appreciated the significance of the cult of personality in today's world, and was only too aware that, had any driver other than Senna been killed, society's response would have been far less trenchant. But it *was* Senna, and that brought motor racing into the public domain.

It didn't matter that much of the outrage was precipitate and ill-informed; inevitably there was pressure on the FIA to make changes to this 'killer sport'. The governing body had not only to take action, but be seen to do so.

Initially, Mosley resisted any knee-jerk reaction, although

some rule changes were introduced immediately, these including a pit lane speed limit. Late in the race at Imola, as it left the pits, Michele Alboreto's Minardi had shed a rear wheel, slightly injuring four mechanics. Given that Senna's accident dwarfed any other event of that day, it received scant attention, but in fact had been a miraculous deliverance.

Ten days later we soberly made our way to Monte Carlo for the next race, and on the opening day of practice – the very first day on which Grand Prix cars had run since Imola – Karl Wendlinger crashed his Sauber. Initially it didn't look like a very serious accident, for there was relatively little damage to the car. Braking very late for the chicane, Wendlinger had lost control, and hit broadside the barrier separating the escape road from the track; a few feet either side, and the driver would have walked away. As it was, he was removed to hospital with life-threatening head injuries.

Suddenly it seemed impossible to escape unhurt from a Formula 1 accident, and in some quarters there was evidence of wild overreaction. Particularly reprehensible was the response of *L'Equipe*, a serious sporting daily whose editors should have known better: the following day's front cover was given over entirely to a shot of the Wendlinger rescue operation, with the stark headline, *Arrêtez ça!*.

Now the FIA truly snapped into action. At a press conference, convened on Friday morning, Mosley announced that a whole raft of technical and procedural changes would be phased in, some immediately. In normal circumstances, such a move would have been precluded by the Concorde Agreement.

'For all that,' Mosley said, very statesmanlike, 'the time has come, because of the gravity of the situation, and the force of public opinion, to push aside such considerations, and simply do what is right, in the general interests of the sport.

'It may upset certain interests, but in the end the fundamental duty of the FIA is to preserve the lives and health of all the participants and, above all, the spectators. There will be loud criticism from certain quarters, but it will have to be ignored.'

The rule changes concerned themselves primarily with three areas: the reduction of downforce, and of horsepower, and modifications to the cars to increase driver safety. All these duly came to be.

As well as that, however, there began wholesale changes to circuits, and while many of these were justified, so also many were not. At Barcelona, a month after Imola, practice was delayed so that a temporary, and wholly unsatisfactory, tyre barrier chicane could be inserted before a corner through which the drivers had for years raced without qualm. The change was made late in the day because the driver deputed to inspect the circuit had not bothered so to do.

As the weeks and months passed, so several drivers reflected on the manifold track changes, the slowing of corners, the insertion of chicanes, and allowed that there had been some measure of overreaction on their part. Perhaps that had been all too understandable, but the owners of some circuits, notably Silverstone, became a touch impatient when drivers began to mutter that now the place was boring.

'At that time,' said Gerhard Berger, 'it seemed as if the world had gone crazy, as if, for some reason, Formula 1 had suddenly become much more dangerous. We looked for some common link in the accidents at Imola and Monaco, but really there wasn't one. You look back on it, and you see that it was all horrible coincidence.'

Berger, Senna's closest friend among the drivers, did chastise himself on one point, however. 'After my own crash at Tamburello, in 1989, I said to the circuit people, "Could we not move the wall back at the point, and put in a proper run-off area?" "Not possible," they said, "because there's a river behind it." And I just said, "Oh, OK..."'

Gerhard was right in his affirmation that the disasters were in no way connected. The FIA went exhaustively into the matter, and reached the same conclusion, but that didn't alter the fact of the global response, above all, to the loss of Ayrton Senna.

Ironically, as Bernie Ecclestone has pointed out, *since* Senna's death there has been an extraordinary surge of interest in Formula 1. First, undeniably it was exposed to a wider world; second, in the starkest terms it served to remind a new generation that this was indeed a serious activity, where tragedy could mean rather more than torn hamstrings.

Ecclestone, unlike some in Formula 1, does not deal in comfortable platitudes. In both his assertions he is correct, but of course the corollary of the second is that the *potential* for danger is fundamental to the appeal of the sport. It cannot, surely, be the wish of other than a psychopath to see a driver hurt, or worse, but if it were possible to make the racing of 200mph cars totally safe, the very essence of Grand Prix racing would change.

'In my era,' said Stirling Moss, 'if it was too hot in the kitchen, fine, don't come in the kitchen. What I'm saying is that if you make racing safe, you obviously lessen the challenge. If you watch high-wire artists, you don't get the same feeling if they've got a safety-net, do you? I mean, I'd try to walk on a wire two feet from the ground, but I sure as hell wouldn't across the Grand Canyon! Now, the skill required is exactly the same in both cases, but the challenge is not...'

True enough, but that was then, and this is now, a time when wartime civilian casualties are referred to as 'collateral damage'. When Moss raced, everyone smoked, seat belts were unknown, and kids were allowed to set off fireworks. Self-protection was your own affair. But that is not the way of it in today's society, and if Mosley was shaken by the public response to the accidents in May 1994, so he quickly concluded that racing dare not risk a repetition.

What has since happened to Formula 1 is thus probably no more than inevitable. In the late 1960s Jackie Stewart almost single-handedly began a crusade for safety, and, given the grim statistics of the time, one can well understand why. Any racing driver of the last 35 years is in Stewart's debt.

Different regimes at the FIA took very different attitudes to safety, some paying it lip service, others treating it with outright contempt, others again taking it seriously. But while it ultimately became a fixture on the agenda of the governing body, since 1994 it has become the overwhelming priority, and this has dovetailed with an ever greater emphasis on showbiz, as opposed to sport.

Early in 1996 Mosley announced his determination to eliminate 'life-threatening corners', of which, in the estimation of the FIA, there were 16. This did not sit well with some of the drivers. It wasn't that they relished such corners *because* they were dangerous, but that inevitably it was corners of this kind which separated the great from the good, which gave driving a Grand Prix car its buzz.

'It's a matter of finding the right balance, isn't it?' Ken Tyrrell mused. 'Of working for greater safety, but at the same time ensuring you don't finish up with something no one wants to watch any more…'

By 1997 Jacques Villeneuve, admittedly something of a maverick, had gone so far as to suggest that Formula 1 was now too slow, too safe. Mosley's smooth response was that he well understood Jacques's feelings, indeed sympathised with them, would have expected nothing else from a racing driver, who only ever wanted to go faster. That said, it was the job of the FIA to protect people like Villeneuve from themselves.

We still go to Imola each spring, and what we find there is a circuit very different from the one at which Senna won so many times, the one at which he died. Tamburello had to go – indeed should have gone years earlier, when Berger's accident showed what was possible there – but why was so much else changed?

'It's almost unrecognisable in places, isn't it?' said Professor Watkins. 'And it's ironic that, while it was changed because of Ayrton's accident, he would have hated it, the way it is now…'

So he would. 'If you take away Eau Rouge,' he once said, when the celebrated switchback at Spa was under threat, 'you take away the reason why I do this.' Perhaps the greatest irony is that all the corners renamed in honour of Senna, from Interlagos to Hockenheim, have been the chicanes he so detested.

The bedrock of motor racing philosophy has always been that a driver climbs aboard of his own volition, mindful of all the risks involved, not least that his car has been constructed by human hands. And that, I believe, remains. Ask a Grand Prix driver worth the name to nominate his favourite circuit, and the chances are he will go – immediately – for Spa-Francorchamps.

As of now Spa remains on the World Championship calendar, but much else has disappeared, and we are into an age in which, according to Max Mosley, we should think of a Grand Prix in terms of a chess match. A glaring paradox, in the midst of this 'safety first' era, has been the re-introduction of mid-race refuelling, a wholly unnecessary danger if ever there was one. Showbiz, as I said.

A Formula 1 car, in the hands of a genius, remains for me the most inspiring sight in sport, and that is a constant. But the repercussions of Imola 1994 forced Grand Prix racing into a period of catatonic self-examination, from which it emerged fundamentally transformed. Perhaps there was no alternative; perhaps, as Sid Watkins put it, 'The old panache of Formula 1 was close to being no longer acceptable.'

When Olivier Panis crashed, and broke his leg, at Montreal in 1997, I confess to being astonished by the general reaction afterwards. Certainly it was an unpleasant accident, and the driver was seriously hurt, but it was not as though his life was in danger. Three months later, indeed, he was racing again. But when Villeneuve pointed out that Panis's injury was no worse than that suffered by dozens of skiers on any winter day, he was widely castigated for a lack of sensitivity.

It was nothing of the kind, merely that Jacques, like Bernie Ecclestone one of few folk to use plain speech these days, was attempting to keep a sense of proportion. 'Come on, people!' he said. 'Get real! If we're going to race cars, occasionally someone is going to be hurt…'

So was everything changed after May Day 1994? I rather think it was, in the sense that thereafter the whole ethos of Grand Prix racing shifted, and for ever. It didn't when Jimmy Clark died, or Jochen Rindt or Ronnie Peterson or Gilles Villeneuve. But when Ayrton Senna died, it did. For he died in the 1990s, and in living rooms around the world.

# Maestro

ONCE, IN BRAZIL, I saw Juan Manuel Fangio walk up behind Ayrton Senna, and tap him on the shoulder. Senna, in the middle of a conversation, swung round, clearly annoyed; then he saw who it was, and as he put his arms around the old man, the *grand seigneur*, his eyes were full of tears.

This was Ayrton's earthly god. Jo Ramirez, his close friend, as well as colleague through the McLaren years, always believed that his ambition was to win five World Championships, as Fangio had done. 'I think that then he would have retired,' Ramirez said. 'He had so much love and respect for Fangio that he wouldn't have wanted to beat his record.'

Many consider that Alberto Ascari was the fastest driver of his time, but it was Fangio who *defined* that era. His racing career ended more than 40 years ago, yet across the world the name of Fangio has always meant 'racing driver', just as mention of Pelé registers even with folk who never saw a football match.

It is given to very few people in this life that their fame transcends their own field of endeavour, but this quiet man from a small town in Argentina cast a spell wherever he went, as much with his personality as with his prodigious skills.

In this, the age of cult personalities and instant heroes, awash with money and self-regard, no man of Fangio's stamp is to be seen. There are many more World Championship races these days, and so there are some with no trace of his talent who have won more. He drove in only 51 Grands Prix – but won 24 of them, thus achieving a strike rate unapproached by any other driver in history. And no one but he, of course, has ever won the title five times.

If, statistically, he stands alone, mere figures tell nothing of the kind of man this was. Jackie Stewart once remarked that whenever Fangio came into a room, conversations dried, everyone's eyes and attention suddenly elsewhere. 'He was quiet, he was shy,' said Stewart, 'and yet he had more presence than anyone I've ever known.'

Phil Hill remembered meeting Fangio for the first time. 'It was in Buenos Aires in 1954, and when he walked in, there was this electric presence – I don't know how else to describe it.'

More than anything, perhaps, Fangio stood for dignity in his sport. Motor racing, he always felt, should be a profession for an honourable man. He had no time for the arrogant, the cheap. Undoubtedly the killer instinct was there, as with all the great ones, yet in his driving he was scrupulously ethical. It was important to win, but only in the right way. It was not by chance that his younger rivals worshipped him.

When Peter Collins voluntarily handed over his Ferrari to Fangio in the 1956 Italian Grand Prix, he knew that by so doing he was tossing away the opportunity to became World Champion.

'Peter never gave it a thought,' Louise, his widow, once told me. 'He was only 24 years old at the time, and never felt there was much urgency about winning the championship. For one thing, it always seemed that he cared much more about winning individual races; for another, he felt that, as long as Fangio was racing, no one else deserved the title of World Champion. Peter simply revered him – they all did.'

None more than Stirling Moss. In terms of pure ability, Moss put Senna on the same lofty plateau as Fangio, but there was more to it than that. 'The difference, to be blunt, was that

Fangio never did anything remotely questionable on the track. I thought Senna was an artist in a racing car, a genius, but some of the things he did, particularly to Prost, Fangio would never have countenanced.'

There was class in everything the man did. Through the 1955 season, he and Moss were dominant in their Mercedes-Benz W196s, but only in the British Grand Prix, at Aintree, did Stirling finish ahead. To this day he has never really known whether or not Fangio simply allowed him to win.

Asked the question, Fangio would simply smile. 'I don't think I could have won, even if I had wanted to – Moss was really pushing that day...'

Stirling never discussed the matter with him. 'Certainly I was far enough ahead on the last lap that he couldn't have caught me – but the thing is, did he *allow* me to build that lead earlier on? If he did, it was with great subtlety – but then, of course, it would have been. That was him.'

If Fangio were never to admit to letting Moss win in his own country, the fact remains that he led much of the way, and on only one other occasion was he ever 'beaten' by another Mercedes driver in a Formula 1 race. At the 1954 Berlin Grand Prix, a non-championship race at Avus, he again finished a close second after leading for a long time, and it can have been no coincidence that this time the winner was Karl Kling, a German on home territory.

It is interesting to contrast Fangio's way of doing things with that of Senna, who, having clinched the World Championship that day, braked on the run up to the line at Suzuka in 1991, very obviously 'allowing' McLaren team-mate Gerhard Berger to take the flag.

Less attractive still was Nigel Mansell's conduct at Monza in 1992. Already confirmed as World Champion that year, Mansell had agreed that Williams team-mate Riccardo Patrese should win at Monza. That done, he stormed away in the early stages, established a big lead, then slowed to a crawl so as to let Patrese catch him.

Once Riccardo had gone by, Nigel proceeded to circulate a few inches behind him, in case anyone had missed his earlier point: 'See how much quicker I am, everybody?' Patrese, humiliated in front of his home crowd, never forgot it.

To paraphrase Moss: it wasn't done with great subtlety – but then, of course, it wouldn't have been. That was him.

I never walk down Curzon Street in London without thinking of The Steering Wheel, and I never think of motor racing's most celebrated watering-hole, sadly long gone now, without remembering 2 June 1979. Although I met Fangio on a number of occasions, it was there, then, that I interviewed him at length, and my heart still beats faster at the memory.

Fangio, then 68 years old, was in England to drive a Mercedes-Benz W125 at Donington the following day, and at very short notice I was offered the opportunity of spending a couple of hours with him. Amazing to relate, the very thought made me so flustered that initially I hesitated. Then I went out to buy a new tape recorder. There was nothing wrong with the one I had, but it seemed appropriate, and, anyway, on this day nothing could be left to chance.

Later that day, I came out of the club, into the bright sunlight, my head whirling. There had been no last-minute problems. He had arrived on time, with an interpreter, and seemed, if anything, more shy than I. He responded to my questions as if he had never heard them before, speaking quickly and quietly, the tempo increasing as he recalled events which gave him particular delight. His eyes, as so many have said, were mesmeric, and there was mischief in them.

'At the Italian Grand Prix, in 1953, my Maserati had a terrible vibration all through practice, and it could not be cured. In every team I drove for, I always made sure of having the mechanics on my side. Very important. Whatever I win, I would tell them, you will get 10 per cent. The night before the race, I again complained of the vibration – and on Sunday it was miraculously cured! I have no idea how they did it, but I know Felice Bonetto's teeth fell out during the race…'

Perhaps the most celebrated image in all of motor racing history is that of Fangio, his Maserati 250F on full opposite lock, through the terrifying downhill swerves at Rouen-Les Essarts in 1957. He had never driven there before, and told

Denis Jenkinson he found the circuit much to his taste.

'Before each practice session,' Jenks said, 'he'd be standing by his car, rubbing his hands. Couldn't wait to get out again. He really enjoyed himself that weekend.'

On pole position by over a second, Fangio won that French Grand Prix by close to a minute. So overwhelming was his superiority that there was probably no need to put the car at such extravagant angles, and I have always suspected that he was simply delighting in his art, sliding the 250F this way and that, simply because he could.

He *enjoyed* himself in a racing car. A month after Rouen, he took his last, and greatest, victory, at the Nürburgring, and photographs as he took the flag that day show him to be smiling broadly.

There was also, he told me, a degree of relief. 'People always say that was my best race, and I suppose they are right. After my pit stop, when I was catching Hawthorn and Collins, I beat my own lap record by 24 seconds, and even now I can feel fear when I think of that race. I knew what I had done, the chances I had taken. The Nürburgring was always my favourite circuit, without any doubt. I loved it, all of it, and I think that day I conquered it. On another day, it might have conquered me, who knows? But I believe I took myself and my car to the limit, and perhaps a little bit more. I had never driven like that before, and knew I never would again. Aye, that Maserati 250F … not very powerful, but beautifully balanced, a lovely car to drive. I felt I could do anything with it.'

Fangio was 46 by then, but if retirement beckoned, still he was unquestionably the best. The Italian Grand Prix was a classic race, a rich battle between the Vanwalls of Moss, Tony Brooks and Stuart Lewis-Evans, and the Maseratis of Fangio and Jean Behra.

Brooks retired after setting fastest lap, but for ever remembered the day well. 'I learned a great deal. Monza was a wonderful place to race at that time – there were none of these silly chicanes all over the place, and many of the corners were very, very, quick, but not completely flat. The Curva Grande was especially nice. We'd approach at about 175mph, I suppose, dab the brakes, and go through at about 160.

'I thought I was taking this corner pretty quickly, and in the early stages I was dicing with Fangio for the lead. First time through the Curva Grande, touch the brakes, turn in – *wham!* – he goes by on the inside, oversteering it on the throttle!

'Later in the lap I got by again, and the next time through the Curva Grande – *wham!* – exactly the same again. I don't know, maybe he wasn't braking at all. Anyway, I worked hard at that corner, and it didn't happen again, which made me very proud of myself, I can tell you...'

At the end of 1957, World Champion for the fifth time, Fangio decided to call it a day. 'After I retired, I was never tempted to return. I was very tired, very content to stop, and I did not miss it. I loved my 10 years as a Grand Prix driver, but there had been great sacrifices – necessary, if you are to remain on top, but sacrifices nevertheless. In that time, 30 drivers died, and while I never allowed it to influence me, my sadness deepened. Racing is beautiful when you are full of enthusiasm, but when it becomes work you should stop. And by the end of 1957 it was becoming work for me.'

They say of really great drivers that the fundamental ability never goes away, and whenever Fangio periodically appeared in a racing car, even into his seventies, it was apparent that the magic was intact, that the light touch remained.

When he drove the Mercedes at Donington, the day after our meeting, he came out of the chicane on his first lap, and – being unfamiliar with the car, and its supercharged 5.6-litre engine – dabbed the throttle a little too early. Out skipped the tail, and momentarily I held my breath, fearful that he was about to embarrass himself.

Not a bit of it. The slide was instantly checked, and on went the power again. Behind me, Dan Gurney and Mario Andretti whooped with delight.

It was the same at Monza in 1981. The day before the Italian Grand Prix, Fangio had a run in an Alfa Romeo 158, similar to the car which took him to the first of his championships, and on race morning he was out in a Lancia D50, the first Grand Prix car with which this nine-year-old fell in love. Every time, he fairly hammered past the pits, and the spectators, stirred once more by the sight of that yellow shirt and brown helmet, were in rapture.

In 1991, to mark Fangio's 80th birthday, a celebratory dinner was organised at the Dorchester Hotel, in London. Everything was pleasantly understated. There were no sponsors' banners or anything of the like, no dry ice. The clues, though, were in place: an Alfa 158, in traditional purply-red, sat next to a scarlet Maserati 250F.

We chatted, and waited. 'Apart from when he was with Mercedes,' Tony Brooks said, 'Fangio's cars were no better than anyone else's – not like today. He won his races in an era when the driver made a much greater contribution. He was so good that when he changed teams, he made the difference.'

No argument about that. The five World Championships were won in four different makes of car. 'But still the main reason we're all here tonight,' Brooks went on, 'is that he was a great man off the track, too. He set an example in everything he did.'

Phil Hill agreed. 'If you ask me about his greatest quality, I would say it was the way he behaved through his life.'

After a few minutes, on a big screen there was a flash of Mercedes-Benz W196, a howl of its sound. At the far end of the room a door opened, and Fangio came in, slightly stooped as ever, still with that familiar shy grin. The applause rattled the chandeliers.

Moss introduced him. 'We're here to pay homage,' he said, 'to the greatest ambassador our sport has ever had.

'Why was Fangio so great as a driver? I don't know – except that whatever time you did, he'd beat it. And he'd beat it because he was better. I saw it more closely than most of you – when I was allowed to … In our year at Mercedes together, I considered it a great honour to be number two to him.'

Other, similar, tributes followed, and then it was time for Fangio to speak. 'In the Grand Prix of Argentina, in 1955,' he began, 'the heat was impossible. Drivers were collapsing. I felt no better than they did, but I imagined I was a man waist-deep in snow – it was the only way to go on. And in that way I was able to finish, and win.

'In the same way, I have tried hard to forget where I am tonight, because otherwise I wouldn't be able to speak. When one is old, perhaps one is more sensitive. At the end of some races, you know, I cried, so tonight it's probably as well I'm not racing any more. With all these tributes, I might start to believe my own publicity, believe I was the best.

'My last race, you know, was at Reims, where there were plenty of straights – and therefore plenty of time to think. And that afternoon I thought about my career. I had come to Europe originally for just one year, and I never thought I'd win a race. In the end, I stayed 10 years, and won five World Championships. But now I thought, 'What am I doing here?' And I knew then it was over, and time for the rest of my life. When I stopped racing, I was made President of Mercedes-Benz Argentina – me a lad from a little town…'

It seemed not to have occurred to him how much he personally had contributed to the fortunes of Mercedes across the world, how much the company had benefited from continued association with his name.

That race at Reims, in the summer of 1958, was run some months after Fangio had announced his retirement, and really he took part in it more as a favour to Maserati than anything else. For much of the race, as he battled with Moss and Behra, it was as if he had never been away, but then his clutch failed, and ultimately he fell back to finish fourth.

The race was dominated by Hawthorn's Ferrari, and in the closing laps Mike backed off a touch, aware of who was driving the car he was on the point of lapping, unwilling to subject him to such an indignity.

Some have greatness thrust upon them, and some have no need. 'What matters in this life,' Fangio said, that night in London, 'is not to be important, but to believe you're important…'

# Players versus gentlemen

'ONLY BY ORDERLY BEHAVIOUR and keeping to prescribed routes can speedy exit from the track be ensured. You don't want a traffic jam, and neither do we, so please don't start one.'

Whoever wrote the programme notes for the 1950 Grand Prix d'Europe, the inaugural World Championship Formula 1 race, was clearly not without a sense of humour, for the event attracted a crowd put at 120,000, and we are speaking here of Silverstone. Half a century on, folk in the know take Berlitz tapes when they head for Northamptonshire in July, appreciating that there awaits a matchless opportunity to learn a new language.

Those travelling on someone else's coin arrive by helicopter, of course, but even 50 years ago there were ways around the traffic problem, if you knew the right people – or, more to the point, if you *were* the right people. When the Royal Family came to Silverstone in 1950, it was with some style.

At an auction long ago I picked up two quirky items, and while one of them – a booklet entitled *Hints on Remedying Stoppages in the Lewis Machine Gun* – need not detain us here, the other was a sheaf of foolscap pages, headed, 'Confidential. Proposed time schedule and sequence of events for the Royal Visit, Grand Prix d'Europe, 13th May 1950'.

One is reminded rather of Peter Ustinov's sublime *Grand*

*Prix of Gibraltar*. Their Majesties, plus entourage, were to travel to Brackley in the Royal Train, getting in at 1.45pm. From there – with the Chief Constable of Northamptonshire in the pace car – they were to proceed in a fleet of limousines to the circuit, arriving at 2.05pm. It seems a reasonable bet that 20 minutes from Brackley to Silverstone on British Grand Prix day will stand as a record for all time.

Only when they arrived at the track, ironically, was their speed trimmed. 'It is hoped that Their Majesties will drive around the Race Track. The length of the Circuit is three miles. It is suggested that the Royal Car should travel at approximately 20 miles per hour. Owing to the size of the Race Track, this speed should not be found too fast.'

Quite so. Their lap completed, the King and Queen were then to meet the drivers, during which time the Band of the Grenadier Guards – none of your Jamiroquai in 1950, thank you very much – would play 'suitable music'.

For all its honorary title of 'Grand Prix d'Europe', the race at Silverstone was a quintessentially English affair of the time, everything about it recalling to mind Frank Williams's favourite line from the movies, spoken by Sean Connery in *Murder On The Orient Express*: 'Do you give me your word, as a foreigner…?'

Connery might have been addressing the drivers' meeting that May afternoon. The basic tenet of the British Grand Prix – to finish it before anyone else – was the same then as now, but in every other respect we might be looking at different planets.

For one thing, the organisers then were actively looking for ways to *speed up* the circuit, a concept not easily grasped today. 'As set out now, the course measures 2 miles 1,564 yards, and all artificial restrictions on speed' – chicanes, in other words – 'have been eliminated. Indeed, the corners have been as much eased in radius as practicable.

'Fastest swerve of all is Maggotts, where the aces may be observed in full flight, in that spectacular state of progress known as a "four wheel drift". The drift has to be smartly brought in hand to cope with the Becketts, and then it's wham through Chapel to Hangar Straight, fastest place of all.'

33

Nor was it only in regard to circuit design that attitudes were somewhat different. In the race programme, a few scene-setting fundamentals were listed for the benefit of the spectators.

'The Race Goes On. Motor racing must have its dangers, and though every precaution is taken, and though the drivers competing today are the most skilful in the world, there may be accidents. It is a tradition of Grand Prix racing that whatever happens the race shall go on.

'Pass, Friend. The French were the pioneers of motor racing, and ever since it has been a tradition to use their rule-of-the-road. Therefore, overtaking drivers should pull over to the left-hand side of the road.

'Smoking Permitted. Grand Prix drivers do not normally have to undergo strict physical training. Moderation in eating, drinking and smoking is sufficient, for motor racing is a test of brain rather than brawn.'

So there you are, Michael; put those weights down, and have a Marlboro.

There was also a note of regret. Ferrari may be looked upon as the one team to have participated in the World Championship since its inception, but in fact Enzo was not represented at Silverstone, having withdrawn his cars following a dispute over 'starting money'.

It would happen not infrequently down the years, but on this occasion the absence of the Ferraris was particularly lamented, for the inevitable consequence was that the Alfa Romeo 158s would be unopposed. Juan Manuel Fangio, Giuseppe Farina and Luigi Fagioli were the regular factory drivers, and, in honour of the occasion, a fourth car was entered for Reg Parnell, the leading Brit of the day.

What they faced was a selection of elderly Maseratis, Talbots, Altas and ERAs, so it was hardly a surprise that the front row of the grid – four cars at Silverstone until 1969! – was all dark red, with Farina on pole position.

At Silverstone the previous year, the fine British driver Bob Gerard had taken his ERA to second place, behind 'Toulo' de Graffenried's Maserati. 'I got a lot of satisfaction out of that,' he remembered, 'but it rather flattered me – you've got to remember that Alfa weren't competing in 1949.' So how was it to race against the Alfas? 'Oh,' Gerard chuckled, 'you didn't *race* against them. You just sort of set off for two or three hours at the same time they did...

'Mind you,' he added, 'that was better than the bloody BRM!'

Better than the bloody BRM, indeed. Although the V16-engined car was on hand, it was considered as yet unready to race (a state of affairs which was never materially to change), and its first public appearance was therefore confined to three 'demonstration laps'.

Remarkably, it completed them. In the hands of Raymond Mays, the architect of the BRM project, it went through the corners on the over-run, and made a lot of racket down the straights, which was its party piece. And the crowds, wishing to believe that here was a British world-beater, cheered it to the rafters.

As a child, I was given an EP record of the V16 on full noise, and once mentioned it to Stirling Moss. 'I'm surprised,' he said, 'that it ran long enough to fill an EP.' It was a fair point.

Even its much vaunted exhaust note, while undeniably arresting, was no match for the cultured eight-cylinder scream of an Alfa 158, the car at which it was vainly aimed.

The reverence in which this first BRM is held by some has always been a source of mystery to me, for it was surely one of the silliest racing cars ever conceived. It may have had huge power – ultimately perhaps as much as 600bhp, at 12,000rpm – but it never gave it for very long, and when it did, delivered it in such a way as to make the car virtually undrivable. Unlike the Roots-type blowers used by Alfa Romeo, which peaked, and then tailed off, the Rolls-Royce centrifugal supercharging used by BRM just kept on coming.

For the wartime aero engines for which the Rolls blower had been developed that was fine, as they ran at virtually constant speeds. For a racing car, though, it was a very different matter, for the power increased as the revs did: add in the primitive tyres of the time, and wheelspin became a way of life. The more the wheelspin, the higher the revs, the more the power, the more the wheelspin...

'The V16 was a thoroughly nasty car,' said Moss. 'The brakes were OK, and the acceleration was incredible – until you broke traction – but everything else I hated, particularly the steering and the driving position.' And what of its handling? 'I don't remember it having any...'

Some, though, were always dewy-eyed about it, and none more than Mays. 'The V16 was an awe-inspiring car to drive,' he said. 'You could re-spin the wheels at 9,800 in fourth gear, you know...' It seemed never to cross his mind that a driver wouldn't actually *want* a car which could do that.

Once Mays had run his demonstration laps, and the Royals had taken their seats, the serious business of the day could begin. After a cool and dull morning, by race time the sun was up, the temperature high, and the 22 cars were wheeled to the grid, then situated between Abbey and Woodcote.

The drivers, one or two in overalls, but most in cotton trousers and short-sleeved shirts, climbed aboard. It was not until 1952 that crash helmets were made mandatory in Grand Prix racing, and while several of the British drivers – including Parnell – already wore them, the continental preference remained for the time-honoured cloth helmet. An exception to the rule, the programme observed, was Philippe Etancelin, 'a colourful French veteran, distinguished by his habit of driving in a cap'.

Away they went. As would be the case 42 years on, when Nigel Mansell and the 'active' Williams-Renault disappeared into the distance, the result was a foregone conclusion, but at least on this occasion there were four Alfas to make a race of it.

So, too, they did. From the start Parnell was unable quite to keep pace with the others, and eventually Fagioli, too, was dropped, but Farina and Fangio ran in close company all the way until lap 62, eight from the flag, when Juan Manuel coasted into his pit, an oil pipe broken. Thus, it was only a 1–2–3 for Alfa Romeo, with the Talbots of Yves Giraud-Cabantous and Louis Rosier fourth and fifth, and the redoubtable Gerard scoring the final point at this first-ever World Championship Grand Prix.

In 1950, the mind of Bernie Ecclestone being focused chiefly on keeping his Cooper 500 on the road, FOCA and its attendant blessings were still way in the future; that being so, details of the prize money – 'To be paid in sterling' – were published for all to see, and Farina, in winning, collected £500.

The imperious Italian will be for ever enshrined in racing history as the first World Champion, remembered not least for a gorgeous driving style, and one very untypical of the day, for he sat back from the wheel as far as possible, arms almost straight.

Moss admitted consciously copying him – 'I thought it looked so good, you know' – but in other respects was not an admirer. 'Farina was a great driver, but everyone was very wary of him, because he was dangerous – he had an absolute disregard for anyone else on the track, even inexperienced drivers he was lapping. And if you got involved in a scrap with him, he was completely ruthless; he'd do things that would never even cross the mind of a man like Fangio.'

Three months later the Alfas were back at Silverstone, for the *Daily Express* International Trophy, and this time the victorious Farina pocketed £525. Curious that the rewards should have been higher at this non-championship race than at the Grand Prix; curious, too, that the entry was significantly better, and included Tony Vandervell's *Thinwall Special* Ferrari for Alberto Ascari.

BRM were also there, this time ostensibly to race. The programme wisely sounded a cautious note: 'Today the BRM makes its racing début. Do not expect too much. The drivers are new to their mount; the pit organisation is untried, and the BRM may show the usual temperamental irritations of the thoroughbred.'

Although two V16s were entered, neither appeared in practice, and ultimately one car was flown on race morning from Folkingham to RAF Cranwell, whence it was transported to Silverstone, complete with police escort.

The great Raymond Sommer had somehow been prevailed upon to drive the V16, and, in the absence of any practice in the car, it seemed a sound plan to let him get the feel of it before the race; therefore he drove three laps on a damp track, and that was deemed sufficient to allow him to start. Qualifying, schmalifying…

After Farina had walked the first heat, the other half of the field came to the grid for the second, with Fangio and Ascari at the front, and Sommer necessarily at the back. There were 15 cars altogether, and when the flag went down 14 of them rushed away towards Copse.

No moment ever better summed up the BRM V16. There it sat, transmission broken, bellowing in impotent rage as Sommer vainly stirred the gear lever around, hoping that some drive could be found somewhere. The mechanics, dead on their feet, pushed the car off the track.

In attitude and style and speed, Sommer was very much the Gilles Villeneuve of his time, and this public embarrassment – in which he was blameless – was mortifying for him. Even so, he expressed interest in driving the BRM again, but sadly it was never to be, for he – another devotee of the cloth helmet – was killed at Cadours only two weeks later, when his Cooper overturned.

Mays found the crowd's response to the Silverstone debacle 'hurtful. There was a BRM Supporters Club,' he said, 'and the members had put a lot of money in it. But when the car was pushed back into the paddock, some people very impolitely threw pennies in the seat. Really rather disgusting. If they'd only known what we'd gone through to get that car there…'

Well, yes, but then they had travelled in the hope of seeing the BRM at last *do* something. And as they queued, radiators boiling, through the long evening hours, they had occasion to reflect upon that. Even in 1950, hype had its price.

In an editorial later in the year, *The Motor* put it rather more elegantly: 'There remain barely six months before next year's racing season, and all at BRM must remember that hope deferred makes the heart sick.'

Amen. Fortunately for British motor racing, Tony Vandervell, initially a keen supporter of the BRM project, was soon to dissociate himself from it, to make Formula 1 plans of his own.

# TONY BROOKS

# The unknown genius

AT THE GOODWOOD FESTIVAL OF SPEED BALL in 1998, Chris Mears, the wife of four-time Indianapolis 500 winner Rick, was seated at dinner next to Tony Brooks. By the end of the evening, she was aware that Brooks was a former Grand Prix driver, but this most self-effacing of men had told her little of his career. She wanted to know more, and spoke to Mario Andretti.

'That guy,' said Mario, 'was the best of the best of the best…'

Brooks himself would not agree. Like all his contemporaries, he revered Fangio, but after the great man's retirement (effectively at the end of 1957), he, like everyone else, put Moss in a category of his own. 'There was Stirling,' he said, 'and then the rest of us.'

Undeniably, Moss *was* the greatest of the late 1950s and early 1960s, but in speaking of 'the rest of us', Brooks does himself less than justice: if Stirling was pre-eminent in that period, so, equally certainly, Tony was next in line, well clear of such as Mike Hawthorn and Peter Collins, both of whom were great only when the mood took them.

It may be that the driving of a Formula 1 car, at a place like Spa-Francorchamps or the Nürburgring, never came easier to any man. Physically slight, Brooks was always a fingertip driver, appearing merely to suggest to his car where it might go next, rather than forcing his will upon it, in the manner of a Hawthorn or Mansell. To lap Spa consistently at well over 130mph, in a front-engined car on skinny tyres, brought no sweat to his brow. He was, in every sense, a 'natural'.

His arrival on the Grand Prix scene was, to say the least, unusual. For three years, from 1952, he was a successful club racer, but he had no thoughts of making a full-time profession of it, even after joining the Aston Martin sports car team in 1955. At 23, he was studying at Manchester University to become a dentist, and looming on the horizon were his Finals.

In October came a call from Connaught, a small, perennially hard-up, Formula 1 team of the time. 'They were doing the Syracuse Grand Prix, they said, and would I like to drive one of the cars? Frankly, they couldn't find anyone else and they were scraping the bottom of the barrel. I had never so much as sat in a Formula 1 car before, but I rather absent-mindedly said yes, and put the phone down.'

Perhaps it was fortunate for Brooks that he was preoccupied with his exams. On the flight to Sicily he worked on his books, and didn't give a lot of thought to the race.

Favourites at Syracuse were three factory Maserati 250Fs, driven by Luigi Musso, Harry Schell and Luigi Villoresi. They had been way quickest on the first day, and it is some indication of Brooks's natural genius that he was soon lapping as fast as they, in a car which handled well, but was short of power.

'It wasn't terribly reliable, either,' Tony said. 'That old Alta engine had been developed to its limit, and the team's finishing record was awful. "Don't do too much practice," they said, because there were no spare engines, and they were terrified of not getting the starting money. Quite understandable, but it didn't really help me! When the Grand Prix started, I'd done no more than 12 or 15 laps.'

By the end of it, he had won his first Formula 1 race. After playing himself in, he took the lead from Musso on lap 10, and was never troubled again. 'I was very pleased at the time, but it didn't really sink in. Quite honestly, all I could think about was my exams! I remember swotting on the plane all the way back, too.' A self-effacing man, as I said.

After a wasted season with BRM, Brooks signed as number two to Moss in the Vanwall team for 1957, with Stuart Lewis-Evans as the third driver. Tony had no outright wins that year, but he did share victory with Moss in the British Grand Prix.

A month before, he had been injured at Le Mans, and was by no means fit by the time Aintree came around. 'I didn't break anything in the shunt, but I had very severe abrasions. There was a hole in the side of my thigh, and I could literally have put my fist into it.'

The day before practice began, Brooks was still in hospital, but he reported for duty on time, and remarkably qualified third, behind Moss and the Maserati of Jean Behra.

'I had no problem in going quickly, but I couldn't sustain it for long because I was weak after that time in hospital. In those days, of course, drivers could take over other team cars if their own had retired, and it was agreed that I'd keep going as quickly as I could, and that if Stirling had trouble he would take over my car.'

In the event, that is precisely what happened. After building up a good lead, Moss retired, took over Brooks's fifth-placed car, and put in a fabled drive to come through the field and win.

The Vanwall, according to both Stirling and Tony, was unquestionably a great car, but not an easy one to love. 'Actually, Tony Vandervell thought his cars were a lot better than they were,' Brooks said. 'The Vanwall was quite a difficult car to drive, in that you couldn't chuck it into a corner, like, say, a Maserati 250F, and steer it on the throttle. You had to be very precise with it, and the gearbox was *terrible...*'

Only at the Nürburgring were the Vanwalls off the pace through the 1957 season. Brooks, although fastest of the team's three drivers in qualifying, was 10 seconds away from Fangio, and in the race became ill, almost 'seasick' as his car struggled to cope with the bumps.

This was the Grand Prix that went into legend, of course, as Fangio's greatest, the race in which, after stopping for fuel and tyres, he made up the best part of a minute on the Ferraris of

Hawthorn and Collins, in the process lapping eight seconds faster than his own pole position time. 'Une course d'anthologie,' was how the French press described it, and so it was, but a year on Brooks was virtually to duplicate it, and his drive, the best of his life, has never received due tribute.

It was Vanwall versus Ferrari in 1958, but only Moss and Hawthorn were truly contesting the World Championship, for although Brooks was right there on pace (taking pole position – by a clear second – at Monte Carlo, for example), by the beginning of August there were only eight points against his name, these scored at Spa, where he won a Grand Prix 'on his own' for the first time. Yes, it was eight points for a victory back then, only a couple more than for second. Never did seem right.

'I particularly loved Spa. I'd been there twice before with the Aston Martin, and had won both times. It seemed to me the essence of a true Grand Prix circuit, very quick and calling for great precision, with no margin for error at all.

'Stirling made one of his lightning starts, intent on leading all the way, and I've always believed that that day he was out to beat me as much as the Ferraris. I'd been to public school, where one learned that "the team was the thing" and there was no way I was going to try and pass Stirling even if I might hustle him a bit. But I'm not sure he believed that, and he tore away, got as far as Stavelot and missed a gear!'

Harmony was generally the way of it in the Vanwall team, although Brooks admits to being sometimes mildly irked by the demands of Moss, the team leader. 'I was never allowed as much practice as I wanted, because if I went quicker than Stirling they'd have to let him go out again, and all that did was to wear out the cars. And then he might want my chassis and his engine, or vice versa, which meant more work for the mechanics, so for David Yorke, the team manager, it made sense for them to keep this number two a few tenths slower. Stirling always made sure he had the best car, and if he thought he hadn't, he'd mix it! That said, we were always the best of friends, and still are.'

The situation at Ferrari was rather less clear-cut. Enzo's three full-time Grand Prix drivers for 1958 were Hawthorn, Collins and Luigi Musso, and many have said that, if anything, the friendship between Mike and Peter was detrimental to the team's competitiveness. 'They were such close mates,' Roy Salvadori said, 'that they really didn't care which of them won. That may sound hard to believe in today's world, but it was true. And I don't think it was necessarily good for the impetus of the team.'

Phil Hill, on Ferrari's sports car payroll at the time, was fond of both Hawthorn and Collins, but he was always wise to them. 'They gave Musso a tough time; they ripped him up one side, and down the other, never missed a chance to belittle him. It wasn't that long after the war, of course, and they were still on that "Brits-hate-the-Eyeties" sort of thing. I felt kind of sorry for Musso; he was very much on his own.

'To some degree, it was all a game for Mike and Peter. They hated Le Mans, for example, and in 1958 there was a suggestion that, between them, they deliberately wrecked their car's clutch so they could go home early. Not that Hawthorn would have had to agree to that, mind you – I mean, he did it to a clutch automatically!

'Anyway, the story got out, and Peter was punished by Ferrari. Made to drive in the Formula 2 race at Reims, instead of the Grand Prix. The Old Man came around in the end, and let him race the Formula 1 car, too, but there's no doubt Peter felt under pressure around that time.'

At Reims Hawthorn gave the team its first victory of the season, but 10 laps into the race, Musso, giving chase, crashed at the flat-out right-hander after the pits, and was killed. 'I have won at Reims,' Ferrari said, 'but the price is too high: I have lost the only Italian driver of note.'

So he had. But for all his occasional sentimentality, the Old Man was a pragmatist before all else, and he was much soothed two weeks later, when his cars finished first and second at Silverstone, with Collins this time the leading driver. Peter may not have been a model of consistency, but when he was really on it, he was formidable; in the British Grand Prix he took the lead from the start, held off a predictably stout challenge from Moss, and, following Stirling's retirement, was never threatened.

43

To Germany, then, where Hawthorn took pole position, followed by Brooks, Moss and Collins. Appalling as they may have been at the Nürburgring the year before, the Vanwalls were pretty well sorted now. Problem was, as usual Brooks's practice laps had been restricted, and although his car was handling well with a light fuel load, he had run not so much as a single lap on full tanks. While Moss raced away in the early stages, therefore, Tony thought it prudent to sit back a while.

In the early laps Stirling shattered Fangio's supposedly unapproachable lap record of the year before, but the Vanwall's magneto failed on lap four, leaving the Ferraris in front, followed by Brooks.

'My car was diabolical on full tanks, and by the time it began to handle properly again, after four laps or so, the Ferraris were half a minute ahead. After another five laps, I was right with them.'

Five laps of the Nürburgring was a long way, but even so the magnitude of Tony's accomplishment – making up 32 seconds in a matter of 70 miles – can scarcely be over-praised. 'The Vanwall and Ferrari were pretty evenly matched that day. On handling, there wasn't much in it, on braking I was better than them – we had discs, whereas Ferrari were still using drums – and on horsepower, particularly at the top end, they had the edge on me.

'My problem was that, although I was quicker overall, the last part of the lap was that long, long, straight, and although I knew I could get by them, so also I knew that they could pass me again at that point. My only hope was to snatch the lead very early in the lap, and pull out so much that they'd be too far back to slipstream me at the end of it. And eventually, that worked out.'

At the beginning of lap 11, Brooks outbraked Hawthorn into the South Turn, and then swiftly got past Collins, who had led since the retirement of Moss. That done, he put everything into building the lead he needed to be out of reach on the straight.

'The tragedy was that Peter, trying to stay with me, overdid it and had his fatal accident. Obviously, I felt pretty bad about it at the time, although I didn't feel responsible or anything like that.'

Collins crashed at Pflanzgarten, turning into the uphill right-hander a little too fast, a little too wide, a little too late. The Ferrari went off the road, hit a bank and somersaulted, throwing the driver out against a tree. Eventually, he was flown by helicopter to a hospital in Bonn, but did not survive the journey.

Phil Hill, driving a Formula 2 Ferrari in the race that day, suspected that brake problems may have contributed to the accident. 'Where Peter bought it, I always thought that was a really hairy place. If you didn't get a certain amount of slowing down done before you went in there, it could really get hairy 100 yards up the road or so.

'We were using drums, of course, and I know that I was completely out of brakes by the end of the race – and my car was lighter than the Formula 1 cars. I think it's very possible that Peter just couldn't get the car slowed down enough. He may have been in handling problems, too: we were using those darn Houdaille shock-absorbers, and even though we doubled up on them, they went away so fast that it was pretty awful, really…'

Brooks knew nothing of this. 'I finally reached the straight at the end of the lap, then looked in my mirrors to see if the Ferraris were still in touch. As it was, there was no sign of Peter, and Mike was a long way behind. I assumed that Peter's car must have blown up, and my immediate reaction was one of great disappointment – for me, the Nürburgring was always the greatest circuit, and I was now really into the swing of things, and had been greatly enjoying our battle. It wasn't until much later on, after the prize-giving, that I discovered Peter had died before reaching hospital.'

Having seen Collins's car go over, seen a blur of his friend being thrown out, Hawthorn drove to his pit at the end of the lap, reporting that his clutch had failed, that he had anyway no inclination to continue. Although he was to finish the season for Ferrari – indeed win the World Championship – he decided almost immediately that he would retire as soon as it was over.

The loss of Collins was felt acutely throughout the racing world, not least in Maranello, for he had been one of that handful of drivers – like Nuvolari, like Gilles Villeneuve – for whom Enzo Ferrari developed a deep affection.

'It's true that Ferrari looked upon Peter as a kind of surrogate son,' said Louise, his widow, 'and it was the same with Laura – Mrs Ferrari, that is. They had lost their only son, Dino, in 1956, and they kind of adopted Peter.

'When I think of Ferrari now, it is with sadness. He always seemed like a very tragic character to me. As for Laura, there was something sinister about her, although she was kindly to me. She always wore black, very forbidding, and she and Ferrari went to the cemetery every day. I don't mean to sound hard, but it struck me as very theatrical somehow.

'The loss of their son certainly clouded them, and there seemed no end to it. Eventually, Peter went in to see Ferrari, and in effect told him to snap out of it. It made him angry that Ferrari wasn't using his authority to run the place the way he should have been, because he was spending so much time in this endless mourning.

'At the time people couldn't believe what Peter had done – that anyone would have the guts to say something like that to Ferrari. But he accepted it, and he was much lighter after that.'

Remarkably, only five weeks after her husband's death, Louise Collins attended a Grand Prix again. 'I never doubted that Ferrari truly was upset when Peter died, and if it seems odd that I went to Monza, it was because he begged me, and said he would go with me. In fact, I don't believe he had any intention of going. And he didn't!

'It was good, though, that he tricked me, because, although it wasn't a great weekend, it was important to see all my friends. When you lose someone, what's really difficult is to do the things you did before – but without them. You have to do it, though, because otherwise you can't wipe out the old picture.'

In Italy Brooks won again, with Hawthorn second, and Moss retiring. Three victories in 1958, then, and all of them at classic circuits: Spa-Francorchamps, the Nürburgring, Monza. Only Moss, with four, beat Tony's tally for the year, and yet both were beaten to the World Championship by Hawthorn, who won but once.

The matter was settled at Casablanca, where Stirling could

have done no more, winning the Moroccan Grand Prix, and taking the point then on offer for the fastest lap; in the closing stages, Hawthorn's new team-mate, Phil Hill, moved over, allowed him by for the six points he needed to take the title. Six years later, in Mexico City, Lorenzo Bandini would do exactly the same for John Surtees.

Moss has said that it was the loss of that particular championship which caused him, if not exactly to lose interest in the title, at least to put it into proper perspective. For one thing, World Champion or not, no one questioned that he was the best; for another, Stirling was one for whom the overriding priority was winning *races*, here, now, today. To drive primarily with points in mind was anathema to him.

At the end of 1958, Tony Vandervell, sick at heart after the death of third Vanwall driver Stuart Lewis-Evans at Casablanca, decided to disband his racing team. And while Moss signed to drive for Rob Walker, Brooks became the latest Englishman to go to Ferrari.

It was a difficult year in many ways. Cooper's 'rear-engine revolution' was under way with a vengeance, and Ferrari, still front-engined, were hard-pressed to keep up on all but the quick circuits. For all that, Brooks remembered the 1959 season well.

'It was a gorgeous car to drive, that Dino 246. Rather like a Maserati 250F in that you could drive it on the throttle through the corners. And its gearbox – after those two years with Vanwall – was a revelation.'

He won at Reims, as Hawthorn had done, and also at Avus, site of the German Grand Prix that year, and he went off to Sebring, for the last round of the World Championship, still in with a chance of winning, like Moss and Jack Brabham.

'Amazingly, we set the three best times in practice, but I had to start fourth, because a faster time was "found" for Harry Schell, who was in an old Cooper. Actually, he'd taken a short cut on the circuit...

'On the first lap, I was hit by Taffy von Trips, my team-mate, in the rear wheel, and a change in my philosophy may well have cost me the title.'

Brooks, like all the Grand Prix drivers of the time, literally never discussed safety. 'The attitude was that the spectators had to be protected at all costs, and that was it. The big attraction was driving a racing car on closed roads, and we accepted that the name of the game was keeping the car on the island. If you went off, you were in the lap of the gods. You might get away with it, you might not. Nobody will persuade me that there isn't more of a challenge to the driver if he knows he might hurt himself if he goes off the road.'

For all that, Brooks did not believe in adding to the dangers of his profession. 'My philosophy changed somewhat when I was thrown out of the wretched BRM at Silverstone in 1956, and completely after the Aston flipped at Le Mans the year after. In both cases, there was something wrong with the car, and I knew it. Eventually I made a firm mental decision never to try to compensate for a car's mechanical deficiencies: if something wasn't working properly, too bad.

'I always felt that it was morally wrong to take unnecessary risks with one's life because I believe that life is a gift from God. I don't want to get theological about it, and thousands will disagree, but that's my view: I felt I had a moral responsibility to take reasonable care of my life.

'After von Trips had run into me at Sebring, my natural inclination was to press on. Believe me, that would have been the easiest thing to do, but I made myself come in to have the car checked over. I lost half a lap doing that, and still finished third. As it turned out, Moss retired that day, and Brabham ran out of fuel near the end, so probably my coming in cost me the World Championship. Still, in my own mind, I think I did the right thing.'

Brooks was never to win another Grand Prix. He admits he never had the dedication of a Moss, and by the end of 1959 was already looking to a life beyond motor racing. To that end he bought a garage in Weybridge, Surrey, and decided, in the interests of building up his new business, it would make more sense to drive for a British team. Therefore, much to Enzo's regret, he left Ferrari, and drove outdated Coopers for the British Racing Partnership in 1960, outclassed BRMs the following year. Third in his last race, at Watkins Glen in 1961, he announced his retirement.

Today Moss says that if he were running a Grand Prix team, and could have any two drivers from history in his cars, they would be Jimmy Clark and Tony Brooks. 'I suppose that my choice of Tony would be a surprise to some people, but to my mind he is the greatest "unknown" racing driver there has ever been – I say "unknown", because he's such a modest man that he never became a celebrity, as such. But as a driver, boy, he was top drawer.'

# PHIL HILL

# American in Maranello

A LETTER FROM DAN GURNEY after the Goodwood revival meeting in the autumn of 1998. 'The weekend,' Dan wrote, 'was moving on so many levels. I felt the ghosts of yesterday hovering above the starting grid, so many ambitious and talented young men … so long ago.'

Somehow one doesn't expect lyricism from a racing driver, even one of Gurney's generation. To be kissed by genius – which he was – and to be a gentle man is to be blessed indeed. Dan was the only driver Jim Clark feared, and to this day has not an enemy in the sport.

When I think of Gurney, in the same beat I think of Phil Hill. Contemporaries, friends, both synonymous with California, one-time Ferrari team-mates. One won the World Championship, and the other should have done. Chat with one, and the name of the other will come up before long.

Hill and Gurney both entered Enzo's employ after making their names with Ferraris in American sports car racing, but they overlapped at Maranello only for a single season, 1959, after which Dan left for BRM. Phil was a Ferrari driver for the long haul. I could listen to either man all day long.

Black humour was an inevitable part of racing in the 1950s and 1960s. I have observed it in virtually every driver of the

50

period to whom I have spoken. 'Just like in the medical profession,' Innes Ireland used to say. 'It wasn't a matter of being disrespectful, but we used it as a kind of defence mechanism. It didn't do to dwell on things too much, because if you did you'd soon reach a point where you couldn't get in a car again. It used to happen pretty frequently, after all.'

It did. Hill began driving sports cars for the Ferrari factory in 1955, graduated to the Formula 1 team late in 1958, and left at the end of 1962. In that time, Alberto Ascari, Eugenio Castellotti, Alfonso de Portago, Luigi Musso, Peter Collins and Wolfgang von Trips all lost their lives in Enzo's cars, yet somehow, in the course of a remarkable career, Hill never once hurt himself.

'Sometimes it's difficult to figure out how or why,' he shrugged. 'One thing I was always careful about was not to get embroiled in the whole Ferrari thing – the Old Man loved to pit his drivers against each other, you know, and that accounted for a lot of them.

'Don't ask me why, but we never even *discussed* safety back then. At Monza, for example, we used the banked section of the track, as well, and it was very fast, and rough as hell. But we just didn't contemplate suspension failures, or whatever, mainly because it was unthinkable! I mean, what were you going to do about it if you thought about it?

'We didn't want to talk about safety, I guess, because if you went on about it too much, someone would start legislating, and then you wouldn't be able to have your precious racing any more. Even inside the sport, we never talked about it. There was already enough of that – people on the outside posing these questions: "How can you do this? Your friends are dying, and yet still you go out and do this…" It was little different from wartime, where you just had to do it – and you wanted to do it.'

Hill concedes that to have come through an era like his without ever being hurt owes much to luck. In his early days, before coming to Europe, he says the thought never entered his head. 'When it did, I developed an in-built caution factor, and that was one big difference between Trips and myself.

'There was something you had to have going for you in those

days, which was a part of your brain sorting out where it was safe to mess around, and where it wasn't. I was highly selective about where I was going to go off. For example, I was the master of spinning at the Thillois corner at Reims, but if it had been lined with trees, I never would have made a mistake there! And, of course, you didn't mess around at a place like Spa – although, for some reason, I was not intimidated by Spa, whereas some people were.'

Like Gurney, Hill is an immensely civilised man, and a cultured one, too; I doubt that anyone more intelligent ever climbed into a racing car. Unusually articulate, by any standards, it is no surprise he writes better of this sport than any driver who ever lived. Of working at Maranello: 'When you come to see that the emperor has no clothes, you are more comfortable with your own nakedness...'

His powers of recall are astonishing, delivery of one-liners reminiscent of Bob Newhart. On Ferrari again: 'La Scala may have lost a great star when Ferrari went into cars...'

Milan's celebrated opera house meant a lot to Hill in his days of living in Italy, for classical music has been one of the enduring loves of his life. But, as Ferrari's number one driver, the World Champion of 1961, was he not mobbed on these outings to hear Joan Sutherland, pestered for autographs all the time?

He said it was never a problem. 'Apart from Stirling Moss, drivers weren't widely recognised back then – there was hardly any Grand Prix racing on TV, remember. And ... probably it didn't hurt that I arrived in a Peugeot!

'It was a different time,' he smiled. 'Just a different time. I read somewhere that Michael Schumacher is making $30 million or whatever from Ferrari – and still they gave him a Maranello coupé as a reward for winning something or other! I didn't even have the *use* of a Ferrari road car. Mind you, I'm not sure I'd have wanted it; they were not the most sanitary things back then, especially in traffic. No, when I was there, my road cars were always Peugeots.'

In the mind of the enthusiast, at least, that period of Ferrari history, perilous as it was, has an irresistible romance. The cars of the time dripped with charisma, yet few originals remain, thanks to the Old Man's policy of either breaking up last year's cars, or modifying them into next year's.

In 1961 Ferrari dominated with the 156 'shark-nose' cars, and Hill has always regretted that none survives today. This was, after all, the car which took him to the World Championship.

Years later, when rock musician Chris Rea was working on a movie about his childhood hero, von Trips, he commissioned the building of a replica 'shark-nose', and I happened to be on the spot at Goodwood when Phil laid eyes on it for the first time. 'Well, I'll be darned…' he murmured, and then he stood silently, stunned by this apparition of a time gone by.

When Hill won the World Championship at Monza, and von Trips died, much was made in the press of their close friendship, and Phil went along with it because, he says now, it would have been churlish to do otherwise. 'We got along fine, but we were very different types. Trips was much more extrovert than me, for one thing, and he knew *nothing* about cars, except how to drive them – and at Ferrari they really liked that, because they didn't think it was the driver's place to do anything else!

'All year long, it was him or me for the championship, and if we'd been really close, it would have been a hell of a lot harder to be sufficiently competitive with him. Face it, it's not a normal situation race drivers are in: you try to beat the other guys on the circuit all day, and then at night you're supposed to forget all that.'

To go to a colleague's funeral was not an unusual event for the Grand Prix driver of the time, but memories of the days following von Trips's death linger with Hill yet.

'You can't imagine what it was like. I mean, the Vatican pitched in, like always when anyone got killed in a Ferrari, and it seemed like everyone in the damn country was milling around at the factory, and there's Ferrari, with three days' beard growth, and wearing a bathrobe and everything, to appear … distraught, I guess. He'd been through it dozens of times.'

Von Trips's funeral Hill not surprisingly remembers as a day of unremitting gloom, but the black humour surfaces as he recalls the build-up and the aftermath. Laura – Mrs Enzo

Ferrari – had unaccountably taken a sudden interest in racing at the time, travelling to most of the races, a practice long since abandoned by her husband. She was, by Phil's account, the bane of the drivers' lives. The source, too, of one of his best stories.

'Ferrari himself didn't go to the funeral – no, he sent the old lady! I went up with Richie Ginther, and I have to admit that it was something I dreaded. For all the Germans, Trips was going to be the new World Champion, and I had to go as this terrible disappointment...'

Hill and Ginther did not travel to Cologne by private jet. They drove up to Milan, where they caught a train.

'When we got there, we met up with Amerigo Manicardi, who was in charge of sales, worldwide. Good guy, about the best guy in the whole place. He'd been deputed to take Mrs Ferrari up there, keep her out of trouble.

'After the funeral, all of a sudden Mrs Ferrari said, "Pheeleel, are you going back now?" She'd decided she didn't like Manicardi – because he didn't like her! – and maybe Richie and I would let her go back with us. "Where are you going?" she said.

'I panicked – I said, "We're going to ... Stockholm!" She said, "What a shame," and meanwhile Manicardi's standing behind her, winking and everything. I mean, that was the way you treated her.

'Well, Richie and I took this endless train trip back down to Milano, got in the car, and we're bombing down the Autostrada del Sole. This was in my Peugeot 404, which had very high backs to the seats, and all of a sudden Richie says, "Duck! Duck! It's the old lady!" And we're supposed to be in Stockholm...

'The next day we get to the factory, and we see Manicardi. I said, "Christ, Richie saw you at the last second! I didn't even see you – I just ducked..." And Manicardi told us that Mrs Ferrari had said, "Manicardi! Non e la macchina di Pheeleel?" And Manicardi said, "I don't know – there's nobody in it!" And she said, "Oh..." That was what it was like, living with Mrs Ferrari.'

First in sports cars, then in Formula 1, Hill drove for the Old

Man for an unusually long time. He thinks of him still as a dominating force in his life, a *power*, but admits that as the years have passed he tends to remember him more benevolently than at one time seemed possible. They did not part amicably.

If he found him sometimes intimidating, Phil was always wise to Ferrari. 'It kind of amuses me that people talk about rent-a-drivers in Formula 1 as if they were some recent phenomenon. Ferrari was on to that pretty quickly, let me tell you.

'When I first met "Fon" de Portago in early 1954, he knew absolutely nothing about race cars. *Nothing*. Never even driven anything with a manual shift.

'He was also ahead of his time, in that he was the first guy I ever met who deliberately ... dressed down, let's say. He wore this scruffy leather jacket, shaved about every four days, looked like he had nothing. Then I saw his card one day, with his address on Avenue Foch in Paris, and that's when I realised you could be fooled by appearances.

'Anyway, Portago was a natural athlete, and he learned to drive – and he got into Formula 1 before I did! Ferrari was working on a shoestring in those days, so if you had something other than driving ability to offer, it could serve you well.

'The first time I ever went to the Nürburgring, Portago said he'd take me round in a road car. He had a certain reputation, you know, and I wasn't keen, but eventually I said OK. We got in this Mercedes sedan, set off – and he spun the thing at the Foxhole! "OK, stop right here," I said. "I'm getting out." How did I get back to the pits? I walked. Later I went round with Fangio, also in a Mercedes, and that was just total perfection. Nothing flashy, nothing dangerous – and much faster than Portago.'

After winning for Chaparral the 1967 BOAC 500 at Brands Hatch, Hill went back to Santa Monica, and never raced again. Typically, there was no formal announcement that he had retired; at 40, he had simply decided that enough was enough.

Unlike some, Phil has never lost his love of motor racing, but he admits that the driving tactics of today leave him bemused. 'They feel they can get away with it, I guess. That's the only possible explanation. If guys drove like that in my time, they usually sorted themselves out pretty quickly. Back then it was just unthinkable, really, to touch another car, because of the potential consequences. I know it sounds corny, but those were the facts. Over the long term, you just couldn't do it, and get away with it.'

There are those who suggest that, whatever the era, the work of the racing driver never fundamentally changes, and in the sense that it always entails beating the rest, getting a car around a circuit faster than anyone else, that holds true. In other respects, though, it seems to me that the demands on a driver are very different now.

At Spa in 1998 Martin Brundle drove some demonstration laps in a 1955 Mercedes-Benz W196. Drove them pretty quickly, too. Afterwards, exhilarated by the experience, he allowed that it had given him pause for thought.

'What's never changed about Grand Prix racing,' Brundle said, 'is that the limit is the limit is the limit. In other respects, though, I'm starting to understand there are huge differences in the job of the driver from one era to another. Physically, I found the car easy to drive, because the g-forces are low, but mentally it was incredibly hard.

'When you're up around 150, going through fast corners, you begin to think about the absence of seat-belts, roll-over bars, and the like. In a modern car, if you're going to crash, you make sure you do certain things beforehand, but in this case I really had no idea what I'd do.

'All right, in the back of a current driver's mind is the acceptance that he might get hurt doing this, but then it must have been right at the front of your mind, I'd have thought.'

Stirling Moss, who raced the car in its heyday, reckoned otherwise. 'No, it wasn't like that. Racing was dangerous, and you knew that when you went into it. It had never been safe – and it never crossed your mind that it ever could be. So you had two choices: do it, or don't.'

Hill agrees that that was very much the way of it. 'Whatever else, no one could be accused back then of doing it for the money! For one thing, there wasn't any; for another, you'd have had to be crazy to do it unless it was something you *had* to do.'

He told me of something he witnessed in early 1954, when he was 26 years old, and on the brink of his international career. It occurred during the Buenos Aires 1000 Kms, and the track used for the event involved part of the *autodromo*, and some of the dual-carriageway outside.

Hill's Ferrari had retired early, and he hitched a lift on the back of a policeman's scooter. As they neared the *autodromo*, an Aston Martin DB3, driven by expatriate Englishman Eric Forrest-Greene, spun as it came out on to the *autopista*. Initially, Hill said, it looked harmless enough, but then the car hit a kerb, and flipped over into a ditch.

'I was digging this policeman in the ribs to get him to go faster, but finally I threw him and the scooter away, and ran the last 10 yards – it was quicker. As I got towards the car, there was this tremendous "Whump!" and it just exploded. There was burning fuel everywhere, including in the ditch. And somehow Forrest-Greene got himself out of the cockpit, crawled out of the ditch, climbed the bank, and emerged on the road, staggering towards me. He was burning from head to foot. They snuffed out the fire with blankets and stuff, but it was hopeless, of course. I've never forgotten it. There is just nothing like fire.'

Phil self-deprecatingly ascribes his survival in a hazardous time to the fact that he wasn't as brave as some, this despite being always at his absolute best on circuits like Spa-Francorchamps and the Nürburgring, places where, as he says, 'You couldn't afford to mess about.'

I confess, though, that I shivered as he talked of that day in Buenos Aires. And later I considered that Hill, as a young man on the brink, had witnessed something as appalling as this, seen how easily it could happen to you, yet never wavered in his desire – his need – to race cars.

Not long afterwards, someone in the paddock, seeking to excuse a driver's behaviour on the track, said to me, 'Well, of course you have to bear in mind that the pressures are so much greater today…' Ah.

# 1967

# The last simple year

Ah, 1967, THE YEAR of my 21st birthday, the year of moving to London with my new Mini-Cooper S. The world was young, and anything was possible, and all the clichés of youth made sense. Everything mattered, and nothing did.

I wasn't yet working in motor racing, but always at the back of my mind was the belief that one day I would. It was a blissful time, all in all, but I find it strange, looking back, that although I went to Le Mans in June, I did not venture to a single foreign Grand Prix. Perhaps it was that the calendar included so many non-championship events in England; by the end of April I had already seen three Formula 1 races.

For me 1967 was somehow the last simple year in Grand Prix racing, when the cars had a purity of line, uncluttered by wings and other aerodynamic devices, to say nothing of the dog's dinner paint jobs which would come with the advent of commercial sponsorship. A Lotus was still green with a yellow stripe, a Ferrari scarlet with a yellow and black badge. Whatever, I wonder, would Enzo have made of Tic-Tac Mints?

That said, he might have been glad of the money. It was not until 1970 that Fiat began sending big cheques to Maranello, and the Old Man meant it when he said that the building of road cars was a necessary evil to finance his racing. You drove for him not because you were looking to get rich, but because he was Ferrari. For 1967 Chris Amon's contract was worth $1,000 a month, plus 50 per cent of whatever money he won.

In addition to Formula 1, Ferrari, unlike the other constructors, had a World Championship sports car programme to fund, and budgets were carefully apportioned. In fact, the team missed the opening Grand Prix of the year, at Kyalami, concentrating instead on the forthcoming Daytona 24 Hours.

Today's World Championship is all very orderly, in the sense that teams nominate their two drivers before the start of the season, and there essentially they stay. But it wasn't that way in 1967. Enzo Ferrari operated as he had always done, signing several drivers (to take care of the long-distance sports car races), and assigning them a Formula 1 car as the mood took him.

'The Old Man,' Phil Hill has observed, 'always liked that situation – more drivers than cars. You knew if you didn't deliver, someone else might be in it at the next race. Brutal, really.'

For 1967 Ferrari had Lorenzo Bandini, Lodovico Scarfiotti and Mike Parkes under contract, as well as Amon, and it was obvious – even though the team sometimes ran three cars – that there could not be regular Formula 1 drives for all of them. 'Not a nice situation,' commented Amon, 'because of the uncertainty. However, it was fairly obvious that Bandini was always going to get a car, and that the Old Man wanted to use me more than Scarfiotti or Parkes; he never thought of "Lulu" as a Grand Prix driver – and he didn't really want Mike to race at all, because he was so valuable as an engineer.'

Elsewhere, the situation was rather clearer. At Lotus Jim Clark was joined by Graham Hill, who had left BRM after seven years, Mike Spence taking his place, alongside Jackie Stewart. Brabham was unchanged, with *Le Patron* and Denny Hulme, and Pedro Rodriguez came in to partner Jochen Rindt in the Cooper-Maserati team, John Surtees having left to drive the lone Honda. Richie Ginther was number two to Dan Gurney at Eagle, and Bruce McLaren was the sole driver in the fledgling team bearing his name.

Then there were the privateers, still a commonplace in the Formula 1 of the day. Tim Parnell had a semi-works BRM for either Piers Courage or Chris Irwin, Bob Anderson continued as the owner/driver of an ageing Brabham, and there were further Cooper-Maseratis for Jo Siffert (Rob Walker), Jo Bonnier and future team owner Guy Ligier. By no means were all these cars to materialise at every race; back then financial considerations obliged you occasionally to skip an event, and when you did, nobody gave you a hard time.

Compared with today it was all rather minimalist. To look after two cars, Gurney's Eagle team, for example, employed just five mechanics, one of whom was Jo Ramirez, now Team Co-ordinator at McLaren, and something of a legendary figure in the paddock. Working at Cooper, meanwhile, was another young mechanic, who would later employ Ramirez: one Ron Dennis.

So to the start of the season. While the Ferrari drivers put endless testing miles on the P4 sports cars, most of their colleagues went off to South Africa. After three days of practice, the last of them on New Year's Eve, the race was run on Monday 2 January, and, given that only two months had passed since the final Grand Prix of 1966, it was not surprising that few new cars were on hand. Indeed, the Kyalami grid was something of a ragbag, the 18 starters including four local drivers.

One of their number, though, was John Love, a Rhodesian veteran of considerable ability, and he amazed everyone by qualifying his own Cooper (with elderly 2.7-litre, four-cylinder, Climax engine) fifth, ahead of such as Surtees, Rindt, Stewart and Gurney. On race day he would do better yet.

Brabham, in the car which had taken him to his third World Championship the year before, took pole position, with team-mate Hulme next up, and then the Lotus of Clark.

It was an impatient time for Lotus, this. On the horizon was a new car, the 49, and a new engine, the Ford-Cosworth DFV, but for now Clark and Graham Hill were saddled with BRM H16 motors. One might have thought that memories of the V16 would have persuaded BRM that maybe 16 cylinders were a few too many, but no, here was another doom-laden project, along similar lines: too heavy, too complex, too unreliable.

Already the H16 had had its only day in the sun, powering the Lotus 43 to one of Clark's very few inherited victories, at Watkins Glen the previous autumn. But at least Jimmy and Graham had the DFV to look forward to; BRM drivers Stewart and Spence were stuck with the lump.

All four of them retired that day, and the race was largely dominated by Hulme, who led from the start until 20 laps from the end, when his brakes began to disappear. No car-to-pit radios in those days, of course, so Denny dashed in, screamed that he needed brake fluid, and dashed out again, putting another lap on the board while the Brabham mechanics got themselves ready.

Next time round he came in once more, but the stop took a minute and a half – and, worse, made no difference. Completely brakeless, Hulme could only canter the last 20 laps, but was still to finish fourth. This was a high attrition day.

It was Love, remarkably, who took over the lead. For much of the race he had fought with Gurney's Eagle-Climax, but Dan, too, was out by now, and the old Cooper found itself 20 seconds up on the factory car of Rodriguez, which had lost second gear.

For a dozen laps Love extended his lead, but with six left came in for fuel. He had equipped his 'Tasman spec' car with an extra tank for this long race, but the auxiliary pump would not pick up the last three or four gallons. By the time he rejoined, Rodriguez was half a minute up the road, and thus they finished, the spectators mortified, the blushes of the establishment spared. Pedro's first Grand Prix win was to be Cooper's last.

Kyalami done, there was a four-month wait for Monaco, but in the interval several lesser races were run, and these the teams used to try their 1967 cars. Far and away the best entry was for the Race of Champions, run at an arctic Brands Hatch on 12 March. Gurney's new Eagle, with Weslake V12 engine, won on its début, beating Lorenzo Bandini in the latest Ferrari 312 by less than half a second.

Then, at Oulton Park, came the Spring Cup, this assuredly the only 'charity event' in the entire history of Formula 1. In fact, it was for a cause understandably close to the drivers' hearts, all the proceeds going to the newly established Grand Prix Medical Service, whose fully equipped unit – literally a hospital on wheels – was on display. The plan was to take it to all the European circuits, where on-site medical and rescue services were invariably lamentable. A grotesque reminder was but a month away.

Brabham narrowly won the race, from Hulme, and the third round of this English mini-series, the International Trophy at Silverstone, went to Mike Parkes, whose lone Ferrari led all the way, beating Brabham comprehensively.

There were not anything like full fields at any of these events, however, one notable absentee on every occasion being Clark, who was spending a year in Parisian tax exile, and, as such, was allowed but one short visit to the UK, this obviously to be for the British Grand Prix.

Jimmy's move was hardly a surprise, given the punitive income tax regime of Harold Wilson's Britain; Stewart, indeed, was in the process of going a step further, buying a house in Switzerland, and putting down roots there. 'It had occurred to me,' Jackie said, 'that, nine weekends out of ten, I was risking my life for the Chancellor of the Exchequer.'

As Monte Carlo approached, the Lotus 49 was still not ready to race, although Hill had tried it at Snetterton – and been astonished by the power of the DFV – before flying off to join Clark for testing at Indianapolis.

Graham, Jimmy and Colin Chapman arrived in Monaco on Thursday morning, having left 'The World Capitol Of Auto Racing' (a claim which never ceased to madden Chapman) the previous afternoon. In the Principality Lotus were to race a pair of old 33s, each with 2-litre V8 engines (Clark's a Climax, Hill's a BRM), and they were not without hopes, for a nimble car, even one short of power, was worth something here.

Twelve months earlier, in the first year of the 3-litre Formula 1, Stewart had won comfortably in a 2-litre BRM, and the team popped one in the transporter this time, too, together with the

H16s. Jackie tried both in the opening session, set fastest time in the smaller car, and opted to stick with it. Ultimately, though, neither he nor Clark could match the fastest of the 3-litre cars, Brabham taking pole position, ahead of Bandini, Surtees and Hulme.

The bare facts of the race, on 7 May, are that Brabham blew up immediately, that Stewart led, then retired, that Clark – who somehow never won here – spun off when a shock absorber broke, that Amon took a fine third on his Ferrari début, that Hill – ever the man for Monaco – finished second, that Hulme superbly won his first Grand Prix.

'Guess I wasn't too famous at that time,' Denny remembered. 'Louis Chiron was the Race Director, and as he takes me over to meet Rainier and Grace, he leans over. "What's your name?" he says … Mind you, considering everything else that was going on just then, maybe it wasn't surprising.'

Half an hour earlier, Bandini, chasing Hulme, had come to grief at the chicane, then a left–right flick, taken at more than 100mph. After clipping the chicane itself, the Ferrari ran wide at the exit, and hit the straw bales which stood between the track and the harbour, into which both Alberto Ascari and Paul Hawkins had in earlier years plummeted without hurt.

Bandini's car, though, did not go through the bales, but skimmed the top of them, then struck a marine bollard, and somersaulted back on to the track. In the impact a fuel pipe was severed, and at once the Ferrari was engulfed in fire.

'Nothing got a car upside down as quickly as straw bales,' said Hulme. 'Lorenzo was horribly unlucky. One time during the race I got a bit tweaked coming out of the chicane, and hit the bales, but fortunately for me the car straightened itself out again.'

They didn't stop races in those days, for any reason, and the six surviving cars continued to circulate. At first it seemed that two cars had crashed, for the straw bales were also burning. Amon, running third, realised that his team-mate was involved, for he could see a gold wheel, and, knowing that Hulme and Bandini had been in front of him, wondered if they had had an accident together.

'Just for a second I thought, "Perhaps I'm *leading*", and then,

"Christ, if I am leading, what a hell of a way to win a race..."
The pit signals disappeared for a few laps, and then I saw I was
second, behind Denny. Then I got a puncture from the debris,
and came in for a long stop – the mechanics were in a trance, of
course.'

Amon had been past the fire several times, and it never
occurred to him that Bandini could still be in it. 'There didn't
seem to be much activity around there, so I assumed he'd got
out all right. It wasn't until after the race that I realised he
hadn't.'

A week later, in *The Observer*, Tony Brooks wrote a piece
entitled 'The Cruel Death of Lorenzo Bandini'. It had been
that, and more. 'Fire,' Brooks said, 'is the consuming dread of
the racing driver. To crash, to be killed outright, is one thing; to
be burned to the point of death is the supreme horror.'

A supreme horror, too, was that the rescue operation had
been so ineptly handled. The situation confronting the marshals
– a car upside down, on fire, with the driver trapped beneath –
was admittedly nightmarish, but had they been properly
equipped, there might have been some chance of saving
Bandini's life, at the very least of sparing him agony.

The marshals – one of whom had a pipe in his mouth – had
only ropes with which to right the car. None wore fireproof
clothing, and such extinguishers as they had were virtually
useless. Nearly five minutes went by before they managed to
put out the fire, turn the car over, and clumsily drag Bandini
from the cockpit.

As they carried him away, a TV helicopter hovered low over
the scene, its rotor blades fanning the fire into life again.
Unprotected, the marshals ran clear, dropping Bandini as they
did so.

Still the race went on, despite the fact that the accident had
occurred near the end, on the 82nd of 100 laps. There was thus
no means of getting an ambulance to the area, and eventually
the mortally injured driver was taken across the harbour on a
launch, thence by ambulance to the Princess Grace Clinic.

It was exactly the procedure followed, a year earlier, in the
making of *Grand Prix*, when Scott Stoddard crashed at the

chicane. Bandini, ironically, had been among the drivers involved in the filming of the scene.

Although somehow alive on arrival at the hospital, he was clearly not going to survive, with third-degree burns over 70% of his body, as well as serious internal injuries. 'Without the other injuries, maybe there was a remote chance he might have made it,' Amon said, 'but … it was probably better that he didn't.'

It was Amon's first season with Ferrari, and initially he had been wary of Bandini, suspecting that this proud Italian, team leader at last after years as number two to Surtees, might resent another foreign driver. 'In fact,' said Chris, 'he was utterly charming, one of the nicest people I ever met.'

Bandini, handsome and charismatic, had been a Ferrari driver for five years. He won the Austrian Grand Prix in 1964, and in Mexico the same year inadvertently resolved the World Championship in favour of his team-mate, Surtees, by running into one of his rivals, Hill.

At Christmas Graham responded by sending Lorenzo an LP of driving lessons! A more violent time it may have been; a more generous one it undoubtedly was.

By 1967 everything seemed in place for Bandini. At 30, he was Ferrari number one, and, partnering Amon in the P4, won both the Daytona 24 Hours and the Monza 1000 Kms. To complete the picture, his wife Margherita, the daughter of his former mentor, awaited the birth of their first child.

For all that, Amon remembered with disquiet his friend's mood a few days earlier. 'I was never a great one for believing in premonitions, but the Wednesday before the race made me wonder. We went off for lunch in the mountains, and on the drive back Lorenzo seemed very reflective, very aware of the simple things in life – you know, flowers, the fact that it was spring, and so on.

'On the way down, he saw an old man fishing by the side of the road, and he stopped, just to watch him quietly for a while. It's difficult to convey what I'm getting at, but it was almost as if he were savouring life, as if he knew something was going to happen. I'll never forget that day.'

Amon believed exhaustion was the reason for the accident. 'It was hard work, that car round there, and the race was much longer back then. I was deadbeat at the end, and I remember being freezing cold – because of dehydration – at about the time he went off. You run low on body fluids, and your concentration starts to go. Lorenzo was very fit, but I was probably stronger, and he'd been going quicker than I had, so he'd taken more out of himself. And it wasn't a big mistake he made – he was a few inches out, no more.'

Bandini was to die three days later. Throughout the sport there was revulsion at what had befallen him, amplified further when his wife, suffering from shock, was herself admitted to hospital, too late to save her child.

It was indeed a seminal accident in the history of motor racing, coming at a time when safety was a subject rarely even discussed. The morning after the race some of the drivers had a meeting with the organisers, and their mood was angry, not least because the hospital authorities had declined a request that burns specialists from East Grinstead be flown in to assist with Bandini's care. Ten years later, Professor Sidney Watkins would take charge of all medical matters in Formula 1; it was not a moment too soon.

Among the drivers' demands was that guardrail should replace straw bales at the exit of the chicane. Twelve months on, it was duly in place, and Johnny Servoz-Gavin hit it. 'He made the same mistake as Lorenzo,' said Amon, 'and he didn't even lose his lead.'

\* \* \*

A month later the clans solemnly gathered at Zandvoort, where some response to the Monaco disaster was in evidence: at every corner there were fire marshals in silver asbestos suits, the best protection then available.

New in Holland, too, situated at the trackside, was photo-electric equipment, which gave an instant read-out of each passing car's speed. Developed by Maurice Gatsonides, it provided motor racing with its first speed trap, but unfortunately the ex-rally driver did not leave it there, going on to produce the 'Gatso', for which we are all so grateful today.

In the paddock all attention was focused on the new Lotus 49, and its Ford-Cosworth DFV. It took me a little time to get used to that; although by then well accustomed to the name at Le Mans, and so on, the snob in me was appalled by the thought of 'Ford' in Grand Prix racing, alongside a name like 'Maserati'. Amazing how your perceptions change.

Amazing, too, in the context of today, was that Henry had given Keith Duckworth and his people a mere £100,000 to design and build engines for both Formula 1 and Formula 2. When the DFV became available, it sold for £7,500; by the mid-1990s each Renault V10 engine cost the *Régie* 30 times as much.

It may have lacked an exotic name plate, but the Ford-badged V8 immediately made obsolete every other engine in the business. Small and light, it gave around 400bhp, a figure approached only by the prodigiously heavy Honda V12. A Ferrari V12 of the time produced around 370, but sat in a weighty car, and the same was true of the Eagle-Weslake and the Cooper-Maserati. While Brabham's Repco V8 was worth little more than 340, on power-to-weight ratio it was probably closer to the Lotus than anything else, and on handling had a definite edge.

Initially, in fact, the 49 was anything but an easy car to drive. Clark, unable to visit England, had not so much as sat in it until he got to Zandvoort, and even he – while, like Hill, highly impressed with the horsepower – found the handling 'tricky…'

Part of the problem stemmed from a combination of the engine's characteristics and the fact that Lotus were using what was essentially a fixed-ratio gearbox from ZF; it wasn't that ratios could not be changed, more that it was a complex and hugely time-consuming task. Therefore the drivers invariably had to make do.

'The DFV is much more powerful than any Formula 1 engine I've driven before,' Jimmy commented. 'That's not a problem in itself – except that it comes in with a bang at 6,500 revs. All right, ideally we shouldn't be down at those revs, but sometimes – because we can't change gear ratios – it's unavoidable.'

Photographs of the Lotus 49 in its début season show it at all manner of angles, from terminal understeer to lurid full-lock slides. As Clark put it, 'Life can get a bit hectic at the exit of a corner when it suddenly hits on all eight...' Four hundred horsepower may not seem like much nowadays, but it has to be viewed against a backdrop of primitive tyres and zero downforce.

Firestone (contracted to Lotus, Ferrari, Cooper and Honda) and Goodyear (Brabham, Eagle, McLaren) were the tyre companies involved in 1967, and Clark felt that the Firestones, while perhaps providing a touch more ultimate grip, tended to exaggerate the handling shortcomings of the Lotus-Cosworth package. 'Unless you're on full power, getting the 49 out of line is liable to lead to trouble,' was his delightful throwaway line.

Goodyears, Jimmy reckoned, were more progressive – and this he came to know positively later in the season, at Mosport, for he tried a set in practice! Things were a little more laid back once upon a time.

Sundry 'new car' problems hampered Clark through practice, and he qualified only eighth, but Hill resoundingly took the pole, a clear half-second faster than Gurney. Graham then led the first 10 laps of the race – until his engine failed, at which point Brabham briefly took over, with Rindt's Cooper-Maserati in close attendance, until Mr James Clark, now becoming more familiar with his Lotus 49, dispensed with both in a matter of a lap, and proceeded to draw away.

Seventy-four laps remained at this point, and that, given what had befallen Hill's car, made for a nervy afternoon for Chapman and Duckworth, but although Clark's engine, too, was not in the peak of health through the closing stages, it held together, and Jimmy won comfortably.

When I think of him now, and the life which he led, he is always in a 49. It seems to me quite inappropriate that history tends to shackle his memory to the 1.5-litre era of 1961–65; with around 200 horsepower, these were hardly Grand Prix cars for the Gods, and the full majesty of a Clark was always best seen in a car which must be tamed. There has been none better than Jimmy.

It was one thing for a new car and engine to take pole position, but victory first time out caused every other team in the paddock to reassess its situation. Many remembered the début of the Mercedes-Benz W196 in 1954, when Fangio won at Reims, and certainly there were comparisons to be drawn, not least that now, as then, the best driver had also comfortably the fastest car.

Fortunately for the rest, though, the reliability of the 49 was to fall way short of Mercedes standards, and the World Championship was not necessarily a lost cause, particularly if you were a Brabham driver. Jack was second at Zandvoort, and Hulme third, after a race-long battle with Amon, who lapped his Ferrari team-mates, Parkes and Scarfiotti, a detail which did not escape Enzo.

For all that, the three of them were entered for the Belgian Grand Prix, two weeks later, having done the Le Mans 24 Hours in the interim. It was a full life for a Ferrari driver back then.

When we speak of Spa in 1967, of course we speak of the *old* Spa, the full 8.76 miles of public roads, embracing the glories and horrors of Burnenville, Malmédy, and the rest. Perhaps most daunting of all was the kink in the middle of the Masta straight, this something of a misnomer for two very definite corners, a left, then a right, approached downhill, and taken almost flat out.

Hulme was a little concerned about the siting of the guardrails there: 'They seem to have been placed so that if you hit them, they're going to deflect you into a house...'

Clark took pole position by three seconds, his average well over 150mph, but Gurney, always brilliant at this circuit, was on a high after winning Le Mans (with A. J. Foyt) for Ford, and qualified the Eagle-Weslake second, ahead of Hill. Fourth and fifth, with identical times, were Rindt and Amon.

From the start Clark led, but at the completion of the first lap Stewart, second, was more than four seconds adrift, and Amon, third, a further five seconds yonder. The gaps were too big: something must have happened, and something had.

As they had neared the end of the opening lap, the order was Clark, Stewart, Parkes, Amon, Rindt and Gurney, but at Blanchimont there was calamity. Stewart's BRM H16 emptied its oil catch-tank into the path of Parkes, whose Ferrari slid out of control at close to 150mph.

'The BRMs always dropped oil at the beginning of a race,' said Amon. 'I was right behind Mike, and I had a bad moment on it, too. He spun, and I backed off – which was a mistake, actually, because you're better to keep your foot in it. He spun backwards across the road, and hit the bank, but then, instead of coming back into the road, rolled along the bank. It was like a toy car somersaulting over and over – just the most horrific bloody shunt you could imagine.

'Later they hung out a board telling me he was OK, but I didn't see it, and drove the whole race assuming he was dead. Coming so soon after Bandini's accident, that had a profound effect on me, and it totally destroyed poor old Scarfiotti. I was probably in a better position to take it, because he was under a certain amount of pressure from his wife to stop racing. He never raced a Formula 1 Ferrari again after that day.'

The commentator told the crowd that the accident 'wasn't at all serious', but that was far from the truth. Although Stewart, following his serious accident at Spa the previous year, had taken to using seat belts, he was the only driver to do so, and as Parkes was thrown from his car, he suffered dreadful leg injuries. In time he recovered well, but there would be no more Formula 1.

As they took Parkes to the Grand Prix Medical Unit, Clark continued to pull away from Stewart, and Amon, distracted by what he had witnessed, was passed by Gurney.

For once the BRM H16 was running tolerably well, and by lap 12 it went into the lead, for both Clark and Gurney came in, Jimmy to have a disintegrated plug changed (which took a couple of minutes, and dropped him to seventh), and Dan to report that his fuel pressure was low. Although the Eagle went back out directly, it was by now 15 seconds adrift of Stewart.

Gurney's engine periodically misfired for the rest of the race, but he was in better shape than the leader, whose gearbox was beginning to play up. 'On one lap,' said Stewart, 'it jumped out of sixth at Stavelot, and I *so* nearly went off.'

For the last 10 laps Jackie had but fourth and sixth available, and then only when he held the lever in. Who can imagine how it was to drive Spa-Francorchamps – Eau Rouge, Les Combes, most of all the Masta kink – one-handed, and to do it, moreover, at competitive speed? It was hardly surprising that Gurney caught and passed him, with seven laps to go, but those heaping opprobrium on Stewart for his increasing safety concerns had cause to keep quiet that day. At this, the circuit at which he had crashed horrifically a year earlier, he was magnificent.

So, too, in the circumstances, was Amon, who gathered himself together in the second half of the race, repassed Rindt and Rodriguez, and finished third. Twenty-three years old, he would be Ferrari's only driver for the rest of the season.

On the podium the perennially luckless Gurney looked a little dazed. Two wins in seven days! Clark, who always considered Dan his only true rival, was delighted for him, and if he were mortified to be leaving Spa with only one point, there was consolation in the fact that both Brabham drivers, most unusually, had failed to finish.

Round five: Le Mans. A dozen of the Grand Prix drivers had taken part in the *Vingt-Quatre Heures* three weeks earlier, but what they found on offer now was bland fare indeed. No matter that Rouen-Les Essarts, Reims and Clermont Ferrand were available for the French Grand Prix, Gallic politics had decreed that the 1967 race should be run at Le Mans's short 'Bugatti' track.

'It's a Mickey Mouse circuit,' commented Hill, and thus a new phrase entered paddock *patois* for all time. 'To have a race at a track like this is an insult to Grand Prix racing.' Oh, Graham, whatever would you have made of Junior Nürburgring?

If the drivers loathed the new venue, so also did the fans. After recently witnessing perhaps the greatest Le Mans 24

Hours of all time, they had little taste for a Formula 1 race around a fiddly little track, and the race day crowd was estimated – generously – at 15,000.

Probably it didn't help that there were only 15 cars on view, Ferrari now being down to a single entry, and Honda staying away, due to a shortage of engines. For the same reason – BRM were late in delivering their promised V12s – Bruce McLaren withdrew his car, but was invited to drive a second Eagle, Ginther having retired from racing precipitately after failing to qualify at Monte Carlo.

The mood in the paddock was generally low-key, and at Lotus downright surly, for Clark and Hill had to miss the first practice session altogether, after French customs officials held up the transporter at Dieppe. 'Apparently they weren't sure of the purpose of the cars in the back,' growled Graham. 'What did they think we wanted to do with the bloody things? Sell them?'

By the Saturday the 49s had arrived, but both persistently misfired, to the point that Clark was able to qualify only fourth. At the very end of the session, though, Hill's engine suddenly went on to eight cylinders, and one unhampered lap was enough to give him pole position, ahead of Brabham and Gurney.

The race, like the place, was dreary. Although the Lotuses asserted themselves at the front, both had crownwheel and pinion failures and departed early, leaving Brabham to fend off Gurney (who retired at half-distance), and Hulme to battle with Amon (whose throttle cable broke).

By the time Jack and Denny came in, after two and a quarter hours, the stands were virtually deserted. Stewart finished third, after reverting temporarily to the 2-litre V8 BRM. 'By the time I came in, everyone had gone home!' he said. 'Can't say I blamed them.' The Le Mans experiment was over and done.

Going into the British Grand Prix, Hulme led the World Championship, with 22 points, followed by Brabham (16), Rodriguez (12), Amon (11) and Clark (10). 'The 49 was proving pleasingly unreliable,' Denny said, 'but we all knew that if they held together at Silverstone, the rest of us were in a different race.'

He was on the mark. Clark may have been allowed only a single brief visit to Britain in 1967, but it was like the plunder of a pirate: fly in, take the pole, win the race, fly out. His public could have wished for nothing more.

Hill was second on the grid, but immediately after setting the time, his car's rear suspension broke, fortunately as it was coming into the pits, rather than negotiating Woodcote (then flat out, of course) or Stowe or ... pretty well anywhere at Silverstone, really. Even so, the Lotus hit a wall, which destroyed the chassis, and the mechanics set to the building of a new one for race day. They also gave Clark's car a very thorough check.

Interestingly, Jimmy worried about the fragility of the 49 as he never had about any previous Lotus. While Colin Chapman's reputation as an innovator of genius remains unchallenged, he did, in the words of Bernie Ecclestone, 'take things to the edge a bit.

'I remember, when I was managing Rindt in 1968, that at the end of that year we had the choice between the Goodyear deal with Brabham, or the Firestone deal with Lotus. And I said to Jochen, "If you want to win the World Championship, you've got more chance with Lotus than with Brabham. If you want to stay alive, you've got more chance with Brabham than with Lotus." It wasn't a bad thing to say; it was a matter of fact.'

On pace, certainly, nothing could live with the 49s at Silverstone. With Clark in front from the outset, Brabham briefly got ahead of Hill, but by lap eight Graham was past again, and gone. By lap 26, indeed, he had taken Clark for the lead, and there he stayed until lap 55 – when he abruptly slowed, and came in, left rear wheel out of kilter. A suspension bolt had come out, and although Hill was back out within a couple of minutes, it cannot have been in an easy frame of mind.

Clark duly won, with Hulme arriving 13 seconds later, and Amon four seconds behind the Brabham, having fought the whole race through with the team's proprietor.

'It was one of the most enjoyable races I ever had,' Chris said, 'but frustrating, too. Every lap I'd come out of his slipstream before Stowe, and then have to drop back in again, because the Ferrari just didn't have the steam to get by.

'Old Jack was adjusting his mirrors early in the race – in fact, one fell off, and whistled past my head. He lost the other one, too, and I've never quite known whether he was adjusting them, or trying to tear them off! He said he had a wheel out of balance, and the mirrors were shaking...

'It was a *very* wide car, that Brabham, and Jack was throwing everything in the book at me: stones, grass, dirt – and mirrors, of course! I finally got him when he ran a bit wide coming out of Woodcote on lap 77, with three to go. After that I started to catch Denny quickly, but we ran out of laps.'

Stewart agreed that, of all the drivers, Brabham was way the most difficult to overtake. 'He'd have fitted into Formula 1 in the late 1990s perfectly! These guys today know *nothing* about keeping people back, compared with what Jack knew. I'm not sure he would actually run into anybody, but he didn't need to, you see – he was much more subtle than that! It's only the unsubtle who actually have to run into people.

'Racing was generally very clean in that era. I'd happily race all day with Jochen or Bruce or Chris or Denny, but Jack was a bit different. He'd block you, use pieces of road that he'd never used before – and you got more chips in your visor following him than anybody else, that's for sure. You couldn't talk to him about it, though; he'd just smile!'

Amon was unfortunate enough to spend the whole of the next race behind Brabham, too, but this time – at the Nürburgring – he was unable to pressure him into a mistake, and the pair of them finished second and third, four-tenths apart.

The German Grand Prix looked on paper like a walkover for Clark, the best driver, in the fastest car, at the most difficult circuit. He beat Hulme to pole position by over nine seconds.

Given the length of the Nürburgring – 14.19 miles – and the consequent long wait between laps, the race organisers sought to pad out the field. To that end, they ran a Formula 2 race concurrently with the Grand Prix, albeit with separate grids, the smaller cars starting immediately behind the Formula 1 brigade.

On this occasion, it was as well that they held to this policy, for it spared a good many blushes: third fastest overall, and only half a second slower than Hulme, was Jacky Ickx, at the wheel of Ken Tyrrell's Matra.

Certainly Ickx already knew the circuit better than most; undeniably, too, the Nürburgring put a premium on handling, and the Matra, with around 210 horsepower from its Cosworth FVA engine, was especially nimble. But even taking all that into account, here was clearly a boy of exceptional talent: Jackie Oliver, second fastest of the Formula 2 runners, was 21 seconds away.

If the regular Grand Prix drivers were impressed with Ickx's times, they were rather less so by the manner in which they were achieved. Jacky had the fearlessness of youth, and his antics – clouting banks with abandon, and so on – caused onlookers to worry for him. At one point, indeed, Stewart earnestly recommended to Tyrrell that he slow him down. Ken's response is not on record.

Given the staggering of the grids, Ickx effectively started 18th in a field of 25, but by lap four was already up to fifth overall, having dispensed with the likes of Rodriguez, Rindt and Surtees. Later he fell back a little, and eventually retired with three laps to go, but the point had been well made. The following year he was to be a Ferrari driver.

Given the degree of Clark's superiority in qualifying, he might have been expected to come by the pits alone at the end of the opening lap, but both Hulme and Gurney were in close attendance. Perhaps, at this extremely bumpy circuit, thoughts of his car's fragility were uppermost in his mind. On lap four Jimmy cruised slowly into the pits, and this time a Lotus 49 had suffered a *front* suspension failure: buckled wishbone, to be precise.

Later in the race, Hill, who never figured, retired when his rear suspension collapsed. This was getting to be a matter of routine.

As Clark disappeared from the scene, so Gurney overtook Hulme, and pulled away conclusively, the Eagle lapping six and seven seconds faster than the Brabham. Like Tony Brooks, another truly great driver underrated by history, Dan's skills were never better displayed than at the Nürburgring or Spa, drivers' circuits *sans pareil*.

His luck, though, could never keep pace. On lap 13, with a 45-second lead, and only 30 miles to the flag, the Eagle had a driveshaft failure, and Hulme was left with a big advantage over Brabham. One-two they finished, with Amon third, Surtees fourth.

Now there were four races left, and unless Lotus made some radical progress on reliability, Denny was going to walk this World Championship. The rules of the time counted a driver's best five scores in the first six races (up to, and including, Silverstone), and his best four from the remaining five. Hulme had 37, followed by Brabham (25), then Clark and Amon (19), Rodriguez (14), and Surtees (8).

Eight days after the German Grand Prix, Bob Anderson lost his life in a testing accident at Silverstone. The shoestring privateer, who had missed the Nürburgring, was running alone, in circumstances unthinkable today. Like Parkes, he was not wearing seat belts, and he suffered terrible chest injuries on impact with the steering wheel. With no doctor on hand at the circuit, half an hour passed before any medical help arrived. Eventually, the unfortunate man was taken away in the circuit's ramshackle ambulance, which had neither siren nor bell. He died shortly after reaching hospital in Northampton.

\* \* \*

Next on the calendar was something of a novelty. Since 1961 a 'Canadian Grand Prix' had been run for sports cars at Mosport Park, but 1967 was Centenary Year in the country, and, that being so, the race organisers applied to the FIA for a Grand Prix date, which was duly granted.

Thus, the Formula 1 circus went to Canada for the first time, and at a point in the season inconceivable in the post-Ecclestone era: the cars ran at Mosport on 27 August, were then returned to Europe for Monza, on 10 September, then transported back across the Atlantic for Watkins Glen, on 1 October, and Mexico City three weeks after that.

Still, it was the date the Canadians wanted, and most of the teams turned up for this race on one of the world's great natural road circuits, 60 miles from Toronto. Honda, working on a new car, did not make the trip, and Richard Attwood subbed at Cooper-Maserati for Rodriguez, who had seriously injured himself in an F2 race at Enna. Clark, in close attendance at the time, was amazed Pedro had survived: 'That's the first time I've ever been passed by someone going up the road on his backside...'

On the opening practice day at Mosport, Jimmy himself had an accident, spinning into the bank backwards at the first turn. By the time of impact, most of the speed had been scrubbed off, and Clark was somewhat disconcerted by the amount of suspension damage incurred in what seemed a minimal shunt.

Chapman was also disconcerted, but for a different reason. Lotus were now in the rent-a-car business, with a third 49 available for any local driver able to pay for it, and it was in this car that Clark had crashed. In Canada, Eppie Wietzes had come up with the requisite loot, and Colin was very keen for the deal to go through. The mechanics – there were but four on hand, to look after three cars! – set to work, and by Saturday afternoon Wietzes was able to qualify, albeit more than eight seconds from Clark and Hill, who were first and second on the grid, followed by Hulme, Amon and Gurney.

After fine weather in practice, race day turned out foully wet, to the point that Brabham, who usually eschewed such things, for once wore a face mask. Through most of his career Jack's approach to racing garb was unconventional; often he did not wear gloves, and the frequent passing up of ear plugs would lead to deafness in later life.

The forecast for the balance of the afternoon was mixed, so that, mysterious as it may seem today, rain tyres were not an automatic choice for the drivers. The advent of slicks was still four years distant, and the dry tyres of the day were conventionally treaded, a rain tyre differing merely in tread pattern and (softer) compound. Mid-race tyre changes were not the norm, and a pit stop could be costly.

Folk who were in the race at Mosport that day asserted that

never anywhere had they driven on such a slippery surface. 'Like grease on a glass door knob,' was how Hulme eloquently put it. There was also a thick mist hanging in the air, and that, combined with the spray, made for visibility which at times verged on dead reckoning. It was hardly surprising that lap times were around half a minute slower than in the dry.

This was the first wet race of 1967, which meant, of course, that it was the first such for the Lotus 49, and Clark and Hill were swiftly to discover that in these conditions the abrupt torque curve of the early DFV made for sweaty palms. As well as that, the Firestone tyres were not the equal of the Goodyears on offer to Brabham, Eagle and McLaren, and by lap four Clark had surrendered the lead to Hulme, who – for all his avowed distaste for racing in the rain – proceeded to disappear.

All told, it was a chaotic afternoon. There was no 'two-hour limit' back then, and for the drivers – particularly those on Firestones – the 90-lap race seemed interminable; at first Hulme seemed to have it made, pulling clear of Clark at more than a second a lap.

If any true opposition looked to be coming Denny's way, it was from McLaren, whose M5A was making its début. It was something of an irony that BRM, while themselves plugging on with the lumbering H16s, should supply the first of their new V12 engines to another team, and Bruce was impressed with it. Having qualified sixth, he spun down to 12th on lap three, but thereafter made the most of the engine's smooth power delivery, to say nothing of his Goodyears. By lap 22 he was past Clark, and hard after Hulme.

Then the rain abated for a while, and as the track began to dry, the pace to pick up, McLaren's engine began to misfire. Before the race he had decided, in the interests of saving weight, to remove the alternator, deeming it unnecessary as the BRM V12 had only a mechanical, rather than electric, fuel pump. He could have used an alternator now, though, for his battery was going flat, boiled almost dry by the hot oil catch-tank situated above it. On lap 69 he had to come in for a new battery, and the long stop dropped him to seventh.

Had McLaren's car run trouble-free, he would probably have

won, for when the rain started again Clark retired, ignition system drenched, and Hulme, barely able to see, made stops on consecutive laps, for new goggles, then a visor. By this time, his canny boss had taken a lead he was to hold to the end.

Gurney finished third, followed by Hill, Spence and Amon, but the Brabham 1–2, as well as clinching a second consecutive Constructors' title for the team, also effectively distilled the World Championship to a fight between Hulme (43) and Brabham (34); next up, with three races remaining, were Amon (20) and Clark (19).

Having collected his cheque ($10,575), Brabham, together with Rindt, Stewart, Hill and Irwin, dashed away for a 'red eye' flight to London, for all were competing next day in the F2 race at the Bank Holiday meeting at Brands Hatch. The organisers graciously allowed them a practice session in the morning, and in the afternoon Rindt won, with Stewart second. In 1967, who needed sleep?

Monza came next, and a strange Monza it was, with only a single Ferrari down to run. Already it was known that Ickx was to join the team the following year, which led to speculation that he might drive a second car in Italy, but in fact Jacky made his Formula 1 début in a Cooper-Maserati, Rodriguez not yet fit to drive.

Scarfiotti, winner of the Italian Grand Prix for Enzo the year before, reappeared for this race, but now at the wheel of Gurney's second Eagle, while Giancarlo Baghetti, who had triumphed for Ferrari on his Grand Prix début (at Reims in 1961), then never won anything again, was at the wheel of the 'Hertz' Lotus 49.

The *tifosi* therefore looked to Amon alone, and before the race, for which he qualified fourth, Chris was quite optimistic. 'From the Nürburgring on, they'd managed to lighten the car quite a bit, and then for Monza we finally had the 48-valve engine, which was certainly better than the old 36-valve, and gave about 390 horsepower. That said, the Lotus was still a lot quicker; although the DFV only had about 15 horsepower more, it didn't suffer from the oil scavenge problems we had – but which we didn't *know* we had at the time!

79

'In fact,' Amon concluded, 'that was the only thing really wrong with that V12, in all its guises, but they never did get it really sorted out, and it cost a load of power. Still, I thought I had a pretty good chance at Monza – until we got to the start, which was the biggest cock-up you've ever seen. We trundled up to the dummy grid, then got the green flag to move to the grid proper – and Brabham just dropped the clutch, and took off! In the end, everyone sort of followed him, and in the confusion I over-revved, and took the edge off the engine right there...'

If the spectators were therefore robbed of a competitive Ferrari that day, they were privileged to witness perhaps the greatest drive of Clark's life, which is to say as great as ever there has been. In the early stages of the race, though, there was no sign of such a thing – indeed no sign that it might be called for; Jimmy, as usual starting from pole position, led more often than not, but at this circuit – then a flat-out slipstreamer, devoid of chicanes – it was difficult to break away, and the two Brabhams, together with the other Lotus of Hill, remained close at hand.

There was something else, too: as in the early laps at the Nürburgring, Clark felt that his car's handling was awry, and once more he had a slow puncture in the right rear. Brabham could see the tyre deflating, and pointed to it as he passed the Lotus. After driving most of the 13th lap at reduced pace, Jimmy came in for a new tyre, and by the time he rejoined, 15th, he had been lapped.

So now it began. By lap 25 Clark had caught and passed the leaders as if they were not there, and put himself back on the same lap – but none could have anticipated that later in the afternoon he would pass them again.

At the time there were those who, while not seeking to play down his achievement, put emphasis on the fact that this was a horsepower track, and the DFV had more of it than any other engine. True enough – and it was also the case that Monza was not a driver's circuit, in the Nürburgring sense of the word. But it was for this very reason, paradoxically, that Stewart, who was to drive a similar comeback race there six years later, considered it Clark's best.

'That was the whole thing about Monza – *anyone* could go fast there, so if you were making up time on them, you were doing something very special. The secret of that place was not to make the tiniest mistake, because if you did, you scrubbed off speed, and your lap was ruined. Therefore, it was extremely difficult to keep the momentum going. The 1973 Italian Grand Prix was certainly my best drive, and I think the same was true of Jimmy in 1967.'

When Clark caught the leaders (for the first time), he hooked up with Hill, and, working together, they towed themselves well clear of the Brabhams. When Hulme retired with overheating at half-distance, and Brabham began to suffer with a sticking throttle, Graham looked set for his first win of the year. For some time he and Jimmy, although a lap apart, continued to run together, each benefiting at a circuit where slipstreaming was all.

Leading as comfortably as he was, though, Hill eventually backed off, and Clark went away on his own. At 50 laps, with 18 to go, he was up to fifth, his immediate targets Rindt, whom he passed on lap 54, and Surtees.

Although John had qualified only ninth, he was finding the latest Honda a much more wieldy proposition than its predecessor. In essence, the RA300 was not a Honda at all, but a Lola IndyCar adapted to meet Formula 1 regulations, and to take the Honda V12 engine and gearbox, Surtees having persuaded his Japanese employers that his close links with Lola could be put to good use. Still a heavyweight by comparison with the opposition, it was yet 100lb lighter than the original car, better aerodynamically, and easier on its Firestones. From the start, Surtees had been thereabouts, and as the race went into its late stages, he began to catch Brabham.

By lap 58, an extraordinary showdown was taking shape, for although Hill looked secure enough, 17 seconds clear in the lead, Brabham now led Surtees by only four seconds – and the mesmeric Clark was but three seconds behind the Honda! He clearly wasn't going to catch his team-mate, but a Lotus 1–2 was on the cards.

A lap later, it was no longer a fight for second place. On the approach to Parabolica Hill's engine suddenly let go – crankshaft broken! – but if there was a swift word of sympathy for Graham in the pits, Chapman and the rest were already focused only on Clark, who had gone by Surtees, and was hard after Brabham. By lap 61 Jimmy had the lead, and, once there, was content to sit two or three seconds ahead.

As it went into its last lap, though, the Lotus was misfiring, and now leading only by a second; at the Curva Grande Surtees and Brabham swept by, their battle now for the win.

John had a plan. The weighty 'Hondola' had tremendous top-end speed, but the Brabham was stronger in the mid-range, and he knew that if he came off the last corner behind Jack, he was unlikely to get by him before the line; equally, if he emerged on to the pit straight only marginally ahead, there was every chance that Brabham would tow past him.

Hill's earlier blow-up had left an oil slick on the inside line at Parabolica, but Surtees suspected that if he left the door open, Brabham would nevertheless go for it. He was right. The Honda led down to the corner, held to the conventional line – and Jack took the bait, snaked wildly under braking, and ran wide. Surtees beat him to the flag by a car's length.

In the stands, they erupted, of course, for the ex-*Ferrarista* remained a folk hero in Italy, but they saved yet greater applause for Clark, who coasted in – engine dead – 25 seconds later. When he braked the Lotus to a halt, he was mobbed.

Not for the first, or last, time, Chapman's obsession with lightness cost his team dear, as Alan McCall, one of Jimmy's mechanics, remembered.

'After practice, Mr Chapman had decided we didn't need much fuel to do this race, so he told me to put in only 31 gallons. Dick Scammell (of Cosworth) took me to one side, told me he thought the old man had got it wrong, and said I should put 33 gallons in. I reckoned they'd both got it wrong, so I put in 35 gallons – and, because Jimmy had to drive so hard for so long, it *still* wasn't enough!

'Mr Chapman questioned me after the race, and I told him I'd put extra fuel in – and his response was that he would sack me immediately if ever I disobeyed him again! If we'd gone with his suggestion, Jimmy would have run out seven laps from the end…'

It was a fine thing that both Chapman and Hill clapped Surtees as he returned in victory to the pit lane; a fine thing, too, to see John accept the trophy from Margherita Bandini, widow of his former team-mate.

As the Milanese hordes made their way finally home, the Brabham drivers knew that one of them would now be World Champion, for in the end Clark had scored only four points, giving him a total of 23; with only two races to run, Hulme (43) was out of reach, and Brabham (40) effectively so.

If it were possible, though, Jimmy's legend gained another layer that day in the old park. In the course of 46 laps, he had made up a whole lap, and more, on Brabham, taken 99 seconds from him, which meant an *average* lap time 2.15 seconds faster. No damned lies there.

Clark was to win the last couple of races, too, although one of the victories – at Watkins Glen – owed more than a little to fortune, and in several ways. To begin with, Jimmy lost the toss.

A Lotus 49 had qualified fastest at every race in which it had competed, and it was a surety that either Clark or Hill would be on pole position at the Glen. On this occasion Graham had the upper hand, but the powers that be at Ford, dismayed by the way the team-mates had gone at it, were keen to avoid a repetition in the race. This was the USA, and what Henry's lot wanted was an orderly 1–2 parade.

That being so, it was proposed that Clark and Hill flip a coin to decide which of them should win the following day. It went down well with neither man, but reluctantly they acquiesced, and Graham called it right. By way of consolation to the loser, it was suggested that the drivers' finishing positions be reversed in Mexico.

Those aware of motor racing's existence before the 1990s had cause to be amused by the hysteria and venom meted out to McLaren after the Hakkinen-Coulthard 'fix' at Melbourne in 1998.

This pre-nuptial agreement in upstate New York would have counted for more, had the Lotus 49 been a paragon of reliability, but of course it was not so. Although the cars led from the start, swapping around to give the illusion of a race, by half-distance they had Amon in close attendance – and at the same time Hill began to experience clutch problems. That being so, Chapman signalled Clark to clear off, leaving Graham to fight with the Ferrari.

On lap 96, with a dozen remaining, Amon retired from second place, engine blown, but although their cars were now running comfortably first and second, the Ford suits were able to relax only briefly. At the end of lap 106, Clark came by at reduced speed, his right rear wheel much out of true.

'A top rear link brace had broken,' Alan McCall remembered. 'We used to call them "pine trees" – they would break or pull bolts out on a regular basis. Mr Chapman insisted they were strong enough, and that we were at fault, for not fitting them properly.'

What to do? Lapping as much as 20 seconds from his earlier pace, Clark bravely pressed on, and in the end crossed the line six seconds ahead of Hill. Had the Ferrari V12 held together, Amon would undoubtedly have won. 'I was a bit disappointed,' he said, 'but still encouraged by the car's improved performance – it seemed only a matter of time before we'd win one. Little did I know...'

Watkins Glen made Hulme's World Championship a virtual certainty, for he finished third, and took his score on to 47, while Brabham, fifth (after stopping to change a flat tyre), progressed to 42; in reality the gap was more than it seemed, for a driver counted only his four best finishes in the last five races, and Jack, unlike Denny, had already scored four times. To take the title, he would need to win the last race, with his team-mate lower than fourth.

Mexico, though, was all Clark. He took pole position, with Amon alongside on the front row, followed by Gurney and Hill, then Brabham and Hulme. Local boy Moises Solana drove the third Lotus (as at the Glen), and qualified a very respectable ninth, to the chagrin of Rodriguez, who, still hobbling, but not about to miss his home Grand Prix, was 13th in the Cooper-Maserati.

Pedro was John Cooper's only driver at this final race of 1967, Rindt having left the team after Watkins Glen. All summer long Jochen had simmered away, increasingly at odds with team manager Roy Salvadori, and maddened by the Maserati V12's lack of power. At the American Grand Prix his engine had blown up: 'When I realised it was about to go, I gave it 12,000 revs to make sure!' A normal limit back then was around nine-five.

After qualifying, Clark opted to race the earlier 49, as practised by Solana, and a sound decision it was, for while Jimmy had a trouble-free run, the Mexican novice, running an impressive fifth, departed on lap 13 with ... broken front suspension.

For the first 18 laps, Hill, with Amon at his gearbox, ran second, but then departed with a broken driveshaft, leaving the Ferrari well clear of Brabham, who was hurrying, and Hulme, who was understandably not. Jack and Denny were ultimately to finish second and third, for again Amon retired late in the day, this time running out of fuel.

When it was all done, Hulme, the new World Champion, had 51 points, followed by Brabham (46), Clark (41), and Amon and Surtees (20). It was one of those years when victories didn't get the job done, for Clark had four, Hulme and Brabham only a couple apiece. Denny and Jack, though, each scored in nine of the 11 World Championship rounds, and there the difference lay: Jimmy retired five times.

Hulme said he had never worried too much about the Lotus 49s. 'There was no point. They were faster than anything else – we reckoned they had at least 60 horsepower more than we did – and if they lasted, they were going to win. But we definitely had the edge on reliability and handling. To be honest, I thought the best thing about the car was its engine – and its driver, of course.'

Its driver was a disappointed man at season's end. 'Both McLaren and Tyrrell are going to have the Cosworth in 1968,' Clark said, 'and I'm not very happy about that. We had it to ourselves this year, and we didn't make the most of it. Overall, the 49 hasn't really delivered the results we'd expected, and one of the reasons for that is that we haven't done any testing.'

In the context of today, those words come across as almost surreal. 'It might not have mattered so much if we had had a spare car,' Jimmy concluded, 'but as soon as we did, of course, Colin had someone driving it.'

After the Mexican Grand Prix, most of the drivers jetted home (on mere commercial flights, of course) as soon as possible, but Clark, ever the enthusiast, went up to Rockingham, North Carolina, to drive a Holman-Moody Ford in the following weekend's NASCAR race. 'It was something new,' he said. 'How could I turn it down?' In a field of 44, he was running 12th when the engine failed.

One final Formula 1 race remained that year, a non-championship Spanish Grand Prix at the new Jarama track. Against negligible opposition, Clark and Hill ran away, and on New Year's Day of 1968 they also finished first and second at Kyalami, in the first round of the new World Championship. This was the 25th victory of Jimmy's career (scored in only 72 races), and in achieving it he surpassed Fangio's total, which had stood as the record for 11 years.

We were never again to see a Lotus in green, with yellow stripe, at a Grand Prix. By the time of the next round, in Spain, the lone 49 was red and gold, and although it won, by then Colin Chapman's world had changed. Five weeks earlier, on 7 April, Clark had been killed in a Formula 2 race at Hockenheim, and a tremor wrenched through the footings of the sport.

'People used to get killed quite often back then,' said Amon, 'but when it happened to Jimmy, we were all shattered. Of course we grieved – but there was always grief; when we lost him, there was another dimension to it, a selfish thing, if you like. His death *frightened* us: if it could happen to him, what chance did the rest of us have? And his death began that awful "seventh of the month" thing…'

Chapman, demented with sorrow, was initially of a mind to get out of motor racing altogether, but ultimately his obligations, both contractual and to his employees, persuaded him to carry on. Mike Spence, with BRM in Formula 1, was signed to take the place of Clark at Indianapolis. On 7 May, Spence's Lotus 56 turbine crashed at Turn One, and that evening he died of severe head injuries. A month later, Lodovico Scarfiotti was killed at the Rossfeld hill-climb, and on 7 July Jo Schlesser was burned to death when his Honda went off the road in the French Grand Prix at Rouen. It was an unspeakably perilous time to be a racing driver.

To no one's surprise, Chapman did not attend the Spanish Grand Prix, run but five days after Spence's accident. Amon took pole position, and dominated before – as usual – his car let him down, but even he was pleased to see Hill win. 'Graham was remarkable at that time. He'd been at Hockenheim with Jimmy, and at Indy with Mike, after all, and then he came to Jarama, and brought Lotus back from the depths.

'That weekend had an unreal quality about it, though. We were all unsettled because we'd lost our leader. A Grand Prix without Jimmy Clark didn't seem right.'

# ROB WALKER

# Profession: Gentleman

IF YOU ARE A FAN OF P. G. WODEHOUSE, you will know that it was *de rigueur* in the 1920s and 1930s, on an occasion such as Boat Race night, for young blades to remove and steal a policeman's helmet. On a high shelf in Rob Walker's study, there resides just such an item.

'I was at Cambridge, and it was Guy Fawkes' Night. A friend and I worked out a scheme: I knocked the policeman's helmet off, which was caught by my friend, who ran as fast as he could, and then did a rugger pass to me with it. Although the policeman couldn't keep up, someone then did a terrific tackle on me, which brought me down on the pavement. I was unconscious briefly, but fortunately had managed to pass the helmet back to my friend.

'As a result, I was gated for the rest of the term, which was rather a bore. But I suppose I was lucky not to have been sent down. And I've still got the helmet...'

Until the spring of 1971 I had no involvement in Grand Prix racing, beyond that of a fan, but a letter to *Car and Driver*, in New York, had brought an unexpected reply. I had written to offer my services as a Formula 1 correspondent, which the magazine then lacked, and, remarkably, was told to go to Barcelona, write a report and let them have it. If they liked it, they would use it.

After the euphoria had subsided, I panicked. Where to begin? I had no contacts in motor racing, didn't even know how to set about getting a pass. At the Oulton Park non-championship race on Good Friday, I approached Robert Ramsay Campbell Walker for advice.

He was delightful, and endlessly patient, suggesting hotels in Barcelona, giving me the address of the organising club, and counselling me about the right approach: 'They tend to be a bit excitable down there, but you'll be all right if you don't argue with them…'

I followed Rob's instructions faithfully, and duly went to thank him in the Montjuich paddock. He proceeded to introduce me to every member of the team, and that day I felt as though a mountain had been climbed. Next morning I got a similar response from Chris Amon. These two, the first people in the business to befriend me, have not unnaturally remained high in my affections.

When Rob ceased his involvement as a team owner, he continued, out of sheer enthusiasm, to come to races as a journalist, working for magazines such as *Road & Track*. Everyone loves him. He is a gentleman, but, more, a gentle man.

His study is reassuringly chaotic. There are paintings and photographs of favourite drivers and friends, and magazines are everywhere, but immaculately filed are the scrapbooks he religiously kept of every race in which his cars competed.

There were a great many. Easily forgotten is that the first Grand Prix victory for both Cooper and Lotus was scored not by the works cars, but by the private entry of the RRC Walker Racing Team. And each time the driver was Stirling Moss.

'Having Stirling as my driver was marvellous in every respect. Apart from the fact that he was in a class of his own, we were great friends. In all our years together, we never had any kind of contract – it was always just a handshake at the beginning of every season.

'The other great thing about having Stirling, of course, was that in those days there was no FOCA to do a financial deal for all the entrants; it was up to each of us to make our own arrangements. There was very little prize money, and starting money – *appearance* money, in effect – was what mattered. And the one driver every race organiser wanted more than any other was Stirling.'

Restricted to the flat printed word, it is not easy to convey the manner and sound of Rob Walker. But it seems appropriate that he has a passion for honey, considering it a cure-all for afflictions as diverse as burns and hangovers.

He speaks languidly, and when surprised by a piece of news invariably responds with, 'Really?' He can make this word last five or six seconds.

His languor, too, is at the root of his humour. I remember once discussing with him a *femme fatale* of the Grand Prix past. 'Did you like her?' I asked. 'Oh, yes!' Rob replied enthusiastically. 'Everybody did.' Pause. 'That was the problem, really…'

This elegant drawl does great service to his anecdotes; he has a wit as dry as Beefeater, and in the course of a varied, admittedly privileged, life, appears to have met everybody.

Some years ago, on the occasion of the first Long Beach Grand Prix, he booked a room on the *Queen Mary*, by now a floating hotel in a California harbour. Several colleagues were with him, and they were aghast at his reception: 'Mr Walker? We're glad to see you, sir. And you'll be pleased to know we've given you your old suite.'

In the liner's great transatlantic days, Walker had been a frequent passenger. 'I was awfully lucky, really,' he beamed. 'The chairman of Cunard White Star had been a chum of mine at school.'

For years sundry publishers tried to persuade him to write his memoirs, but, for a variety of reasons, it was not until 1993 that the project was finally undertaken. Once he ran through a list of those who had approached him, beginning thus: 'Well, Macmillan asked me.' Pause. 'But then he died…'

Once, at Silverstone, I asked him why he had missed the previous race, in France. 'Oh,' came the reply, 'I was busy that weekend – we were taking Ginger Rogers to Wimbledon.'

Lest I give the impression that Rob is an advanced

namedropper, let me stress that this is not so. From him, taking G. Rogers to the Centre Court for the afternoon sounds like running old Mrs Perkins to the bus station.

Simply, he is a man from a generation increasingly extinct. His grandfather was the managing director of Johnnie Walker, which explains why the family, in his own words, 'has never been short of a penny or two'. He has no business connections with the company now, though, and ironically has no taste for Scotch. 'Probably just as well. My grandfather was quite fond of sampling his own wares. He died of old age. At 33…

'My father was prey to the same temptations, and he only made it to 32. Not long before he died, he took it into his head that the family wasn't very well off, telling my mother she couldn't have the chauffeur drive her to the station, a mile or so away, but would have to walk to save money. And, d'you know, after he'd died, she found she had £50,000 a year for life. Which was a lot of money in 1921.'

Life, not surprisingly, seems to have been idyllic for the young man. There were years of Cambridge, of driving up to London for dinners at the Ritz in a succession of desirable cars. By the time he was 20, he reckons, he had been through as many cars as he had years.

'I suppose I must have had about a hundred now,' he said, speaking with particular fondness of a Mercedes-Benz 300SL. But Rob's passion has always been for racing cars. 'When people ask me about my life,' he said, 'I always say motor racing's all I've ever done – that and the war.' He served as a pilot in the Fleet Air Arm, although this entailed the return of a flying licence which had been withdrawn for life.

'I'd taken a Tiger Moth to a horse race meeting, and during the interval for luncheon, everyone got frightfully bored, so I got back in the aeroplane, and started jumping all the fences. Unfortunately, a policeman gave my number to the Air Ministry.'

In the years leading up to the war, Walker raced a good deal. At Le Mans, in 1939, he drove his own Delahaye for virtually the entire distance, finishing eighth. And even here there was a flourish. 'I started off the race in a pin-stripe suit, but it seemed inappropriate for the morning, so at dawn I came in and put on a sports jacket. And, of course, I'd have a glass of champagne each time I stopped.'

After the war, he raced no more. By now he was married, and had promised Betty he would confine himself to hill-climbs and speed trials. When one of his cars raced, someone else was aboard, and over time drivers such as Peter Collins and Roy Salvadori appeared in the distinctive dark-blue-and-white noseband colours.

In 1958, though, Rob's team moved into a different league altogether. Stirling Moss, at that time Vanwall's number one driver, needed something to drive in Argentina, scene of the opening Grand Prix of the year, for the Vanwalls weren't ready. He called Walker.

'I had a Formula 2 Cooper, with a 2-litre Climax engine, which Jack Brabham had raced for me the year before. Stirling said he'd take it to Buenos Aires, and of course I agreed. But I didn't go myself, which I've always regretted, because Stirling drove an absolutely brilliant race, gambling on not changing tyres, and managed to win. It was the first Grand Prix victory for us – and also the first by a Cooper. And I missed it.'

Vanwall pulled out of racing at the end of that year, and Moss joined Walker full time, with a new Cooper and full-sized 2.5-litre motor. 'I loved going racing with Rob,' Stirling said. 'A small team, very relaxed, yet very professional. It was always a matter of buying cars from another company, of course, but that aspect really appealed to me – trying to beat the factories. And quite a few times we did.'

True enough. Moss's 1960 Monaco win in a Lotus preceded the first by Colin Chapman's team cars by 18 months. And his victories the following year, at Monaco and the Nürburgring, have passed into racing legend. 'There really was no one like him,' Walker said. 'For me, he was the perfect racing driver.'

For Enzo Ferrari, too. In the 1961 Monaco and German Grands Prix – each at circuits where driver ability counted for more than anything else – only Moss thwarted the red cars. The *Ingegnere* didn't like that, and asked Stirling to come and see him.

For years, following a promise broken by Ferrari early in his career, Stirling had resisted entreaties from Maranello, but now he relented, and went to visit the Old Man. 'Drive for me,' Ferrari said, 'and I'll get rid of the other drivers, run a single car for you. Tell me what you want in a Grand Prix car.'

No one else ever received such an offer. But Moss declined, and made his own suggestion. He would drive a Ferrari, he said, and one prepared by the factory – but it had to be painted dark blue, and run, at the circuits, by Rob Walker's team. Astonishingly, Ferrari agreed.

This was early 1962, and arrangements were set. But everything came to nought when Moss crashed a Lotus at Goodwood on Easter Monday. He was never to race at the top level again.

'I was devastated, of course,' Walker remembered. 'The team carried on, with Maurice Trintignant, my second driver, but it wasn't the same. With Stirling anything had been possible, because he was so much better than anyone else.'

Thereafter, Walker's happiest racing days were with Jo Siffert, who joined him in 1965, and stayed five years. He remembers 'Seppi' with huge affection, and cites his victory in the 1968 British Grand Prix as perhaps the most satisfying of all.

'This is no disrespect to Stirling, who was quite obviously the best driver I ever had, but that day at Brands Hatch was unforgettable, for a number of reasons, not least because it was the British Grand Prix, which we'd never managed to win. Before that, for the outside world it had always been largely a matter of Stirling winning, and I think Seppi's victory was seen more as one for the whole team.

'Betty and I adored Seppi. A wonderful man, with unbelievable courage and a great sense of humour. Earlier that year I'd bought a new Lotus 49 for him to drive, and at our first test – at Brands – he wrote it off. That was bad enough, but when the wreckage was taken back to the workshops, a spark from one the mechanics' drills ignited fuel vapour, and the whole lot went up. I lost what remained of the Lotus, of course, but also my ex-Seaman Delage, as well as scrapbooks and souvenirs collected from 30 years of racing. It was heartbreaking.

'Still, we carried on, for a while with an ex-Tasman 49, and then a new one, which arrived just in time for the British Grand Prix. In fact, the night before practice, the mechanics stayed up to finish building it. And then Seppi won, after the most fantastic battle with Chris Amon's Ferrari. There was never more than a second or two between them, and I thought that race would never end.'

Siffert had originally joined the team as number two to Jo Bonnier, Rob's regular driver for two years, and quickly asserted himself over the steady Swede. 'I don't think Jo liked being beaten by his team-mate, and at the end of the year he suggested I should revert to running only one driver in 1966. "I quite agree with you," I said to him, "and it's Siffert…"'

Having been around motor racing so long, Rob has seen everything, so that any incident of today triggers a memory. No fan of Schumacher, he was delighted when Michael was black-flagged in the 1994 British Grand Prix, not least because Damon Hill then went on to win.

We discussed it on the phone a few days later. 'Nigel, have I ever told you *my* black flag story?

'It was at Casablanca in 1957. Brabham was in my Cooper, and it had something wrong with it. The Clerk of the Course was "Toto" Roche, a very fat man, who sometimes used to start races with his flag while standing in front of the grid.

'I saw him reaching for the black flag, and guessed it was for my car, so what I did, I engaged him in conversation every time Jack was due to come past. Roche was on the track, of course, with his flag, and I was in the pits. Several times it worked perfectly: as he turned round to answer me, he'd have his back to the track – and Jack would go past, behind him.

'Eventually, though, he realised what was going on. "I know what you're doing, Rob," he said, "and next time round I'm going to give your driver the black flag." He really didn't know what he was doing, though, and he waved it at the next driver through – which was Fangio!

'It was awfully bad luck on Fangio, but he was terribly nice about it afterwards. And it's significant that, when he got the black flag, he simply obeyed it without question, even though he hadn't a clue why they were giving it to him. Not like bloody Schumacher...'

There is a hint of good-natured cynicism in much of Rob's laconic speech, but his sense of wonder, remarkably, has never left him. I remember watching his face as Ayrton Senna worked through one of his all-or-nothing qualifying laps, and finding him lost for words afterwards.

'I was a tremendous fan of Ayrton's,' he said. 'I thought we were incredibly lucky to have two really great drivers at the same time. Ayrton and Alain Prost were in a different class from the others, and what fascinated me was that these two artists achieved very similar results in such different ways. Prost's overtaking manoeuvres were beautiful in themselves, weren't they? So graceful and sure, almost like ballet...'

One on his own, Rob Walker.

# A game for two players

JACKIE STEWART ALWAYS SPEAKS WISTFULLY of Silverstone 1969. Maybe he doesn't count it as his greatest victory, but certainly it stands in his memory as the most enjoyable race of his life.

'The great thing about racing with someone like Jochen Rindt or Chris Amon or Denny Hulme – or virtually any of the stars from that era – was that it was so clean,' Stewart said. 'We were all very good friends, for one thing, and when you passed someone coming out of their slipstream, there was no point in weaving or trying to block them because they were going to pass. And, in fact, if you let them pass your lap times were quicker – because then you got them on the next bit of straight.

'At Silverstone the places to pass were down the Hangar Straight, to Stowe, and then between Abbey and Woodcote. If you got everything right, if you didn't screw up Becketts or Club, you'd pass twice a lap – and it was quicker to do that, so you'd let him through, and that way you'd keep the gap to the guy behind. In the large majority of races, when there's attempted passing going on, everyone goes slower…

'The British Grand Prix in 1969 was special, though. How many times in your career are you going to have a race like that? There was as good as no difference in ability between Jochen and myself, and the same was true of my Matra and his

*It is May 1950, at Silverstone, and Giuseppe Farina has just won the very first World Championship Grand Prix. (LAT)*

*Silverstone 1950. Stirling Moss and Peter Collins prepare to meet the Royals. (LAT)*

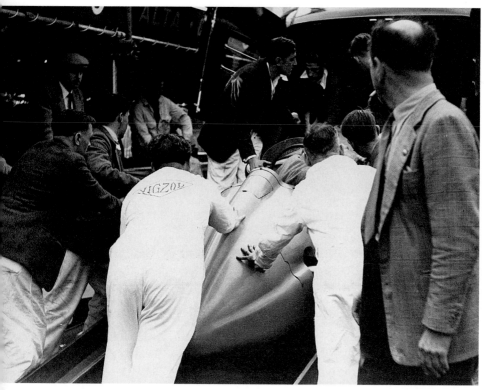

*Silverstone 1950. Raymond Mays (right) looks on as the BRM V16 is unloaded. It would have been better left in the transporter. (LAT)*

*Silverstone 1950. A practice shot of Farina in the glorious Alfa Romeo 158. It was this relaxed driving style that Moss was consciously to copy. (LAT)*

*Not your average Formula 1 circuit backdrop. Luigi Villoresi's Ferrari in the 1952 Turin Grand Prix, run through the city's Valentino Park.*

*Image of the 1952 and '53 seasons: Ascari's Ferrari, in the lead, beyond challenge. This is the French Grand Prix at Rouen in '52. (LAT)*

*Left* Alberto Ascari won every Grand Prix in 1952, save the Swiss. That day the great **Milanese** *was driving this 'Ferrari Special' in the Indianapolis 500, then a round of the World Championship.* (Indianapolis Motor Speedway)

***Below left*** *Monza 1953. One of the closest Grands Prix ever run featured Fangio (Maserati), Ascari (Ferrari), Onofre Marimon (Maserati) and Farina (Ferrari). Only Fangio came through a multiple shunt at the final corner …* (LAT)

***Right*** *Eugenio Castellotti – archetypal Italian racing driver of the fifties.*

***Below*** *The racing car with which the author first fell in love: the Lancia D50, posing for a publicity shot at Monza in 1954, Castellotti at the wheel.* (LAT)

101

*Far left Pit-to-car communication in 1954. An intrepid Mercedes mechanic holds out a board to Fangio during the British Grand Prix at Silverstone. The flag marshal (in white coat) may be even braver ...* (LAT)

*Left Image of the mid-fifties: Fangio, with yet another laurel wreath, and Alfred Neubauer, Mercedes-Benz team manager of legend.* (Mercedes)

*Below left Through the downhill swerves at Rouen in 1957. Jean Behra's Maserati 250F is at the limit of adhesion; Fangio's similar car is venturing beyond, into a realm of its own.* (LAT)

*Right June 2nd 1979. Juan Manuel Fangio signs the wall of the lamented Steering Wheel Club in Mayfair.* (David Winter)

*Below Before they built the Loews ... Monte Carlo is elegant in 1955, as the Lancias of Castellotti and Ascari lead Behra's Maserati into the Station Hairpin.* (LAT)

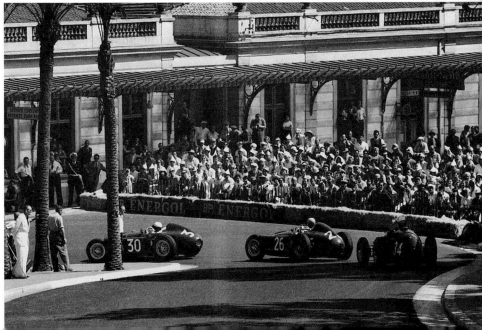

**Above** Safety? What safety? Farina's Ferrari chases the Mercedes at Spa in 1955. (LAT)

**Left** Not for those of nervous disposition. Maserati 250Fs tackle the Monza banking in the 1955 Italian Grand Prix. (LAT)

**Above right** Jacques Pollet's Gordini on the banking, while Carlos Menditeguy's Maserati hurtles towards the bridge beneath. (LAT)

**Right** Ye Gods, Grand Prix drivers joking on the grid! Stirling Moss (nearest to camera), Harry Schell, Juan Fangio and Mike Hawthorn, before the International Trophy at Silverstone in 1956. (LAT)

*Silverstone 1956. In the British Grand Prix Tony Brooks struggles with the BRM, a car he loathed. At Abbey Curve a sticking throttle led to this debacle, but Brooks was virtually unhurt. (LAT)*

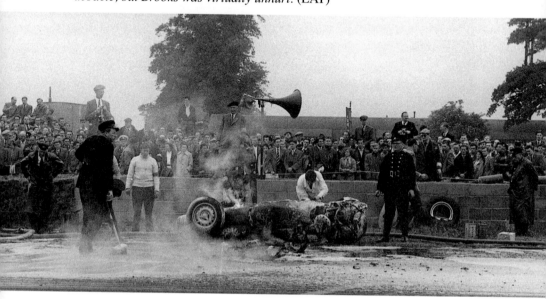

*The first Grand Prix victory for Vanwall. Brooks and Moss share the trophy at Aintree in 1957.*

*Pescara 1957. In an effort to spare the drivers the worst of the heat, they started the race at nine in the morning; as noon approaches, Moss's Vanwall heads for victory.* (LAT)

*Above left* Nürburgring. Tony Brooks at the scene of what would be his greatest victory. (LAT)

*Above right* Nürburgring 1958. After his greatest win, Tony Brooks is happy and relaxed, as yet unaware of the consequences of Peter Collins's accident. (LAT)

*Below* Reims 1958: Fangio's last race was worthy of the man. Here, fighting over second place, his Maserati leads Schell's BRM, Moss's Vanwall and Behra's BRM. (LAT)

*Right* Casablanca 1958. Moss, winner of the race, has just learned that his World Championship is lost. After that season, Stirling was never again to care too much about the title. (LAT)

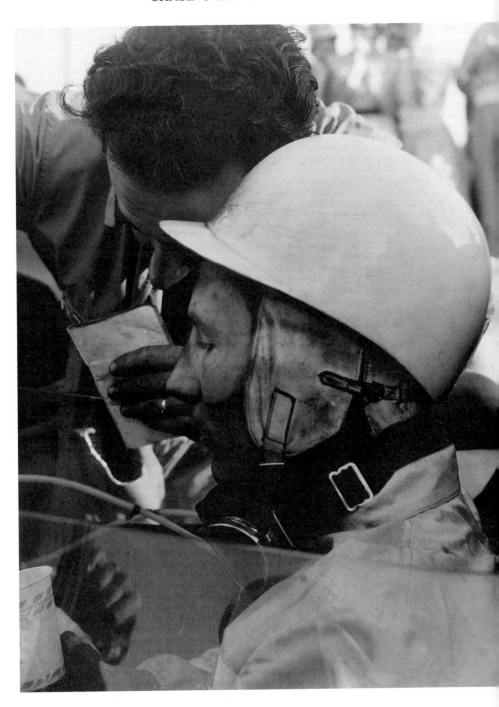

*Far left* Phil Hill, America's first World Champion, and as intelligent and articulate a man as ever sat in a racing car.

*Left* Monza unplugged. Phil Hill, a Ferrari 156, and a park in northern Italy, in September 1961. Hill became World Champion that afternoon. (LAT)

*Right* Not always in agreement, but nevertheless firm friends: Innes Ireland and Denis Jenkinson.

*Below* Watkins Glen 1961. Innes Ireland leads Graham Hill's BRM on the way to Team Lotus's first Grand Prix victory. He was sacked by Colin Chapman shortly afterwards. (LAT)

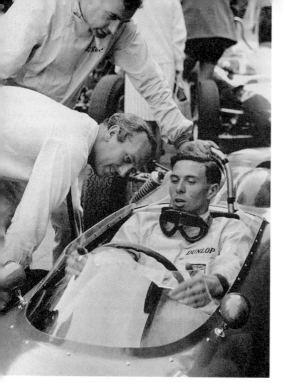 

*Above left* "Hell, Colin, this cockpit feels like a bathtub, compared with the Lotus …" Jimmy Clark samples a Ferrari at the Nürburgring in 1962. (LAT)

*Above right* Watkins Glen 1966. Pedro Rodriguez and Lorenzo Bandini look sceptical as they listen to James Garner, star of Grand Prix, filmed through that season.

*Below* Not a great car, nor a great engine: simply a great photograph of a mesmeric talent in action. Jim Clark and the Lotus 43, powered by the BRM H16, at Oulton Park in 1966. (Nick Loudon)

*The consequences of a small mistake. Lorenzo Bandini, watched by sundry folk in blazers, at the chicane during the 1967 Monaco Grand Prix. Late in the race he would crash at the same point, suffering burns which could not be survived. As the straw bales blaze, the Ferrari lies in the middle of the track. (LAT)*

*Driver's eye view of the Monaco chicane in 1967, as Jackie Stewart takes his BRM through at over 100mph. Lorenzo Bandini crashed after clipping the 'Shell' apex point on the left. (LAT)*

*Somehow Clark never won – never even finished – at Monaco, but none was ever better through the streets. Here is Jimmy on opposite lock at the entry to Casino Square in 1967. (LAT)*

*A poignant moment at Monza in 1967. John Surtees, who has just won the Italian Grand Prix for Honda, is greeted on the podium by Margherita Bandini, widow of John's friend and former team-mate.*

*This is what they call insouciance. Denny Hulme, World Champion of 1967, lifts his left hand from the wheel while opposite-locking the Brabham. And this is Monza, at the Curva Grande … (LAT)*

**Above** *Oh, if only they hadn't invented downforce … Chris Amon steers his Ferrari on the throttle at Oulton Park in 1968. (LAT)*

**Left** *Monaco 1969. A delighted Piers Courage has just finished second to Graham Hill's Lotus in Frank Williams's Brabham. (LAT)*

**Above right** *Rob Walker and Jo Siffert at Silverstone in 1969. Moss apart, 'Seppi' was Rob's favourite of all those who drove for him. (LAT)*

**Right** *Watkins Glen in 1969, and Rindt has finally won his first Grand Prix. Close friend Piers Courage took second place in the 'Frank Williams Racing Cars' Brabham. (LAT)*

*It wasn't the smoothest of relationships, but the genius of Chapman and the genius of Rindt could not be denied in 1970. With the Lotus 72 not yet up to speed, Jochen reverted to the 49 for Monaco (below), and drove a staggering race, pressuring Jack Brabham into a mistake at the very last corner. (Maureen Magee and LAT)*

*Brands Hatch 1970. A Brabham mechanic (by the name of Ron Dennis) kneels by the car, as Jack prepares to go out.* (LAT)

*Monza 1971, some years before Max Mosley decided that overtaking was boring. Amon's Matra leads the gaggle past the pits at the Italian Grand Prix.* (LAT)

*Above* The way they were. Ferrari drivers Mario Andretti, Clay Regazzoni and Jacky Ickx, in 1971. (LAT)

*Below* The glory days of Tyrrell. Jackie Stewart leads team-mate Francois Cevert at Monaco in 1973. (LAT)

*Right* "I never really liked it when I was doing it …" As a commentator, and race analyst sans pareil, James Hunt came to love motor racing a great deal. We saw the best of James the man after Hunt the driver had retired. (LAT)

*Left* Fuji 1976. Niki Lauda, less than three months after his accident at the Nürburgring, has withdrawn from the race on the second lap, judging the torrential conditions unacceptable. (LAT)

*Above* And you wonder why the crowds loved him? Gilles Villeneuve's Ferrari 126C at Zandvoort at 1981. (LAT)

*Below* Until the last couple of weeks, Gilles thought they were friends. Pironi and Villeneuve at Long Beach in 1982. (David Hutson)

*US Dallas Grand Prix, 1984. This is a Grand Prix circuit the evening before the race? Engineers go to work on one of several corners, but their quick-dry materials didn't dry quickly enough ... (LAT)*

*There are marbles – and there are marbles. Niki Lauda's McLaren-TAG was one of many cars to finish up in the wall. (LAT)*

*Strange that a Finn should be so at ease in the heat. Physically, as well as metaphorically, Keke Rosberg was the coolest man around at Dallas. (LAT)*

*The Patreses and the Cheevers pose with a Benetton-sponsored Alfa at Southfork Ranch. (Author)*

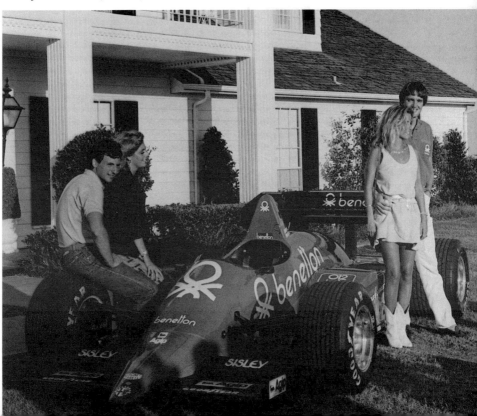

**Left** *A trick of the light creates a not wholly appropriate halo effect around the Old Man of Maranello.*

**Below** *Professor Sidney Watkins, soon after his arrival in Formula 1. The safest pair of hands in the history of the sport.* (Maurice Hamilton)

**Right** *Not a dry eye in the house. Jean Alesi wasn't the only one in tears when he finally won a Grand Prix, for Ferrari at Montreal in 1995.* (LAT)

*In another life, Max Mosley and Bernie Ecclestone were anything but well inclined towards the FIA. (LAT)*

*Schumacher chats with Ecclestone at Montreal in 1998. Bernie has always regretted Michael's insistence on a subservient team-mate. (LAT)*

Lotus. From the start we both went hard at it, and the battle went on and on and on! Off the track Jochen was probably my closest friend; and on it he was a man I trusted implicitly – which is something you need to feel about another driver before you're absolutely comfortable racing with him. Yes, all told, the ingredients were perfect that day.'

Stewart, given hindsight, is right. But qualifying – most of it, anyway – had scarcely suggested a memorable fight between these two. Through the summer of 1969 JYS and the Matra MS80, his favourite car, were on a roll, and in practice little suggested any disruption of the pattern. Rindt and the Lotus 49 had threatened, yes, but Jochen came to Silverstone in July without a point on the board. The thing never held together.

In all ways the season had been disastrous for him. At Barcelona he had started from the pole, and for the first quarter of the race was untouchable – until one of the flimsy rear wing supports buckled, which pitched the 49 into the barriers at 150mph, flipping it on to its back. Bloodied and concussed, Rindt was not fit enough to run at Monaco five weeks later, but he returned for the Dutch Grand Prix, qualified fastest, and led until a driveshaft broke. At Clermont-Ferrand he retired, sick and groggy, a combination perhaps of the track's ups and downs and his bang on the head in Spain.

At Silverstone, though, he felt fine and eager. Earlier in the year, at the International Trophy, he had driven a mesmeric race in the rain, lagging with drowned electrics in the early laps, then sweeping through the field when the problem cleared. On the line he all but caught the victorious Jack Brabham. He liked Silverstone, had good memories of it.

On Thursday morning Jochen's good humour evaporated. When he arrived in the paddock, there was no sign of the Gold Leaf Team Lotus transporter. We should remember, at this point, that 30 years ago there were no 'unofficial' practice sessions. All were timed, and all counted. And at Silverstone the first was on Thursday morning – *sans* Lotus.

Rindt was incensed. I can still see the expression on his face as he stood, in civvies, watching the rest go out. And while Jochen stomped around, fuming, team-mate Graham Hill made other arrangements for the morning. While Lotus had two drivers and no cars at Silverstone, Brabham's problem was precisely the opposite. A couple of BT26s were on hand, but Jack himself was off games (having broken an ankle in a testing shunt), and Jacky Ickx was late in arriving. Ron Tauranac therefore asked Hill to step aboard, and Graham was happy to oblige.

Difficult to imagine now, isn't it? – a driver skipping from car to car in the course of a meeting. Mind you, difficult to imagine, too, is the non-arrival of a major team for the first morning of practice.

When the transporter did front up, finally, the drivers were dismayed by its contents. Out rolled two of the four-wheel-drive 63s, plus a single 49B for Rindt. On the passenger seat of Colin Chapman's Piper Navajo was his secondhand car dealer's hat. Still warm.

Hill was appalled to learn that his regular 49 had been sold to South African John Love, while the spare car had been moved on to Jo Bonnier. The Swede, a close friend of Graham's, recognised his predicament at this, the British Grand Prix, and gallantly agreed to hand back his car for this one race, instead taking over one of the dread 63s, then seen by Chapman as 'the future'.

Four-wheel drive was much in Formula 1 vogue in 1969. In addition to the Bonnier car, Lotus also ran one for John Miles at Silverstone; there was a similar McLaren for Derek Bell, and Matra brought over their MS84, albeit without the intention to race it.

It was good they did. In the final qualifying session, on Friday afternoon, Stewart crashed. Conclusively quickest the day before, Jackie had just improved further, and was about to complete another lap, still faster. At Woodcote – the old Woodcote – he clipped the broken inside kerbing, blew the right rear tyre and spun hard into the bank at the exit of the corner. He was out of the light blue Matra in an instant: 'I knew the car had had it, but I was OK, and uppermost in my mind was that Helen and other members of my family were in the pits, and would have seen the whole thing. I wanted them to know I was OK as soon as possible.'

If the accident was bad news for Stewart, it was rather more than that for his team-mate, Jean-Pierre Beltoise, who had now to surrender his own MS80 to the master, pass the rest of the weekend in the heavy four-wheel-drive car.

In JPB's hastily renumbered machine, Stewart rushed out again, and got within half a second of his previous best. But it wasn't enough: by now Rindt had lapped in 1m 20.8s, which put him on the pole.

Jochen, I recall, was delighted. One thing to be on the pole; more important, he suggested, was the financial aspect of the thing. Through the final two-hour session, there was a bonus of £100 awarded to the fastest man in each 30-minute segment. Stewart took three of the four, but the last went to Rindt. Ah, what a man would do for a hundred quid back in 1969. For that matter, there was only a thousand for the race winner.

Hulme's McLaren joined Rindt and Stewart on the front row, but after Copse he never had a clear view of them again. At the end of the first lap Jochen led narrowly from Jackie, with Denny already more than three seconds adrift. The two leaders were setting up a pace impossible for the rest to sustain.

There was actually quite a gaggle disputing fourth place. At first Pedro Rodriguez, having a rare outing for Ferrari, ran there, chased by Bruce McLaren, Chris Amon (racing a Formula 1 Ferrari for the last time), Piers Courage (in Frank Williams's Brabham), Hill, Jo Siffert (Rob Walker Lotus) and Ickx. But for most of the afternoon all were quite incidental to the race. There was only a single point of focus: at the front.

Nothing to choose between them, really. Rindt's Lotus was marginally better on top speed, Stewart's Matra a shade superior under braking and through the turns. Jochen led for five laps, then Jackie was in front for ten.

On lap 16 it was again Rindt from Stewart, but now it seemed a little more settled. Was Jackie thinking ahead, as always, reckoning that 84 laps of Silverstone was a long way, there was time enough? We didn't know. We waited.

Endlessly they ran like that, routinely going round faster than most drivers had qualified. Such as McLaren, Hill, Siffert and Amon were lapped before half-distance. 'You might have expected Jochen to be right on the limit, and Jackie to be neat and calm,' Bruce observed afterwards, 'but when they came past me, it was the other way round.' Maybe Stewart didn't have anything left; maybe he was simply clinging on.

After 51 laps Rindt's lead was out to three seconds, but thereafter it came down, by tenths and slivers; after 61 the Lotus was firmly in Stewart's sights, and next time around the Matra was in front – and by five seconds. One lap later Jochen was into the pits.

It was a stupid thing, his problem, a matter of poor preparation. The left-hand rear wing endplate had worked loose, and through Silverstone's predominantly right-hand corners was chafing the tyre. Unable to find tools suitable for the job, the Lotus mechanics tore off the endplate with their bare hands, and sent Rindt back into the race, still second, but now 35 seconds away from the lead.

'Altogether, I think there were something like 30 lead changes between Jochen and myself,' said Stewart, 'although they didn't necessarily register at the start-finish line, because they happened out on the circuit. I've got a Michael Turner painting of me passing Jochen, and pointing at the rear wing, to alert him to the fact that it was rubbing against his tyre.'

Anger was fired in Rindt, cheated yet again of his first Grand Prix victory. The bulk of the spectators had been plainly with him all afternoon, and they cheered him one last time as he resumed the charge.

It was all for nothing, and he knew it better than anyone, but still he was carried along by the adrenalin of the day until lap 78, just six from the flag. Then he was a minute overdue, and more, and finally he went into the pit lane again, this time crawling, engine dead. The Lotus, incredibly, was out of fuel.

They sloshed a few gallons in, and once more Jochen returned to the race, now fourth and totally disheartened. With three laps left, indeed, he was passed by Courage, but on the last responded to pit signals, and moved past the Brabham again. By now JYS was on his slowing-down lap. The lap of honour, everyone felt, should have been shared.

Stewart went on to win the first of his three World

Championships, and remembers the 1969 season with particular affection. 'It was the height of all the good times, really. After the year before, when we'd had so many accidents and deaths, 1969 was a relatively clean year, a breath of air very badly needed. Then, in 1970, it all started again, and by 1973 I was going off the whole idea…'

# Frank's favourite driver

I REMEMBER THE RELIEF and reassurance we felt when they announced, at Zandvoort that day, that everyone was all right. It hadn't looked that way. At the end of the 23rd lap two drivers – Jo Siffert and Piers Courage – were missing, and on the far side of the circuit a huge waft of black smoke billowed into the gloomy sky.

It was fully an hour later when the announcer said there had been 'a mistake' earlier on. 'We have to tell you,' he said, 'that Piers Courage died in his car.'

This was 21 June 1970. Courage had been running eighth in the Dutch Grand Prix, at the wheel of the de Tomaso run by Frank Williams Racing Cars, a Formula 1 team in its fledgling years. 'In every respect,' Frank said, 'life got very tough the next day.

'I can't tell you that I considered getting out of the business. Not for a second. But after Piers died, it was a matter of going racing for different reasons. I was devastated. And, looking back, I believe every single one of his contemporaries came to his funeral, which says a lot about the bloke.

'In the 1970s,' Frank murmured, 'we buried a lot of drivers, didn't we?'

At the time of Courage's accident, less than three weeks had

134

passed since the death, in a midweek testing accident at Goodwood, of Bruce McLaren. Jacky Ickx had miraculously come out of a blazing Ferrari at Jarama, and Denny Hulme had suffered burns at Indianapolis.

On the rostrum at Zandvoort Jochen Rindt showed no pleasure in victory, for Piers had been a close buddy. And at Monza, less than three months later, Jochen, too, would die. An awful year, as Frank Williams remembered.

I never knew Piers Courage, coming into the world of Formula 1 a year or so after he was gone from it. But over time I've heard so many tales of the man as to feel enormous regret that we never met.

'When I talk about him, I have to be very careful,' Williams said, 'not to make it sound like a eulogy. The first thing about Piers was that he viewed almost everything he did with an amused eye. He was very good at a dinner party, for example, because he could sit with complete strangers, and talk to them about anything – half of it nonsense, of course, as always at dinner parties.

'He had a wonderful sense of humour, and delighted in telling stories against himself – though never at the expense of others. I mention this first, because I'd come from a very poor background, and didn't have anything like his privileges or self-confidence at that time – I was mesmerised by this performance he would put on! And, rightly or wrongly, much impressed by it.'

Piers, indeed, came from a privileged background. The eldest son of the chairman of Courage Breweries, he was educated at Eton, and knew nothing beyond huge wealth – until deciding one day to abandon accountancy (for which he was hardly suited) for a career in motor racing.

'We were sharing a flat,' said Frank, 'and with various other people, at different times, among them Charlie Lucas, Jonathan Williams and Charlie Crichton-Stuart.

'Piers was desperately keen to succeed as a racing driver, but it was a long time before anyone took him seriously. His background rather worked against him, because people thought he couldn't be tough enough. And at the same time they assumed he had access to family money, but that wasn't the case: his parents never supported his racing. He was like the rest of us – broke.

'He had started racing with a Lotus 7, then decided in 1964 he would have a go at Formula 3, which he did for two seasons. It was a very hand-to-mouth existence, I can tell you, a matter of setting off to some little race in East Germany or Sicily or somewhere, towing the car behind his old Ford Zephyr. He used to crash fairly regularly in 1964, I remember, and you'd probably doubt me if I told you we used to try and straighten out the chassis by pushing it against a wall with another car! But that's what we did...

'Very much the English gent, though, Piers, even when he was penniless. We'd share the driving of his Zephyr, towing to and from the races, and when it was my turn to drive he'd sleep on the back seat – but always in pyjamas! In fact, many's the time we stopped on an autobahn at first light, and Piers would head off to the gents with his toothbrush, still in his pyjamas. The locals used to think that very strange, but I'm sure he never noticed.'

It would be very easy, thus far, to get the impression that Courage was merely a dilettante, an escapist playing at being a racing driver. But Piers, according to Frank, was always very dedicated to his career.

'Because he was so different from the popular conception of a racing driver – especially these days – some people found it difficult to take him seriously. But he thought a great deal about whatever car he happened to be driving. He may not have been a great test driver, but he was extremely good at working with an engineer. In 1969 it was essentially just him and me, after all, and I relied on him almost totally for guidance.

'It was a lovely year, that. We had a Brabham chassis, Cosworth engines, and Dunlop tyres. Given the relative paucity of opposition that season, you usually got some points if you finished. We were second at Monte Carlo, second at Watkins Glen, and so on.

'That was the year Piers really found himself as a racing driver. He'd done Formula 1 before, with the Parnell BRMs, but it hadn't worked out very well. At the end of 1967 he came to me and suggested we do Formula 2 together, with a Brabham he knew I had hanging around. He proposed splitting the expenses, and I said, "Piers, that's great – you're on!" He got his confidence back with that, and then we decided to do Formula 1 together the following year.'

Over the winter of 1967/68 Courage decided to put together a team for the Tasman Series, running a Formula 2 McLaren, with a loan from his father, another from his bank manager. Usually, he was hard pressed to stay with Jimmy Clark's Lotus and Chris Amon's Ferrari, but at Longford, a long-defunct true road circuit in Tasmania, appalling weather conditions worked his way. The little McLaren, on Dunlop 'wets', was ideal for the task at hand.

Race morning was chaotic. The circuit at one point crossed over a wooden railway bridge, which was set afire by vandals, then put out. Then a torrential downpour waterlogged the circuit, after which the bridge caught fire once more, needing further extinguishing. The drivers began to debate the wisdom of starting the race at all at this, a track lethal even in perfect weather.

Discussions took place, and there was necessarily some pressure on those taking part: the race, if it were to go ahead, had to be over by a given time, because the track also went over a level crossing…

Courage described it thus: 'Even the most feckless racing driver is unwilling to compete with an express train travelling at right angles to himself. This was the only time I have known the timing of a race to be governed by Bradshaw.' A nice laconic touch he had. And he won the race, too, with Clark second, Pedro Rodriguez third.

After the Formula 1 successes of 1969, Williams reached agreement with de Tomaso to run a new Dallara-designed car for 1970, and of course hoped Courage would drive it.

'These days,' Williams said, 'we see drivers who are … very commercially minded about their five- or ten-year lifespan in Formula 1, let's put it that way. Piers didn't view it quite like that – he wasn't out to make as much as he could while he could.

'For 1970, he got an offer from Ferrari, for both Formula 1 and sports car racing, and he turned it down. He had already verbally agreed to drive for me in Formula 1, and for Alfa Romeo in sports cars, and never thought of going back on his word. The money, in fact, worked out at about the same, but he well knew what moving to Ferrari would do for his career. For the drivers of today, it would have been no contest, I'm sure.

'That period with the de Tomaso was sadly brief, but Piers really flowered as a racing driver at that time. The car was terrible at first – overweight, lousy handling and so on – but after the first race, at Kyalami, he sat down with Dallara and the others, and went through it, point by point. It was like a two-hour debrief, which was unheard of in those days. And the second version of the car was a huge improvement. By mid-season we were getting to the stage of becoming really competitive with it.'

There was always an impression at the time that Courage personified his name perhaps too much for his own good. 'Piers was *very* brave, certainly,' Frank agreed, 'but very skilful, too. He wasn't as good as Jochen Rindt – whom I personally still regard as the best there's ever been – but he was very much a top Grand Prix driver by 1970.'

A mighty unusual one, however. 'It seems to me that one of the advantages of a privileged education, like Piers had at Eton, is that, even if you're not going to be a brilliant physicist or whatever, they try and instil into you the importance in life of history, literature, the world around you. They try and make sure you haven't spent seven years there, just to go out and start screwing.

'I think of Piers, for example, whenever I hear Beethoven's Sixth Symphony – the Pastoral – because it was his favourite piece of music. And in 1969 and 1970 I took to travelling with books of poetry, to be ready for him! Even so, he could always outquote me, which maddened me.

'Racing was a lot of fun then. It still is now, in some ways, but back then it was like being on a high all the time. Piers's career – and the team's career – were coming along very strongly. Everything was looking good for the future. Ford had just bought out de Tomaso, so we had high hopes of more finance and technical backing. We seemed to have it made.

'And here was this society golden boy driving for the team! He was a great-looking fellow, very amusing, devastatingly charming, beautiful wife, title, all that stuff. Sally, his wife, was just like him – nutty as a fruitcake! A very pretty girl, but a very tough-minded one, too.

'I particularly recall one afternoon with them, in Monte Carlo in 1970. We were sitting in a little cheap old café, with everyone stopping by to say hello to them, and I remember thinking that this life was so beautiful and happy for them that it just couldn't go on. I wasn't thinking in terms of his getting killed in a racing car, or anything of the kind; just that their life was almost too good to be true…'

## JOCHEN RINDT

# Working without
# a net

IT WAS A LITTLE RED FIAT, a 500, and it sat in the traffic that morning, anonymous among countless others. An unlikely number of people were crammed into it, together with provisions for the day.

The morning was very hot as they inched along. As usual, the police had lost control, and horns blared in constant discord. An overheating Alfa pulled off, steaming, to the side of the road, the driver loudly at odds with his sweating passengers. In the bedlam, though, the general timbre was good-natured. These people were going to Monza.

The Fiat I have never forgotten. Covering its entire rear window, stuck there with respectful black tape, was a message: *Jochen, non ti dimenticare.*

There were others, lots of them, in cars and vans and coaches, wherever you looked, but nothing sticks so vividly in the mind as that simple and moving message. *Jochen, you will not be forgotten.*

Thirty years ago it is now, and hard to believe so. It was my first time at Monza, and I saw this little car near the traffic lights by the Hotel de la Ville, where I have stayed for virtually every Italian Grand Prix since. And always, as I arrive there from the airport, the image comes back. Oddly, it was some

140

years before I discovered that Jochen had been staying there that last weekend of his life.

I went to Monza only for race day in 1970, and with very mixed feelings. In my flat, late the previous afternoon, there had been some mention of his name on a faint radio in another room, and I thought only that he must have taken pole position, as he usually did that summer. Then, an hour or so later, outside Baker Street station I saw an *Evening Standard* hoarding: 'World's leading race ace dies in crash'.

Monza the following day furnished every emotion Grand Prix racing can muster. From my seat in the stand, I looked over towards the archway into the paddock. Only a few hours earlier I had seen it on the TV news, a truck driving slowly through, Jochen's broken Lotus 72 dangling from its crane.

There were no chicanes at the proud *autodromo* then, and the cars tended to come by the pits in swarms. Clay Regazzoni won that afternoon in the only surviving Ferrari, and the orgy of celebration afterwards was in poignant contrast to how things must have been 24 hours earlier, when that still, so incongruous and eerie at a race track, settled over the place.

I have no personal tales of Jochen Rindt to tell, because I never knew him. At the time of his accident I was on the point of going into journalism, months away from covering my first Grand Prix.

When Gilles Villeneuve was killed, a lot of people wrote to me in their sorrow, knowing he had been a friend, offering sympathy. Some said their lives had been touched by him – they hadn't known him, but, yes, their lives had been touched by him. And I could understand them readily, because I had known exactly those feelings of remote loss when Rindt died.

Probably they have their roots, these feelings, in selfishness. Jochen Rindt put all manner of things in my life that I couldn't put there myself, and now they were gone. My friends and I spent hours in reminiscence of him; whole days spectating in freezing April at Silverstone, simply for those sublime moments when Jochen would teeter through Woodcote in the Lotus 49.

Wings on Formula 1 cars were around for the last three years of Rindt's life, and it was no surprise that he hated them. For one thing, he thought them dangerous (which, in their infancy, indubitably they were); more to the point, they made racing cars easier to drive. Manna for the journeyman, certainly, but necessarily distasteful to an artist. Ayrton Senna and Alain Prost would feel the same way about traction control, and other electronic 'driver aids'.

Curiously, I would not immediately think of Rindt when compiling a list of the best drivers in Grand Prix history, but his name would come up instantly when contemplating the greatest.

When the talk is of Rindt, most people at once think of Monaco in 1970. That day, I would suggest, he drove much of the race in the sort of altered state Senna would later attempt to describe, that sensation of being 'ahead of the car'. Watching Jochen at Monte Carlo, one had the impression of a man leading his car, dragging it behind him at a speed it did not enjoy.

Jochen was peeved at Monaco that year: the new Lotus 72, for which there had been so much optimism, wasn't yet working well, so out came the old 49. There seemed little realistic hope of success, and Rindt qualified the car only eighth, his time of 1m 25.90s almost two seconds away from Jackie Stewart's pole lap. He wasn't much interested, in truth, and drove in the same fashion for the first half of the race, picking up places only when such as Stewart, Jacky Ickx and Jean-Pierre Beltoise retired. By 40 laps – half-distance – he was fourth, 15 seconds behind Jack Brabham, the leader. Then he passed Denny Hulme for third, and suddenly his lap times came alive.

It was an incredibly fast race, one way and another, with Brabham lapping consistently under his qualifying time, Amon a couple of seconds behind in the March, and Jochen 12 seconds behind Chris.

Twenty laps left, and Amon retired with broken suspension, and now Rindt had that whiff of the leader's scent. Fourteen seconds to make up, and Jochen began to pare it away, albeit not by enough to catch Brabham; all he could do was maintain the pressure, hope that Jack might be flustered into a mistake. With four laps left, though, the gap was still nine seconds. Hopeless, apparently.

Or maybe not. On lap 77 Brabham was disastrously held up by an ailing Jo Siffert, so that as he crossed the line, with three laps to the flag, he led Rindt by 4.4 seconds. On the next lap, agitated still, he lost another couple. Two laps … 2.4…

Jack collected himself now, and his 79th lap was his fastest of the race – but still Jochen gained over a second! One lap … 1.3…

In the end Brabham blew it at the last corner. All round the final lap Rindt was gaining, gaining, but on the approach to the Gasworks Hairpin was not quite in range. Brabham, though, was thoroughly unnerved by now, and decided he had to lap Piers Courage's de Tomaso before the corner. In so doing, he got on the marbles, locked up, slid straight on into the guardrail.

The following morning there was one of the great photographs on the front of *Nice Matin*: Stewart, who had retired while leading, was out on the road by the finish line, cheering Rindt in. If he couldn't win, there was pleasure in his friend's success.

The aftermath of that race was extraordinary. I had my tape recorder running, and even now the animated buzz of the crowd brings back the day. Announcements, in French, Italian and English, added spice, and eventually the full force of Rindt's achievement came into perspective.

'Un record du tour sensationnel! Au quatre-vingtième tour! Jochen Rindt, sur Lotus numero trois! Une minute vingt-trois seconds, deux-dixièmes!'

There were gasps at that, but there it was. On his last lap, Jochen had done 1m 23.2s. What we didn't know at the time was that the one before had been 1m 23.3s. And this after going on two hours around Monaco. He had qualified, remember, at 1m 25.9s.

Even dry statistics come alive when they are such as these, but they cannot hint at what Rindt was doing with that Lotus in the closing stages. You could believe, watching him, that he was in some kind of trance.

And afterwards, too. Up in the Royal Box, with the Rainiers, tears ran down Jochen's cheeks as the Austrian national anthem was played. It was a spontaneous release of emotion, a man who had come suddenly back to earth, begun to understand the enormity of what he had done.

Later, much later, we saw him again, relaxed now and laughing. It was after midnight when he and wife Nina walked from the Gala Ball at the Hotel de Paris, across Casino Square and down to the Tip-Top Bar, swinging the trophy between them. There was simple joy in his face, and he wanted everyone to savour the moment with him. It was so easy to share his pleasure.

I remember this race particularly because it was a day when a racing driver transcended his car, and I have seen only a handful like that. Most of my memories of Jochen are tied to the Lotus 49, for the 72 – once it had become homogenised – was more a car to drive on rails. That summer he won with it at Zandvoort, Clermont-Ferrand, Brands Hatch and Hockenheim, and undoubtedly it was the class of the field. 'A monkey,' he said, after beating Ickx in Germany, 'could have won in my car.'

Jochen had a face which was easy to read, and as a fan I always loved that about him. On the victory rostrum in Holland, there was no hint of a smile, and nor should there have been, either, for his pal Piers Courage had been killed in the race. But elsewhere, when Rindt won, his elation was vivid. And when the car let him down, as at the British Grand Prix in 1969, you knew this wasn't the time for autographs.

He could be arrogant, they say, and certainly didn't suffer fools, but those who knew him well recall a gentleness, too, a vulnerability. Through that summer of 1970 he began to worry increasingly: 'Things are going well – almost too well, in fact.'

Two weeks before Monza he drove the 72 at the Oulton Park Gold Cup. In time-honoured Lotus style, everything was a little haphazard, and in the first heat he was only third, hampered by a low top gear ratio. They changed it for the second heat, and this one he romped.

Immediately after taking the flag, he pulled off at Old Hall, where I happened to be watching, and my last sight of him was as he climbed into a Piper Aztec, which immediately took him to a connecting flight for Vienna. The next day he had promised to run his F2 Lotus in an Austrian hill-climb.

What do we recall of him now, the only posthumous World Champion, the man Frank Williams regards as the greatest ever? The mesmeric car control, certainly, the deep voice, the boxer's nose, tousled hair. But those who saw him remember Jochen chiefly for this: he made them catch their breath.

# This slipstreaming lark

WHEN THE DRIVERS ARRIVED at Monza, in September of 1971, there was nothing – save a Grand Prix victory – at stake. At Zeltweg, three weeks earlier, Jackie Stewart had put a lock on his second World Championship, for Jacky Ickx and Ronnie Peterson, the only threats to his title, had failed to score. Such was Stewart's domination with the Tyrrell that summer – five wins from eight races – that, with Monza, Mosport and Watkins Glen still to come, his total was beyond reach.

For all that, the Italian Grand Prix promised to be something, because it always was. Monza was then a slipstreamer circuit, uncompromisingly fast, and as close in concept to an IndyCar oval race as ever Formula 1 has seen. 'OK, you had the Curva Grande and you had the Lesmos, which were testing corners,' said Stewart, 'but for most of the lap you were flat out.'

Although the track was routinely denigrated as no real test of a driver, nothing more than a temple of raw speed, still the feeling was that, like Monte Carlo, it had a place in the Grand Prix calendar as a maverick event. Even 30 years ago, though, before safety became an overriding issue in motor racing, it was considered perilous.

The 1971 season was my first as a racing journalist, and everything was fresh. In the course of that summer, I had got to

146

know most of the drivers, and of particular help to me was Chris Amon, whom I still count among my closest friends.

I have never been a natural supporter of the 'underdog', for the sake of it, yet undeniably Amon had this quality about him, by virtue of his appalling luck. Down the years I have never seen greater car control than his, and time and again he led Grands Prix consummately, only for something to go wrong.

It is undeniable that many of the attributes considered desirable in a racing driver make them sometimes unattractive as human beings, which explains in part, perhaps, why Chris never achieved the success his ability warranted, and also why he was, and is, such wonderful company. If he had talent to throw away, what he didn't have was the blind dedication to go with it. For Amon, motor racing was merely one of the good things of life, and he wasn't going to live in a monastery for it.

Fitness was thought a good thing back then, but no more than that. 'Tell you what,' Chris confided at the end of that season, 'I'm really going to try and get back to where I was in 1968, with Ferrari. Go for runs, cut down on the booze, and keep the cigarettes under some sort of control.' When last I saw him, two years ago, he was still working on it.

In 1971, Amon was with Matra, who had perhaps the best-handling chassis in the business, but a V12 engine lamentably short of horsepower. So pathetic had it been at the Nürburgring that the team opted to give Austria a miss, and concentrate on resolving the problem, which centred around the oil system.

'It worked, too,' Chris said. 'Everyone thought we had a new engine, but it wasn't that at all – they'd simply solved the oil churning problem. My engine at the Nürburgring had had only 395bhp, whereas the one they gave me for Monza had 460, which was on a par with Cosworth, if not Ferrari and … er, the best BRM engines.'

BRM looked good for Monza, having recently hit a period of unaccustomed reliability. Following the death of team leader Pedro Rodriguez in a sports car race at mid-season, Jo Siffert had stepped nobly up to the plate, and won at Zeltweg, another high-speed track. Monza was expected to favour the V12s, with the Cosworth V8 brigade for once up against it.

During the practice days in Italy, the crowd was down, perhaps because the World Championship was already resolved, in favour of Stewart, rather than Ickx, and clearly the organisers hoped for a Ferrari driver on the pole. Timekeeping was a somewhat haphazard business back then. There were no TV screens, showing order changes, no TAG-Heuer automatic timing system, and at Monza there were six hours of practice, all official, all counting for grid positions.

After each session, you waited endlessly for the sheets to be issued. Late on Saturday afternoon, Ickx – and Ferrari – were shown as fastest, and the Italian journalists wrote suitably rabid stories, imploring the locals to come, give their support on the morrow.

After the papers had gone to press, amazingly, someone discovered a time faster than Ickx's. Half a second faster, in fact. 'Throughout practice, when I was running on my own, I was lapping nearly a second quicker than anyone else,' Amon smiled, 'and I got pole quite easily. As well as that, Ickx's time was cooked, I think.'

Thus, when the devoted poured into the old Monza Parco on Sunday morning, they were disappointed to find that a blue car, rather than a red, would be on pole position. But they were mollified when Clay Regazzoni, on the fourth row with his Ferrari, made the best start.

Comfortably the best start. Before the rest had moved, Gianclaudio was in second gear, at least, but in those halcyon times to penalise a Ferrari at Monza – particularly one driven by the previous year's winner – would have been unthinkable, and at the end of the first lap the red car had a sizeable lead, cheered to the echo, of course.

Most of the early leading, though, was done by Peterson's March-Cosworth, Ronnie hounded by the Tyrrells of Stewart and François Cevert, Siffert's BRM, Regazzoni and Ickx. Inevitably, with so many long straights, the attrition rate was high, and by lap 18 Stewart was gone, together with – tragedy for the locals – both the Ferraris. So engrossing, though, was the lead battle that the *tifosi* stayed put. Monza used to be like that.

Next to find trouble was Siffert, whose BRM jammed itself in fourth gear, but others were coming through by now, including Mike Hailwood, who had not been near a Formula 1 car for six years, and was making a return with Surtees. On lap 25, 'The Bike' – who had qualified 17th – came by in the lead! 'I didn't know what this slipstreaming lark was all about,' he grinned afterwards. 'I'd never done it before.' A close friend of Amon's, he endorsed the same hearty lifestyle: 'This is supposed to be a sport, not a bloody religion...'

As the end of the race neared, the protagonists shook themselves down, tried to prepare themselves for the final sprint to the flag. It was all a matter of being in the right place at Parabolica, the last corner, of getting through it well, of slingshotting by the rest just before the line. No one wanted to lead *into* Parabolica, in other words.

Cevert and Peterson arrived pretty well together, both leaving their braking a mite too late, and getting out of shape as a consequence. At this point, Peter Gethin, fourth going into the last lap, took a deep breath, dived past them, and took his BRM V12 a thousand revs over its limit before snatching top gear. At the line, Gethin – who somehow had the confidence to give a victory salute – was perhaps a couple of feet ahead of Peterson, with Cevert third and Hailwood fourth. Howden Ganley, fifth for BRM, was six-tenths behind his team-mate.

And Amon? He was sixth, half a minute later. 'I got a pretty poor start, and the temperatures started to go up a bit, so I just sat back, and waited until I'd got rid of a bit of fuel. Once I'd done that, I had no trouble in getting up to the front.

'I led for several laps, without any problem, until nine laps from the end, when I lost my visor... In previous races, I'd been losing tear-offs, so this time I'd taped it more firmly – too firmly, as it turned out, because when I pulled it off, the whole bloody visor went! Actually, it wouldn't have made a lot of difference, because then I started to get fuel starvation, as well. It was a bit disappointing, all in all.'

In American racing circles, they are very fond of statistics. After a race, they like to reel off the number of leaders, of lead changes, and things like that, but in Europe such things are never mentioned, perhaps for the sound reason that lead changes are not something we take for granted in contemporary Formula 1.

Lest you believe otherwise, though, it was not always so. At Monza that day in 1971, the lead changed 25 times, among eight drivers, and perhaps the most remarkable fact of all is that on only eight of the 55 laps was the order as it had been the previous time around. Gethin would never score another World Championship victory, but assuredly his name will be in the record books for ever, as the winner of the fastest Grand Prix ever run: 150.754mph.

It was, however, very much a last hurrah for Monza. When the teams went back, a year later, chicane blight had attacked the circuit, and changed its character utterly, serving to break up the field, to reduce the lap speed by 20mph. Amon and Ickx shared the front row again, but neither finished, and it was left to Emerson Fittipaldi's Lotus to win comfortably from Hailwood's Surtees.

'A better result than last year,' Mike observed, 'but no fun at all. They've ruined the place with these poxy chicanes...'

# DENIS JENKINSON

# The little man with the beard

DENIS JENKINSON'S STANDARDS were always exacting. At Silverstone, years ago, a bunch of us were given a ride in a factory Porsche 935, and at the wheel was a man who had won a Grand Prix. Jenks – of course – was first to go. Afterwards, we asked how it had been, and his expression told its own tale. 'Fantastic!' he said. Pause. 'Just think what it would have been like with a proper driver…'

He was overdoing it, of course, and knew it, but then everything was relative in Jenks's world. 'I've never been interested in who won a race,' he would say, 'until I know who was behind him.'

Like anyone involved in racing journalism, Jenks well knew that to admire the driver was not necessarily to like the man. He had his villains, as well as his heroes, and once you were into either file, there you stayed for ever. That said, though, there remained a fundamental esteem for anyone who raced, be it in cars or on motorcycles.

He came from a hard school – this, after all, was one who hung out of a sidecar through Burnenville and Malmédy – and while he would grieve when a driver died, so he accepted it as a natural, if unwelcome, adjunct to a sport which could never be safe, in any workaday sense of the word.

Significantly, it was the loss of Mike Hailwood which affected him most of all: for one of his greatness to die on a track, running at 'full noise', would have been one thing; to perish in a road accident, through the fault of another, was unacceptable.

Jenks took so much simple joy in motor racing. He might be crotchety as hell, for whatever reason, in the traffic on the way to a circuit, but once into the paddock – around racing cars – his mood would be transformed, and he never lost that. After Gilles Villeneuve had won the 1981 Monaco Grand Prix, I walked down the hill to Ste Devote, and there encountered DSJ, literally dancing a jig of delight. Drenched through, glasses misted up, he was the same way, too, when Ayrton Senna won in the rains of Estoril four years later.

Although his chief interest in the sport always lay with machinery – with engines, above all – Jenks was fascinated by the genus racing driver in all its forms, and if Grand Prix racing was obviously his first love, he was never one to denigrate other areas of the sport. One time, over breakfast in Long Beach, he saw someone coming into the room, and urgently asked who he was. 'He's a racing driver, isn't he?' It was Cale Yarborough. 'Knew it!' said Jenks, triumphantly. 'Didn't know who he was, but I could tell he was a racing driver. Something about his walk, the look in his eyes...'

I tried for years to get him to come to Daytona or Indianapolis with me, for Jenks, above all things, loved raw speed. 'Don't think I could stand the excitement,' he would say. 'It would all be too much.' He never did go to either 500, but eventually visited Indy, and babbled about it like a schoolboy afterwards.

During dinner at the Autosport Awards, only a couple of days after Jenks's death in 1996, Stirling Moss called for a moment's quiet, then asked us to raise our glasses to the little man. 'He was,' Stirling affectionately said, 'a wonderful bloke, and without doubt one of the true eccentrics.'

No argument there, as anyone can attest who ever visited his home. Jenks's domestic arrangements were ... unorthodox. You got used, for example, to the lack of electricity: power, such as it was, came from a small generator, and was insufficient to provide illumination for two rooms at once, so that if anyone needed to use the loo, everyone else was in total darkness until his or her return.

This Jenks saw as nothing out of the ordinary. 'Blackout time,' he would cheerfully announce, and there was the same insouciance when once I questioned the siting of a Daimler V8 engine at the foot of his bed. 'Nowhere else to put it,' he said, as if that explained everything. 'No space in the sitting room.' Indeed there wasn't; that was given over to a selection of motorbikes, in various stages of repair.

That really was the whole thing about Jenks. His great charm – and a source of endless amusement to his friends – was that he truly believed that his was the logical way, that the rest of the world was curiously out of step. Bliss was fettling one of his cars or bikes, to the accompaniment of Sidney Bechet.

The absence of electricity never bothered him, but he would have been lost without his telephone, which was used with abandon, and around the clock. Countless times I would be on the point of sitting down to eat, and the phone would ring: 'I've been thinking about that lap of Senna's on Saturday...' the quiet voice would say, and you knew that supper was a lost cause.

Other than cars and bikes, Jenks cared absolutely nothing for material possessions, but he loved good food and wine, and would sleep like a child after a hearty dinner: the great storm of October 1987 may have devastated southern England, but it failed to awaken the guest in Stirling Moss's spare bedroom.

His favourite period of racing, certainly in relatively recent times, was the height of the turbo era, when boost was unlimited, and such as Renault and BMW laid around 1,400 horsepower at their drivers' backs for qualifying. That, combined with 'one lap' tyres, and the ability of a Senna, made for drama as distilled as Grand Prix racing has known, and Jenks revelled in it, particularly at what he considered a 'proper' circuit, like the Österreichring or Spa-Francorchamps.

Ayrton was one of his great heroes, a man whose artistry could, and occasionally did, move him to tears. It pleased him enormously to receive a Christmas card each year: 'To friend Jenkinson, from Ayrton Senna'. And although he would probably have denied it, I don't believe he ever felt quite the same about racing after Imola in 1994. It was good he wasn't there that day.

'May the first,' he murmured sadly on the phone the following week. 'We won the Mille Miglia on May the first, and I always associated it with such pleasure. Now this...' His diary entry reads simply, 'Absolute bloody disaster'.

Gaining entry to Jenks's personal hall of fame was not the work of a moment: 'In my teens,' he said, 'my hero was Bernd Rosemeyer, and *everybody's* hero was Nuvolari.' And since the war? 'It's a waste of time comparing different eras; you can only go for drivers supreme in their own time. There are just five in my top bracket: Ascari, Moss, Clark, (Gilles) Villeneuve and Senna.'

Arguing with Jenks – on this or any other subject – was not a rewarding experience. 'What about Schumacher?' you'd say. 'Does nothing for me...'

In a certain mood, black was white, and that was the end of it. He took a special delight in playing devil's advocate. 'Hang on a minute,' you'd splutter, 'how can you criticise Prost for doing no more than necessary to win a race, and then praise Fangio for always trying to win at the slowest possible speed?'

'Different,' he would reply, studying the menu. 'Well, how is it different?' 'Just is...'

A minute or two later, once he had got you to the point of apoplexy, there would come a sly grin, and you would realise once again that you'd been had. He could, on occasion, be maddening, and none of his friends would claim otherwise, but neither would they suggest that, at heart, he was other than the kindest of men, who liked nothing better than to share his enthusiasm for motor racing, his experiences in the sport.

'Jenkinson!' you would hear all the time if you were in his company in Italy. Even 40 years after that Mille Miglia victory with Moss, he was widely recognised in this country he adored. And sometimes, at the end of a day, I would drive with him into the hills near Imola, where the road signs read 'Futa' and

154

'Raticosa', and the spirits abide of Nuvolari and Varzi, Castellotti and Taruffi.

In the summer of 1995, Mercedes-Benz brought a 300SLR to the Goodwood Festival of Speed, and although Stirling and Jenks had made guest appearances in similar cars on previous occasions, this was the first time in chassis 0004 – the actual car in which they averaged almost 98mph around Italy that day in 1955. 'The last time I saw it,' Jenks said, 'was in the square in Brescia that evening.'

They ran it up the hill several times over the two days, Moss gunning the car hard wherever possible, so that one heard again the unmistakable 'thrummy' bellow of the 3-litre straight-eight, a sound quite unlike any other in a weekend of gorgeous sounds. At the end of it all, Jenks's eyes were moist. 'I can die happy now,' he said.

When I was a kid, I would read his writings in *Motor Sport*, and, even more than his race reports, I relished 'Continental Notes', in which he would discuss anything that touched his world. Quite often, there would be a detailed description of a journey on open and uncluttered roads, by Porsche 356 or E-Type Jaguar, to a race somewhere, and I would think to myself that life could scarcely be better than this.

If anyone fired in me the desire to write about motor racing, it was this little fellow with the beard. When a piece had those initials, DSJ, at its foot, you knew it was the real thing. Like so many of my contemporaries, I owe him more than I can say.

# Leaving the party early

THINKING BACK, my table at the Autosport Awards evening in 1992 was a particularly fine one. Round about me, among others, were Patrick Head, who couldn't be boring if he tried, Bobby Rahal, among the most articulate and civilised racing drivers I have known, James Hunt and Innes Ireland.

It was a memorable evening, with tongues well loosened by red wine, and I wish now I could remember more of it. When we went back to the Grosvenor House, a year later, both James and Innes were gone.

Hunt's death came as a particular shock, for he was only 45, and had latterly changed his way of life, given thought to his health, even taken to using a bicycle to get around.

Only a few weeks before the London dinner, he had arrived in this fashion for Denny Hulme's Memorial Service in Chelsea. We were standing around outside the church when the former World Champion hove into sight – his bike an old-fashioned sit-up-and-beg type, complete with basket on the front.

'Morning, chaps! Back in a minute...' And with that he briefly disappeared. It had not escaped us that James was less than suitably dressed for an occasion such as this, but soon he was back, immaculate, having popped round the corner to change. After the service, he went through the procedure again.

Hunt died, of a heart attack, on the Monday evening after the Canadian Grand Prix the following June. I flew back from Montreal that night, and the following morning watched the tape of the race. The BBC had not sent James and Murray Walker to Canada, and instead they had performed their inimitable double act from a studio in London; Murray later told me that James had been quite his normal self, good-humoured and ebullient. Certainly he sounded that way on the commentary.

At lunchtime I had a call informing me of the awful news, and at once set to the writing of an obituary for that week's *Autosport*. It was not until the next morning that I got around to playing back the messages on my answering machine. After three weeks away in North America, there were many, and the last one set me trembling: 'Nigel, J. Hunt speaking. Six twenty-five, Monday evening. Just calling for a gossip. If you're back tonight, give me a shout – failing that, tomorrow perhaps. Bye...'

It was only after his retirement from Formula 1 that James and I became friends – indeed, truth to tell, in his racing days I never much cared for him. At the height of his fame, in the mid-1970s, he had about him a posse of hangers-on to set your teeth on edge.

These were not, in any important sense, offensive people, but they maddened you with their vacuous self-importance. The McLaren motorhome was like a school common room of the worst kind, but there always lingered the suspicion that James himself did not really belong.

Glamorous, successful, loose and free, he was an obvious target for celebrity leeches, but when he gave up racing, in 1979, they mercifully evaporated, and what remained was a man urbane, charming, lucid, kind.

There was, in fact, nothing of James Hunt that was phoney. Later he began a second career in racing, as a broadcaster and journalist, and I was one of many former detractors who came to hold him in great affection, as well as respect.

Despite a rather ungainly gait, James was a natural

sportsman in his youth, but motor racing caught his interest only when friends took him to Silverstone. 'I was 18,' he said, 'and, for the first time in my life, thought that here was something I might be able to do well.'

He began with a Mini, and progressed through the ranks, much of the time a bull looking for a china shop. But his ability was obvious, and in 1973 he was hired by Alexander Hesketh to drive for his lordship's newly-founded Formula 1 team.

'In fact,' Hunt said, 'the plan was to do Formula 2, but at the start of the year we did the Race of Champions at Brands with a rented Surtees, just for the Lord to get a taste of Formula 1, and that went pretty well. So he suddenly took the rather intelligent view, we all thought, that we might as well do Formula 1, his philosophy – very simple, really – being that, "If we're going to mess around at the back, making fools of ourselves, let's do it in the real thing." So, because we were no good at F2, we moved up to F1!'

In 1974 James won his first Formula 1 race, the International Trophy at Silverstone, and the following year his first Grand Prix, holding off the then dominant Ferrari of Niki Lauda at Zandvoort. In 1976 he joined McLaren – and became World Champion.

Hunt was an instinctive racer: 'I was never much of a worker, never that much involved with my racing, outside of when I got in the car, and started to drive it. It's the same with squash – but put me on a court, and I give everything. I turn on in a competitive situation.'

He would admit willingly that his approach to racing was not particularly deep, and that he believed both good and bad. He was never a man to 'think himself' into a Grand Prix for a week beforehand, never one to allow distractions to get to him. 'Conversely, in bad times some drivers will get stuck into the root of the problem, and regenerate enthusiasm in the team. I was never the man to do that.'

It was in such circumstances that James retired, and, typically, he did it in the middle of a season. Following his Championship year, he won several races for McLaren in 1977, but after a poor season in 1978 left to join Walter Wolf's team.

At the Monaco Grand Prix of 1979, his car broke down, and he walked away from it without a backward glance. 'It was over,' he said. 'I knew this was my last race, and I hated that car, anyway. I felt no sadness at all, just immense relief.'

If Hunt always raced with consummate bravery, he was well aware of the risks in an era far more perilous than this one. Often he was sick before a race, but from tension rather than fear. Once in the car, he was all business.

There has always been a sprinkling of drivers prepared to fight as hard for 10th place as for first, but Hunt was emphatically not of their number. 'I always needed to feel I could win,' he said, 'and in my last couple of seasons I didn't have the car to do it. I wasn't prepared to go on risking my life to finish seventh, or whatever.'

In a car, his natural ability was high, his audacity considerable, his racing brain unusually sharp. Tactically, James was always strong in a race, and this was also to serve him well in his BBC TV work.

He became, to my mind, one of the great sports commentators, the mahogany voice and dry humour meshing perfectly with M. Walker's more overt delivery. As an analyst of Grand Prix racing, he was unmatched. There was always the substance of personal experience.

Hunt never artificially romanticised motor racing. 'I won't compromise myself by saying things I don't mean,' he said. 'What tends to happen, in fact, is that I compromise myself by saying exactly what I think.' So, too, he did. James was always honest, not least with himself.

He was a rich man when he retired, but the 1980s were to deal harshly with him. There was a costly divorce, and a series of poor investments progressively dissipated a considerable fortune. There remained, however, his beautiful, slightly tatty, house in Wimbledon, where he lived in splendid anarchy. Invariably the front door, like the French windows, would be open, and a variety of folk would wander through the sitting-room in both directions. Presumably James knew most of them. With his beloved Alsatian gnawing at the sofa, and one of the parrots squawking unsuitable English, he would sit back and smile.

It was an irony that towards the end of his life Hunt worked hard at his fitness, and had given up both cigarettes and booze. 'Quite simple, really,' he cheerfully acknowledged. 'The tail was starting to wag the dog.' And in the same way he made no attempt to hide that – in his terms – he was close to broke. Whatever his turmoils, his demeanour never changed, and it was perhaps this quality his friends most admired. He had not a grain of self-pity.

Ultimately James came to love racing a great deal, but it wasn't always so. While he was actually doing it, he once told me, he didn't really like it very much. He retired young, a few months short of his 32nd birthday, and never regretted it.

It takes a brave man to admit to fear. 'I was getting scared of hurting myself,' he said. 'I don't think that would have happened if I had been in a car that could win, because that's the way I am: in a competitive situation, everything else goes out of my head. But I didn't have that for my last couple of years, and I was never the type to get pleasure from simply being a racing driver. Driving a racing car, when you've got the ability, is like riding a bike. You don't get worse at it. It's only your head that moves around, right?'

After his retirement, the drivers Hunt most admired were Senna and Prost. Not only did he consider them the best, he also had boundless respect for their staying power. 'To run at the front in Grand Prix racing – and to stay there – is mentally exhausting. The brain gets tired before the body does.' A pause. 'I mean, you've only got to look at some of the geriatrics tooling around nowadays to see who's got tired brains...'

For all his laid-back irreverence, however, James could be intensely serious when the moment demanded. That was what made him such a gem of a commentator. The mellow voice helped, of course, but he was never bland, never followed party lines. A great performance from a driver or team received due tribute, a poor one stinging rebuke.

Like all journalists, admitted or not, he had his likes and dislikes, and sometimes rattled a cage or two with his observations. On these occasions, when confronted by the object of his criticism, he would fight his corner vigorously, but always with good humour.

I still miss the visits to that lovely house in Wimbledon, with the old Mercedes and A35 van outside, the soppy Alsatian, foul-mouthed parrot and bare-footed owner within. In an age made colourless by political correctness, he was genuinely a free spirit; it was a terrible sadness that, personally happier than at any time in his life, he left the party so early. 'It's always the bores that stay to the end, isn't it?' he would say.

\* \* \*

Well, usually, but not always. At any social event of any worth, R. McG. I. Ireland was invariably the last to leave. Innes and James got along famously, and no surprise there, for there was much in their make-up that was similar.

Ireland was feisty and tough, yet essentially a gentleman, and as humane an individual as I have known. One of the very fastest drivers of his generation, in 1960 he created a sensation in the new Lotus 18, with which he won squarely at Goodwood and Silverstone.

A race I recall more vividly, though, is the Oulton Park Gold Cup of that year, when he simply ran away from the field, which included Stirling Moss in Rob Walker's similar car. When the mood was on him, Innes could hack it with anyone, but invariably his luck was poor, and that day was typical in that the car eventually broke.

There was always a strong element of fatalism in Ireland, and it is a fact that his career was signposted by a number of huge accidents. He was under no illusions about Lotuses of the time, accepting, if unwillingly, that if Colin Chapman's radical cars were blindingly fast, they were also fragile. 'Setting off on a lap of Spa in one of those things, lad, it was best to put your imagination on a very low light. Something would break, and you'd come in, and they'd Sellotape it together, and send you out again…'

In practice at Monaco in 1961 there was a particularly huge shunt. 'We had this new wrong-way-round gearbox on the Lotus, and in the heat of the moment I got second instead of fourth, locked the back wheels solid, and that was that. No bloody seat belts in those days, of course. Came out of the tunnel without the car...'

Compounding the problems of a man who crashed many times was his medical inability to tolerate analgesics. His silver identity bracelet bore the legend, 'Innes Ireland – A Rh Pos – Allergic to morphia'. To whisky, however, Innes had no such adverse reaction, and he always asserted that 'Scottish wine' was a pain-killer beyond compare.

Even by the late 1960s, Innes had come to hate increasing commercialism in a sport he always considered a romantic vocation. 'The decision to give up racing,' he wrote in his memorable autobiography, *All Arms And Elbows*, 'has been the most difficult thing I have ever done. Perhaps, if I had not lived with the belief that motor racing was the "Sport of Gentlemen", the decision would have been easier. I have never been able to equate money to motor racing.'

Ireland, one of few drivers to leave racing less well off than when he arrived, had contempt for the avariciousness of contemporary Formula 1. In 1992, after the Italian Grand Prix, I attended the 30th anniversary celebrations of the *Club International des Anciens Pilotes de Grand Prix* in Venice. Around 40 ex-drivers were present, and they had all been at Monza, where the story of the weekend was of Nigel Mansell's near-hysterical announcement that he was leaving Williams.

'To say I've been badly treated is a gross understatement,' commented Mansell, in reference to Frank's refusal to go the extra six million or whatever for 1993. Innes, like the majority of his fellows on the trip, already had his enthusiasm for Nigel fairly well under control, but this exhibition of moaning and greed made him apoplectic, then quietly sad.

'Always thought the bloke was a twerp,' he muttered, 'but how can anyone walk out on the best team for the sake of money? How many millions can one man spend, for Christ's sake?'

Innes was on fine form in Venice. A few of us knew that he was being treated for the cancer which would eventually claim him, but he never so much as mentioned it. For all the scrapes he got himself into in the course of a highly colourful life, his innate dignity was never threatened.

He was a trusting man, too, and a part of him never quite got over being brusquely fired by Colin Chapman, immediately after winning the US Grand Prix in 1961. Times were ruthlessly changing, and even then Innes, a professional racing driver with an amateur's spirit, was considered something of an anachronism.

Years on, Camel, then sponsoring Lotus, organised a party at a race somewhere, and in a master stroke of Public Relations invited every journalist – save the one who had scored the first Grand Prix victory for Team Lotus that day at Watkins Glen. Perhaps more than most of us, Ireland saw the funny side of it. 'It didn't register with Chapman then, so why should it with some bloody PR company now?'

As well as winning in America during his final year with Lotus, Innes memorably beat a squadron of factory Porsches at Solitude, and also won the Austrian Grand Prix in Zeltweg. That evening, doubtless emboldened by strong drink, he climbed the clock tower in the nearby hamlet of Judenberg. On the outside.

Twenty-five years on, now back to cover the race for *Road & Track*, he attempted, after a particularly sociable dinner, to repeat the procedure. My colleague Alan Henry and I – like Ireland, barely able to stand, let alone climb sheer brickwork – attempted to dissuade him. It was around two in the morning, and not another soul was to be seen.

'Same sort of night as 1961, lad! Moonlight and schnapps…'

'Yes, Innes, but you're pissed…'

'Was then, too, but I managed all right.'

'Yes, Innes, but you were 30 then, and…'

'And what, lad?'

'Well, you know, you're a bit older now, and…'

It wasn't working. Resolutely, Innes set about finding footholds, and began to climb. What to do? I invented a policeman, said he was coming this way. The mountaineer growled a very rude word, and continued to ascend.

I remember, too, being driven by him on the motorway from

Budapest out to the Hungaroring. It was one of the early races, when all the hire cars were primitive, and of East German origin. Whatever we were in had a top speed of about 70, and the strength and rigidity of a paper bag. As Innes slalomed though the smoky traffic, with appropriate commentary and without lifting his foot, for the first time in my life I wished I were in a Volvo.

The terror abated, though, once I took in anew that he knew absolutely what he was about. Once a racing driver always a racing driver, and his judgement was perfect.

After retiring, Ireland took up journalism. An unusually well-read man, he could write quite beautifully; no words on motor racing have ever moved me more than his piece on the death of Jimmy Clark.

The last time I saw him was at the Memorial Service for James. The atmosphere was light, for although the sense of loss was still very much there, it had been weathered a little by the passing months. Most poignant of all was the lesson read by Innes, whose own time was near.

When I think of him now, that day comes back to me, and also a moment which crystallised the man.

I was sitting with him on the short flight back from Hockenheim one year, and Heathrow approached before Innes was quite ready for it. As the tyres chirruped on the tarmac, his seat belt was undone, his table down, his seat back. In one hand was a cigarette, in the other a Scotch. There was not, I pointed out, a single rule he had left unbroken. 'Right, lad!' he beamed. I could have said nothing to please him more.

# Second best

'THE BEST DAY OF MY CAREER?' Jean-Pierre Jabouille had no need to think, really. 'Dijon – it must be. For me, everything came together in the one race: first Grand Prix win for Renault, first Grand Prix win for me, pole position … and in France! Fantastic, really. Everyone dreams of it, no?'

Jabouille always had the look of a man who'd walked under too many ladders. He was silent for a few seconds. 'The sad thing for me,' he ruefully grinned, 'is that no one remembers who won the French Grand Prix in 1979 – only the fight for second place! Even an hour after the race I felt that. And when I saw the video, I was not surprised…'

Mario Andretti, in rather more feisty style, always felt the same way about Fuji: 'I won the race, right? My first in a Lotus – a big day for me. But who the hell else remembers? Right afterwards, I'm in the garage area, and all everyone's saying is how Niki quit, and Hunt won the goddam Championship!'

The Japanese Grand Prix of 1976, however, was one thing. The French of 1979 has passed into motor racing folklore. In its closing minutes David Hobbs, commentating for CBS, was virtually lost for words. 'I have never, *never*, seen anything like this in my life – not in open wheel racing,' he spluttered. 'I mean, you'd think they had stock cars out there!'

When René Arnoux retired, at the end of 1989, stories were written about his long career, about his working-class background, his struggle through the ranks, seasons in the vanguard of Formula 1 with Renault and Ferrari, years of decline with Ligier. Appropriate tribute was paid to his seven Grand Prix wins, but none of them springs instantly to mind at the mention of his name. No, for ever, Arnoux will be remembered for Dijon 1979, for his battle there with Gilles Villeneuve.

It was the eighth round of the World Championship, and when they came to the French Grand Prix Jody Scheckter led on points, tailed by Jacques Laffite and Villeneuve.

It had been a strange kind of season thus far. Lotus, dominant the year before, were nowhere, and the first couple of races, in Argentina and Brazil, had fallen readily to Jacques Laffite's Ligier JS11, superbly effective in the new 'ground effect' tradition. Then, at Kyalami, Ferrari's new T4 appeared, and Villeneuve and Scheckter finished 1–2, which result they duplicated at Long Beach. At Zolder it was Jody's turn, this more by reliability than pace, but at Monte Carlo he won squarely.

The only intrusion into the trio's domination had come at Jarama, where Depailler, Laffite's Ligier team-mate, had triumphed. But now Patrick was out of the picture, lying in a Paris hospital with dreadful leg injuries after a hang-gliding accident.

Serious threat to Jody, Jacques and Gilles came from two quarters only. Patrick Head's lovely new Williams FW07 had to win a race soon, with Alan Jones. And Renault – at that time still the only turbo team – were going to be a threat at any circuit with straights worth the name. Dijon was one such.

Reliability apart, throttle lag was still the abiding Renault problem. At Monaco Arnoux and Jabouille had made up the back row of the grid, embarrassing anywhere, but especially so at a French race. A good showing at Dijon was vital to the Régie.

And there the grid was turned on its head. This time the yellow cars had the *front* row to themselves. At Dijon the cars had twin KKK turbochargers, which markedly improved torque and, more importantly, throttle response. With their power advantage, they could run more wing than the rest, and seemed in a class of their own – until Villeneuve produced a stunning lap to join them in the 1m 07s bracket. No one else was close. This would be Gilles against the home side.

'They're only two or three clicks quicker than me through the speed trap,' he commented after qualifying, 'and usually it's about 15kph, so they're using a lot of wing. That's where they're making up the time here – through the turns.

'I need a win here,' Villeneuve went on, 'to close the gap on Jody. I'm not interested in three or four points. If Jabouille once gets into the lead, I think it'll be impossible to catch him, so I have to make a good start. Somehow I must at least split the Renaults on the first lap.'

He did better than that. Both yellow cars got away reasonably well, but the red one sliced between them on the run down to the first turn. And a missed gearchange dropped Arnoux back to ninth.

In the opening stages we had Gilles in his element, at his purest, running away from Jabouille at a second a lap: 'To go for it was all I could do. We had very little downforce, and I knew I was hurting the Michelins, but what was the alternative – run third all the way, and go to sleep?' There are people who drive racing cars, and there are racing drivers.

The French Grand Prix fell into predicted shape finally on lap 15. Still it was Villeneuve from Jabouille, but now Arnoux had the other Renault up into third place, having picked off such as Jones, Laffite, Lauda, Jarier, Piquet and Scheckter with relatively little problem. For Gilles the auguries were not good. Sixty-five laps remained, and he had no one working in his corner. Still, he charged on. 'If you can build up a lead,' he said, 'you just might unsettle the other guy, make him put pressure on himself.'

Jabouille, though, was in calm frame of mind, playing the race like the dedicated fisherman he is, paying out a little, reeling in. He knew the extent of the Renault's superiority, could maintain the gap to the Ferrari without breaking into a sweat. As the 30-lap mark approached, Villeneuve's lead was pared away: 'I looked in my mirrors, and saw I had company.'

Taking quite awesome chances through lapped traffic, Gilles pulled out to four seconds again, but by mid-race his tyres had run up the white flag, and the T4 was all over the place, understeering on left-handers, oversteering on right-handers. By lap 46 Villeneuve had no more cards to play, and Jabouille swept by him at the end of the straight. Gone.

'I could tell his tyres were finished when I passed him,' Jean-Pierre said. 'How he got to the end on them, I'll never understand.'

In the Ferrari pit, they were getting new Michelins ready for Gilles, for Scheckter – lapping at nothing like his team-mate's pace – had already been in for a change. But Villeneuve stayed out. All right, nothing could be done about Jabouille, but now Arnoux was chipping away at the 15 seconds separating him from second place. With 10 laps to go, René had the gap down to four seconds, and Gilles looked like tethered prey. As they went into the last five laps the cars were as one.

The closing minutes of that race at Dijon beggar description. At the end of lap 70 Arnoux came by ahead, and in the stands there was delirium. That was that, we said. Gilles had carried the battle to the Renaults, and the gamble had failed.

But Villeneuve was not like that. 'When René passed me,' he said, 'I thought he'd run away down the straight, like Jabouille had. I was in really bad shape with handling, but still I could stay with him – so he had to have a problem, too.'

He had. In the closing stages, the Renault's fuel pick-up had begun slightly to falter. 'I thought I'd try to get him back as soon as possible,' Gilles explained, 'because he wouldn't be expecting it. At the end of the pit straight I wasn't really close enough, but I went for the inside and left my braking really, really, late...'

Smoke plumed from all four tyres as the Ferrari scrabbled inside the Renault, and they went round the right-hander side by side.

No one – not even the drivers themselves – really knew how many times in those last couple of laps the two cars passed and repassed, how many times they banged wheels, slid wide, went off the road, rejoined, touched again. It was desperate in a manner perhaps not seen in Formula 1 before or since.

Halfway round the final lap, with the crowd now in a frenzy, René seemed to have it done. At the uphill hairpin he felt sufficiently confident of his advantage to take the wide, conventional, line in. Gilles, braking later than late, put the Ferrari through the open door. Now the issue was settled.

In the midst of all this, 15 seconds up the road, Jabouille was coming in for a momentous victory, but his tragedy was that everyone was looking behind him, waiting, waiting. Then it was red–yellow – a blink – over the line. And as they cruised into the slowing-down lap, Villeneuve gave a wave of comradely respect, immediately acknowledged by Arnoux.

We should have expected nothing else. It had been ragged, it had been wild and frantic, but it had been also clean. 'I don't know how many times we touched,' Gilles said, 'but I know it never happened because one of us was trying to put the other off the road.'

'It was fun!' he giggled. 'A real battle. I thought for sure we were going to get on our heads, you know, because when you start interlocking wheels it's very easy for one car to climb over the other. But we didn't crash; it was OK, and I never enjoyed a race more.' Arnoux says the same to this day.

At Silverstone, the next race, Villeneuve and Arnoux were grilled at a Grand Prix Drivers Association meeting by a selection of Formula 1's elder statesmen. Lauda, Fittipaldi, Scheckter and others called them irresponsible, stupid.

'From where they were,' Gilles dryly commented afterwards, 'what the hell did they know? I couldn't believe the things they were saying. Jesus, they're supposed to be racing drivers…'

Andretti, predictably, was not among the critics. As the racer's racer, his response was swift and to the point. 'Nothing to get worried about,' he said. 'Just a coupla young lions clawin' each other.' For most of us, that said it best. More than 20 years on, we have seen nothing like it since.

# Season of turmoil

WHEN SYLVESTER STALLONE began showing up at the races, in 1997, he had plans for a new movie about Formula 1. It would capture, he said, 'All the grandeur and creativity and intelligence which makes this the most exciting sport in the world...'

Hmmm. We thought back to *Grand Prix*, released 30 years earlier. Plenty of fine racing footage, to be sure, but were we really to take seriously a storyline which had a driver bedding down with a rival's wife? Absurd, we had thought. At the time.

And that was really the whole point. The longer one is around motor racing, the more one comes to see that the clichés about life imitating art are actually simple truths. 'Stallone doesn't need a plot,' someone murmured. 'Just make a film based on 1982...'

In so many ways that season was the most disagreeable in memory, and if, by the end of it, the fundamental narcotic of Formula 1 remained, to some degree my feelings for it had shifted, and for ever. It was an ugly year, pock-marked by tragedy, by dissension, by greed, and yet, paradoxically, it produced some of the most memorable racing ever seen: from 16 Grands Prix came 11 different winners, in seven different cars, statistics faintly surreal in the context of today.

The atmosphere within the sport was generally poisonous, but we might have seen that coming, for all the pieces were in place for discord, just as they were for calamity on the track. And while it was hardly a pleasant time, in one sense anyway, for a journalist it was manna, for one had constantly to decide which quotes to leave out. No question of 'filling space' in 1982.

Public Relations had not even the feeblest toe-hold back then. There were no daily press releases, no homogenised quotes, no press conferences, and even had there been a sprinkling of damage limitation specialists scurrying about the place, the free-spirited drivers of the day would have consigned them swiftly to a rubber bedroom. From that point of view, the press never had a better time of it.

In other respects, though, it was rough, and sometimes downright unpleasant, for it seemed that every week some fresh issue would erupt, requiring firm comment, so the only certainty was that, wherever you were in the paddock, someone whom you had recently enraged was close at hand. The tension ran *very* high.

It had been building a while. Through the winter of 1980/81 there had been the FISA–FOCA War, this a locking of horns between Jean-Marie Balestre, newly elected as president of the FIA's sporting arm, and the daunting combo of Bernie Ecclestone and Max Mosley. Time had come, Balestre felt, for the governing body to start governing again, an unwelcome development for the increasingly robust gentlemen of FOCA.

After a lot of empty talk about a breakaway championship, and the like, compromise was reached, because it had to be, and thus the first Concorde Agreement was drawn up, in April 1981. Announced as 'a working document, under which Formula 1 is run', it was swathed in secrecy from the beginning, but its essentials were clear.

One was that 'The FIA is the sole international body governing motor sport. Its Statutes have delegated this power to FISA, which governs the organisation of the FIA Formula 1 World Championship, which is the exclusive property of the FIA.'

Fine. But there was a trade-off, the governing body granting 'The exclusive right for FOCA to enter into contracts with the organisers/promoters of FIA F1 World Championship events, in the best interests of all competitors.' Henceforth, in other words, Balestre would look after the rules, and Ecclestone the deals. Everyone was happy.

Or not. Within the ranks of the constructors there remained deep divisions between those using turbocharged engines and those not. Renault, the turbo pioneer in Formula 1, had arrived in 1977, and while there was an obvious power advantage in their boosted V6, poor drivability – excessive throttle lag – and lamentable reliability kept the establishment from going without sleep.

In 1979, though, Renault won a race, and although the yellow cars still retired more often than not, disquiet was growing among their rivals, particularly when it became known that Ferrari, too, were at work on a turbo motor. In 1980 there were three Renault victories, but still the traditional FOCA teams held general sway, by virtue of superior, lighter, 'ground effect' chassis.

At the end of that year, however, FISA banned the sliding skirts perfected by the best of the British teams. Cornering speeds were getting out of hand – some things never change – and the governing body decreed that, for 1981, there must be a six-centimetre gap between the bottom of the car and the ground. There would be constant checks, and the rule would be rigorously enforced.

Yeah, right. By the second race, in Brazil, Brabham had side-stepped the rule, Gordon Murray devising a hydro-pneumatic suspension system which made for a 'legal' car at rest, but one which brushed the ground at racing speed. The BT49C also had skirts (albeit fixed ones), which had supposedly been banned. At once way quicker than anything else, the Brabham obliged every other team to follow its lead, and there followed a sick joke of a season, in which every car blatantly flouted the rules.

If Formula 1 were not to become a complete laughing stock, FISA needed to show some muscle, but instead from Paris there was abject capitulation. For 1982 the ride height rule was forgotten, and fixed skirts were officially kosher, which meant in turn that suspensions had to be solid. All that mattered was crude downforce, and the cars, nasty to drive the previous year, now became hellish.

At Rio, the second race, the drivers spoke of the wretchedness of a contemporary Grand Prix car at a place like this, bumpy and abounding in high g-force corners. I remember the sight of Nigel Mansell's shins, swollen and bleeding after being bounced against the steering-rack for two hours; many drivers were at the end of their physical tether.

We get ahead of ourselves, however. The opening race, on 23 January, was in South Africa, and the leading players for the new season were Alain Prost and René Arnoux (Renault turbo), Gilles Villeneuve and Didier Pironi (Ferrari turbo), Bruno Giacomelli and Andrea de Cesaris (Alfa Romeo), Jacques Laffite and Eddie Cheever (Ligier-Matra), and the 'Cosworth brigade' of Carlos Reutemann and Keke Rosberg (Williams), Nelson Piquet and Riccardo Patrese (Brabham), Niki Lauda and John Watson (McLaren), Elio de Angelis and Mansell (Lotus), and Michele Alboreto (Tyrrell).

Come the first day at Kyalami, though, not a car ventured from the pit lane. The drivers were on strike.

During the winter they had each received a 'Superlicence' application form, and most had blithely signed without troubling to read the small print. But Lauda noted a clause for which he didn't care, and drew it to the attention of Pironi, then president of the Grand Prix Drivers Association.

What troubled Niki was the proposal that future superlicences be issued to a driver *and team*. The constructors claimed that this was simply to stop drivers from breaking contracts (as when Prost left McLaren for Renault in 1981), but Lauda saw it as a means of subjugating them, putting them in the 'ownership' of their teams. Villeneuve had seen it in ice hockey in Quebec, and he, too, wanted no part of it.

Therefore, when they arrived on the first morning, the drivers found at the paddock entrance a coach, which Lauda invited them to board. Once loaded up, it trudged off to Johannesburg, to the Sunnyside Park Hotel, while Pironi remained at the circuit, negotiating with Balestre and Ecclestone, these two for once in accord.

Bernie, predictably, had snapped into combat mode from the outset: if his Brabham drivers were not on hand for the first session, they would be sacked for breach of contract. But as 10 o'clock came and went, Piquet and Patrese, like their colleagues, were lounging in the sun.

No one was in a mood to compromise, and later the FIA stewards announced that the race was to be postponed, that an application would be made for the suspension of the drivers' licences. And there followed a risible statement from Bobby Hartslief, the Kyalami MD, which said that none of the drivers would be eligible for the World Championship – *ever again!*. The teams, Hartslief added darkly, would be looking for new drivers.

'Twenty-six young persons required for career in motoring. Some experience of a thousand horsepower an advantage.'

At the hotel the drivers pondered their next move. Clearly they would now have to spend the night there, and Lauda reasoned that if they took single rooms, unity would be lost. Therefore he organised a small banquet suite, in which mattresses were installed. And there the drivers stayed, entertained by the piano-playing of de Angelis and Villeneuve, awaiting news from the front.

Only Teo Fabi apparently broke rank. 'He said he was going for a pee,' said Rosberg, 'but he ran like a chicken, and lost our respect for ever – not because he left, but because he betrayed us. He went straight to Ecclestone and Balestre, and told them everything we had discussed.'

Late that evening the stewards declared that if the drivers turned up next day, and that at least 15 of them practised, the race would go ahead, after all. But it wasn't until mid-morning that Pironi called to say that the battle was won, that they should return to the track.

After a night of indifferent sleep, and not really sure what had been agreed, they complied. A brief practice session, then an hour of qualifying, and that was it as far as race preparation was concerned.

It was remarkable, in the circumstances, that the race drew from Prost one of his greatest drives. After leading from the start, his Renault punctured a rear tyre after 41 laps, crawled back to the pits, rejoined eighth, and took the lead again on lap 68, with nine to the flag.

On the podium there weren't too many smiles, though, for during the race – *during* the race – a further statement had come from the stewards: 'For the purpose of running a race, a temporary truce was called in the disagreement between the drivers and officials. The truce lasted until the end of the race, when it terminated. This means that the position which existed prior to the agreement is effectively reinstated. All the drivers named are suspended indefinitely.'

Underhand as this may have been, it was mere posturing, for where were the stand-in drivers to be found for this bastard breed of Grand Prix car? And while the team owners may have been livid about the drivers' behaviour, who were they to get high-minded? Within a few weeks *they* would strike, too. And they didn't relent.

An immediate casualty of the unrest was the Argentine Grand Prix, which should have been run on 7 March, but was called off when its organisers declined to risk last-minute strikes, and the like. Thus, the next punch-up was delayed a fortnight, to race day in Brazil.

Suffering the drivers may have been in practice at Rio, what with the heat and the bumps, but none could say they didn't get to their work, and the qualifying times revealed just how alarmingly speeds were rising: Prost's pole position lap, 1m 28.808s, was 6.27 seconds inside Piquet's mark of the year before.

Even more of a worry was that the drivers were restricted to two sets of qualifying tyres, each good for but one *banzai* lap. Villeneuve told me of his disquiet. 'Qualifying,' he said, 'has become ridiculous. First, with only two opportunities to go for a time, you spend no time on the track, and that's bad for the public.

'Second, it's unnecessarily dangerous. If I have only two chances to set a time, I need a clear track, OK? If it isn't clear, if there's someone in my way, I just have to hope he's looking in his mirrors – I mean, I can't lift, because this is my last chance.

'What the hell do qualifying tyres prove, anyway? That a soft tyre is quicker than a hard one, that's all. In the race, a slow driver is still a slow driver.

'No one outside Formula 1,' Gilles went on, 'can know how bad these things are to drive. The g-forces are unbelievable, and steering is like a big truck with the power steering not working.

'After a while, you ache everywhere, and you become aware of not enjoying driving a racing car. After the race people will be bitching about fatigue, but then we'll go to Long Beach and Imola, where the g-forces will be less, and the thing will get forgotten. Other tracks will be bad, though. Zolder, I guess, will be quite a good killer…'

A throwaway line, this last, but no less chilling for that.

His race next day was the personification of the man. From the start he took the lead, and stayed there for 30 laps, under increasing pressure from Piquet's lighter – *much* lighter, as it turned out – and more wieldy Brabham. A pragmatist would have accepted that his tyres were going away, and let Nelson by, but that was never Gilles, and ultimately he put two wheels on the grass, and spun into the catch fencing.

Piquet went on to win, followed by Rosberg and Prost. On the podium he smiled weakly as his public chanted, but then his legs buckled. While fitness was never Nelson's strong suit – he had also been semi-comatose in Las Vegas the previous autumn – his condition said everything about this generation of Formula 1 car.

At least, though, he had made it to the end, unlike his team-mate, who spun at half-distance, then veered around like a man looking for a breathalyser. In the pits, they lifted Patrese from his car, and he took an hour to recover; after the spin, he said, he had not known where he was.

For the powers that be, though, the drivers' problems were a relative trifle. After the race Renault put in protests against Brabham and Williams, the teams which had finished ahead of them, and when these were turned down, they appealed against the decision, this to be heard at an FIA Tribunal a month hence.

In the meantime, there was Long Beach, and the odd note of levity, gratefully received. Mario Andretti, for one thing, was back, making a one-off appearance for Williams. Had Pat Patrick, his IndyCar team owner, been lukewarm about his accepting the ride? 'Yeah,' Mario growled, 'lukewarm like ice…'

Frank had a vacancy because Reutemann, who had retired at the end of 1981, then changed his mind, was now gone for good. At Kyalami Carlos had been at his very best, splitting the Renaults, but the drivers' strike was disagreeable to a dignified man beginning his 11th season of Formula 1, and these cars, which hardly lent themselves to artistry, were not to his taste. After a poor race in Brazil he had no wish to continue.

Hoping to influence the FIA Tribunal, Ferrari decided to follow the FOCA teams' lead, to see how far you could go with 'deliberate misinterpretation' of the rules. In practice at Long Beach, both cars appeared with double rear wings, one mounted in front of the other, but staggered so that the net effect was of a single wing almost twice as wide as the rules permitted.

Mauro Forghieri struggled to keep the smile from his face. 'Each wing is legal,' he said. 'Where does it say you're allowed only one…?'

As a jape, it was harmless enough, and the drivers said it really didn't make a lot of difference. But Villeneuve's car raced that way, finished third, and was promptly disqualified, following a protest from Tyrrell.

Long Beach was memorable for a dominant victory by Lauda, in only his third race since coming out of retirement. He had looked a cert for pole position, too, but that, amazingly, was stolen by de Cesaris. When you saw the state Andrea was in afterwards – weeping copiously, and shaking so violently he was unable to hold a bottle to his lips – you doubted his readiness to run 75 trouble-free laps in the race.

He took an immediate lead, but soon Lauda was pulling on the line. Aware of Andrea's reputation, Niki was in two minds: better to sit there, awaiting the right moment, or try to get clear as soon as possible, avoid involvement in the leader's inevitable mistake?

Almost at once his predicament was taken care of by Raul Boesel, whom the leaders came up to lap at the hairpin before Shoreline Drive. In de Cesaris's estimation, Boesel was less co-operative than he might have been, and as he accelerated past him, he violently shook his right fist.

It might more usefully have been employed in changing gear. By the time this had been accomplished, Lauda, shaking with laughter, was gone for the day.

Very much the wild card of 1982, the McLarens were sometimes nowhere, sometimes devastating. From race to race the form of the MP4B was unsettled, in part because McLaren alone, among the leading Cosworth runners, were with Michelin, whose bewildering range of compounds was aimed primarily at Renault, their turbo team.

Rosberg took a good second at Long Beach, in what was the last race for the fabled Williams FW07. Due to make its début at Imola was FW08, and Keke couldn't wait, for the new car, smaller, more agile, had flown in testing.

Perhaps Lauda was right: 'I think the problem was that Frank's new car was too quick too soon, and its times frightened people. If it had been maybe 20 kilos under the 580 limit, perhaps nothing would have been said, but it was much more than that...'

Whatever, a month after the Rio controversy, the FIA Tribunal found in Renault's favour, announcing that Piquet and Rosberg had been disqualified, that the new winner was Prost. This was Monday 19 April, six days before Imola. The forces of all hell were about to break loose.

Renault had protested Brabham and Williams on the grounds that they had raced underweight, and about that there was no argument. The FOCA establishment, which had welcomed the Renault turbo with a barely concealed smirk five years earlier, now realised that the Cosworth DFV – after holding sway for a mere 15 seasons – was about to be blown aside. And a hitherto undetected conservative streak in their nature revealed itself: they wanted turbos banned, these same people who perpetually cried that you couldn't stand in the way of progress.

The turbos had always had a considerable power advantage,

but the real fear was that now the teams using them were showing signs of building cars close to the minimum weight limit; from a power-to-weight point of view, therefore, chances were that the Cosworths would be outclassed.

It was easy to be sympathetic. Ferrari and Renault, with all their cumbersome and weighty turbo clobber, could just about get down to the limit, whereas such as Williams, McLaren and Brabham had no difficulty in undercutting it. Therefore they took it upon themselves to restore some semblance of equality, by matching lower weight to their lower-powered engines. This was the situation in Brazil, and we had a very good race.

The problem was The Rules. Rightly or wrongly, all parties had signed the Concorde Agreement, thereby accepting the FISA regulations, one of which was that the minimum weight limit was 580kg. If the rule had been straightforwardly written, there could have been no argument, but it laid itself open to abuse, for it stipulated that this was to be the weight of the car, minus driver, but including normal lubricants and coolants – which could be topped up after the race, prior to the checking of the car's weight.

That being so, for ingenious minds it was the work of a moment to spot a loophole, and what they came up with was 'water-cooled brakes'. The car, equipped with a huge water tank, would go to the grid with the thing full, spray its contents away in the early laps, run the bulk of the race 30kg under the limit, then have the tank refilled afterwards so as to be over 580 for the check.

Clever stuff – if clearly against the spirit of a rule to which they had given their consent. And perhaps, if they had been slightly less holier-than-thou about it, the FOCA teams might have had more sympathy in the press. As it was, they would insult your intelligence, asserting the merits of $H_2O$ as a means of cooling the brakes. Why, then, did they not take enough for the whole race? Silence.

Only Frank Williams came clean about the aim of the water tank, arguing its case solely on grounds of power-to-weight ratio. That was infinitely more acceptable.

It was one thing, though, for the FIA Tribunal to wipe Piquet and Rosberg from the Rio results; on the heels of the announcement came another, declaring that in future the cars would be weighed as they were when they came off the race track. No more adding of 'coolants', in other words.

A bizarre aspect of the Brazilian disqualifications was that Messrs Watson, Mansell and Alboreto were each promoted a couple of places: all had been driving cars as 'illegal' as the Brabham and the Williams, but they, of course, had not been protested.

Rosberg was particularly incensed by that: 'It was crazy to disqualify Nelson and me from Rio – and allow all the other "water tank" cars to stay in the results. That was the only reason Watson was in contention for the championship at the end of the year!

'Having said that, however, I must say I was surprised at Frank not going to Imola...'

Not only Williams skipped the San Marino Grand Prix. Following the FIA announcement, the FOCA teams decided on a boycott, although Ken Tyrrell was given special dispensation to attend, for his much-needed major sponsor was Italian.

The FOCA heavyweights' argument was that routine topping up had always been allowed, a time-honoured custom, if not actually a rule. That being so, if nothing could now be added, the weight limit was effectively being increased, and that constituted a rule change. On that basis, they said, they felt justified in giving Imola a miss, for they 'needed more time to prepare cars to meet the new rules'. Tyrrell somehow managed it immediately.

The vote to skip Imola was not a unanimous one. Even within teams – McLaren, for example – there were differing views, and much of what went on was close to farce. Ligier adopted a weak-kneed position in the middle, having the guts neither to race nor to associate themselves with the boycott. They had decided, said a press release, to miss Imola in any case – for 'technical reasons'. A surprise, this, to those who had seen the transporters heading back to the French border the day before practice.

It was ironic now to look back to Kyalami, to the team

owners' condemnation of the drivers' strike, their insistence that problems be sorted out away from the circuits. Perhaps they believed that the San Marino Grand Prix couldn't happen without them; perhaps, too, the fact that it was an Italian race influenced their decision. If so, it was a gross miscalculation: Ferrari were there, and an Italian crowd needs nothing more. Attendances were higher than the year before.

More surprising than the absent teams' indifference to letting down the public was their assumption of support from the sponsors, many of whose representatives turned up at Imola, and lost no time in making their feelings known.

If Formula 1 were now show business, then how to ignore its first rule, that the show must go on? In the press room the feeling was that they should have sorted out their turbo equivalence and their water tanks and their weight limits in their own time, away from the public gaze. To penalise the fans could never be right.

We wrote as much, too, and it was perhaps a reflection of a muddied world that more than one FOCA man suggested that the attitudes of some British journalists had been … financially influenced by Renault. There again, these accusations were made soon after the attitude of some small teams towards going to Imola had been financially influenced by FOCA, so perhaps the concept was fresh in their minds.

Morris Nunn, concerned that his Colombian backing (for driver Roberto Guerrero) might evaporate if the Ensign were not on parade for an avid local TV audience, had been advised that if he went to Imola, television coverage in Colombia just might disappear for good.

Tyrrell apart, there was a high degree of unanimity and goodwill apparent among the teams which made the trip, and we might have anticipated a race devoid of controversy. Not so.

Only 14 cars went to the grid, headed by the Renaults of Arnoux and Prost, and the Ferraris of Villeneuve and Pironi. Engine failure soon accounted for Prost, so now it was Arnoux against the red cars, and for an hour the action was mesmeric, until René's engine, too, expired, leaving the Ferraris home free, Gilles ahead.

That being so, victory should have been his, for Maranello team orders had always been that, as and when the cars became first and second, the driver ahead at the time should win. Villeneuve, whose integrity was absolute, had always played by these rules, most notably at Monza in 1979, where he sat behind team-mate Jody Scheckter, knowing all the while that if he passed him, he would likely win not only the race, but also the World Championship.

Pironi was a man of a different cut. Unlike Villeneuve, he was obsessed with thoughts of the title, but a year alongside Gilles had established that he was unlikely to get the upper hand at Ferrari by conventional means.

Outwardly, at least, their relationship had always been good, professionally and otherwise, and Villeneuve, whose guileless instinct was always to trust until given cause not to, believed Pironi a friend.

Shortly before the Imola weekend Didier had married Catherine, his long-time girlfriend, and while Ferrari's team director, Marco Piccinini, was present as best man, Gilles and his wife were not so much as invited. He thought that strange, and mentioned it during the practice days. 'Joann says I shouldn't be surprised,' he shrugged. 'She thinks he's just trying to get "in" with Piccinini. She's never trusted Didier…'

When Arnoux made his smoky exit, Ferrari hung out a 'slow' board, and Villeneuve immediately backed off, for now there was no need to hurry, and the Ferraris were marginal on fuel at this very thirsty circuit. Although Pironi immediately passed him, Gilles didn't worry, assuming that he was merely playing to the crowd. More of a concern, though, given the fuel situation, was that Didier picked up the pace again.

This went on into the closing laps. When Villeneuve was in front, the lap time would be around 1m 38s, then Pironi would go by again, and it would be down to 1m 35s. 'I thought it was bloody stupid,' Gilles said, 'but no more than that.'

On lap 59, with one to go, Pironi lifted on the approach to Tosa, and Villeneuve passed him for what he believed would be the last time. 'Even at that stage I thought he was being honest, obeying the original pit signal. He'd left it late, but never mind.

'I went into that last lap so easily you can't believe it, still very worried about the fuel; down to Tosa I was almost cruising...'

There, at the last overtaking spot on the circuit, Pironi darted from Villeneuve's slipstream, and snicked by. Only then did Gilles realise he had been duped. 'It never entered my head to cover the line,' he said. 'Stupid, wasn't I?'

Thus they took the flag, Pironi in front. At the end of the slowing-down lap, Villeneuve came into the *parc fermé* in a welter of revs and tyre smoke, slewing his car to a halt. I went to speak to him, then thought better of it. He looked in Pironi's direction, uttered a single word – English, and of four letters – and, after a token appearance on the podium, strode off to a nearby park, where his helicopter awaited.

'I left,' he said, 'because otherwise I would have said some bad things. He was the hero who won the race, and I was the spoiled bastard who sulked. I knew it would look like that, but still I thought it was better to get away.'

Among those joining Gilles on the flight was Jackie Stewart. 'I'd never seen him angry like that,' Stewart said. 'You know, with him the World Championship was incidental. He told me his one goal was to beat the record for the most wins, which I then held, and this one had been stolen from him. He was *stunned*. There had always been this innocence about Gilles – he didn't have a trace of maliciousness in him, and he couldn't believe what had happened. It was awful that the last days of his life were so tormented and disillusioned.'

So indeed they were. The following week I called the apartment in Monte Carlo, and we talked for an hour and more. It was a conversation which left me disturbed and apprehensive, for Gilles was a good friend. He was never going to speak to Pironi again, he said. 'I've declared war. Absolute war.

'Finishing second is one thing – I'd have been mad at myself for not being quick enough if he'd beaten me. But finishing second because the bastard steals it...'

So there it was. The duplicity was what Villeneuve couldn't stomach. As Stewart said, what truly mattered to Gilles was winning *races* – that, and being known as the fastest driver on earth. It was deeply offensive to him that some believed he had been beaten in a straight fight.

'People seemed to think we had the battle of our lives,' he muttered. 'Jesus Christ, I qualified a second and a half faster than him – where was my problem? I think I've proved that, in equal cars, if I want someone to stay behind me … well, I think he stays behind…'

So what now? I said. 'In Belgium, if we get a repeat of Imola, running 1–2, short of fuel, then I guess we're both going to run out, right? If it's a matter of trying to pass him at the end of the straight, I'll take the same chance as if it were a Williams or a Brabham. I'll do what I should have done at Imola.'

As I left for Zolder, Villeneuve's fury was still much on my mind, and there were other signs, too, that this would be anything but a relaxed weekend. The FOCA lot were back, and decidedly unappreciative of what had been written in the wake of the Imola strike. On the aeroplane to Brussels I found myself next to a Williams man I had known, and liked, a long time. Throughout the flight he stared out of the window, wordless and resolute.

Finally, as we queued at passport control, he exploded, telling me I didn't understand, didn't have all the facts. Quite right, I said. That much was inevitable with any secret society; I didn't know much about the Masons, either.

Up at the track countless similar conversations blazed away, but at the same time one sensed that reality had been faced, that the anti-turbo movement was beginning to melt away – not least because the FOCA muscle-men's own turbo plans were taking shape. Folk from the lesser teams emerged from FOCA meetings with tales of the 'I'm All Right Jack' attitudes suddenly prevalent among the leading lights. 'They make us miss Imola,' said Mo Nunn, 'and then, when it suits them, they put us out on the street.'

The FOCA President, of course, was in the happy position of having a foot in both camps, Bernie's team arriving at Zolder with turbocharged engines from BMW! One thought of Sam Goldwyn's immortal line: 'I was always an independent – even when I had partners…'

Humour was not uppermost, however, in the mind of McLaren's Teddy Mayer, who accused me of having been 'bought' by Renault; that alone, in his opinion, could account for my aversion to what FOCA had done. In a rage, I went off to watch final qualifying from the Ferrari pit.

Ten minutes from the end of the session Villeneuve went out for his third and last run, on a set of mixed, used, qualifiers. One warm-up lap, and then he was on it.

A couple of minutes more, and suddenly there was the ghostly silence one dreads at a race track. The red flag went out. Everyone stood around, apprehensive. Then a near-hysterical voice shouted from the loudspeakers – in English – that the session had been halted because of 'an enormous accident to one of the Ferraris'.

Soon afterwards the surviving red car drifted down the pit lane, engine off, and – there's no other way to say it – my heart sank when I saw it was number 28.

A few of us went to Terlamenbocht, where Gilles had gone off, and what we found there looked like a plane crash. He had been thrown from the car, we were told, clear across the road, and into the catch fencing. He was alive, but could not survive.

As we stumbled back to the paddock, anything else which may have been wrong with Formula 1 took its place in the shade. Everyone wanted news, and a lot of folk were weeping, but still a jolt or two awaited. A driver's girlfriend asked me how bad it was, and I said as bad as it could be. She was silent, then wondered how they would get back to Monaco next day; they had been due to fly with Gilles, she said. Inconvenient, that.

Then a driver took me on one side, wanting a quiet word. Who did I think would get the Ferrari drive? I said I thought probably that decision would be left until after Villeneuve had died.

The accident had come in precisely the circumstances he had described in Rio, those few weeks before. Flat out, on his last run, he had encountered Jochen Mass, cruising back to the pits. Down to Terlamenbocht, Mass had seen the Ferrari in his mirrors, and moved right to give it the line through the corner, but by then Gilles had committed himself the same way.

He died that evening, leaving his fellow drivers distraught, and also angry. 'It's all a matter of luck,' said Alboreto. 'Where Gilles crashed, I overtook slower cars maybe half a dozen times. Some hadn't seen me, some didn't bother to move over. I made it through. I was lucky. Gilles was not.'

For some of us, at a time when so much else was awry with racing, the loss of Villeneuve was almost too much to take in. Lauda said it best: 'He was the greatest driver in the world, with more talent than any of us. And I liked him even more than I admired him.'

He was gone, though, as the gap in the row of transporters poignantly confirmed on Sunday morning. As a mark of respect, Pironi's car was withdrawn; Ferrari had left for home.

In the race the Cosworth brigade, despite now running at 'legal' weight, had very much the best of it. Rosberg and the new Williams led comfortably for most of the way, until the tyres went off, and Keke fell prey to Watson's McLaren, which had qualified only 10th, then came through like a train. The Michelin thing again.

Rosberg was acutely disappointed, but kept his sense of perspective. 'After Gilles's accident, it was difficult for me to concentrate. It sounds callous, but at a race a driver is very absorbed in his own thing, you know. I am there to look after Rosberg.

'That weekend was very difficult. Gilles and I had had so many battles over the years, and now here was I, leading a Grand Prix for the first time – and he had died the day before. I had to work hard to put it out of my mind, but still it didn't really hit me until the day after the race, when I had to go up to the track to do some pictures. All that was left was garbage and Gilles's helicopter...'

As it would be again in 1994, following the death of Senna, the paddock at Monaco was a sombre, edgy, place. Here Villeneuve had lived, had won the Grand Prix the previous year, and the sense of his absence was overwhelming. Perhaps for that reason, the weekend passed quietly enough. Until the closing laps of the race, anyway.

In Renault's early days, Monaco had shown up the

shortcomings of a turbocharged engine like nowhere else, throttle lag being exactly what you didn't need at the track Piquet once compared with 'riding a bicycle in a bathroom'. At the 1979 race, indeed, the cars of Arnoux and Jean-Pierre Jabouille started from the back row.

Three years on, though, Arnoux was on the pole, and from the start he rushed away, followed by Patrese, back in a Cosworth-powered Brabham for this race. Riccardo got much the best of the deal, in fact, for team leader Piquet's BMW turbo popped and banged all weekend, and he was never a factor.

After Arnoux had unaccountably spun on lap 15, Prost took over, with Patrese, Pironi and de Cesaris behind him, and for most of the afternoon the finishing order looked set. Only at the end did the race come alive: in the last three laps, the lead changed four times.

Lapping an unhelpful de Angelis at Ste Devote, Prost clipped the guardrail with his left rear wheel, and this may well have had some bearing on the outcome of the day, for a minute or so later, exiting the chicane, the Renault snapped out of control, and hammered hard into the barriers.

It had been drizzling lightly for a while, and everyone was on slicks, but Prost, who badly bruised a foot in the accident, said he was as sure as he could be that he had not made a mistake.

Whatever, Patrese now led, but on the next lap – the penultimate one – he spun on the slippery approach to the Loews hairpin, and came to rest half on the pavement, beached. Pironi and de Cesaris went by, now first and second, but not all was lost for Patrese, for his car, although stalled, was clearly in 'a dangerous place', and therefore entitled to a penalty-free shove from the marshals.

As he coasted down the incline to Portier, Riccardo was able to bump-start his car, and it was good that he did, for de Cesaris's Alfa used the last of its fuel up the hill to Massenet, coughing to a halt in Casino Square, and Pironi got little further, stopping in the tunnel, half a lap from the flag. Those mindful of the circumstances of his Imola victory were disinclined to sympathise.

Now came 'The North American Tour', beginning with a new race, in Detroit, which found little favour. If they had their enthusiasm for the city under control, though, the drivers reserved their choicest remarks for the circuit through its streets. An extra 'acclimatisation' day of practice was scrapped when the tyre barriers were found to be inadequate, the escape roads too short. On Friday morning guardrails were still being installed, and it wasn't until four in the afternoon that the safety measures passed muster.

Nor, when they took finally to the track, were the drivers much mollified, for they disliked its geometric layout, and were disconcerted by the bumpy surface.

It was also extremely slow, even by comparison with Monaco, the race winner averaging just 78.20mph. In this place – *Motown*, after all – they were not much impressed by that, and the writings of the local press reflected the problem Formula 1 may always have in a country where racing means ovals and drag strips, where raw speed is all.

The day belonged to Watson. Seventeenth only on the grid, he found his McLaren working supremely in race trim, and picked up a momentum early in the race which simply wafted him up the order. In a single lap he disposed of Pironi, Cheever and Lauda, which took some believing, but the facts were there: on lap 32 he was fifth, and on lap 33 he was second.

All told, John's was one of the most assertive drives ever seen. 'Now you're going to ask me why I can't do it all the time,' he smiled. 'I wish I could answer...'

At this stage, with seven races run, Watson led the point standings, with 26, from Pironi (20), Prost (18) and Rosberg (17), the low scores illustrating that no one was about to rush off with this World Championship; already five drivers had won races.

A sixth – Piquet – was added to the list in Canada, and that was some surprise, for in Detroit, the previous week, he had failed even to qualify! Over the border, though, and on a cold day, BMW's four-cylinder turbo behaved itself, and Brabham scored a rare 1–2, Patrese – still in the Cosworth car –

following Nelson in, and Watson consolidating his championship lead with third place.

On the strength of qualifying, Pironi had looked like the favourite, for revised front suspension had finally made a great car of the Ferrari 126C2, and he took pole position at this circuit newly named for Villeneuve. 'I want to dedicate it to Gilles,' he said over the PA, 'because I think we all know that if he'd been here, he would have been on pole.'

I was talking to another driver, and we paused to listen. 'If it hadn't been for him,' he murmured, 'Gilles *would* have been here…' Harsh, perhaps, but a reflection of what many people were feeling.

At the same time, though, they were beginning to see Pironi as the likely World Champion. He may not have been the equal of Villeneuve, but animosity towards the man did not colour judgement of the driver. In the cockpit Didier was more than good; he was coming to be great.

The crowd was very small in Montreal that year. With Villeneuve, a nation's idol, so recently gone, that was inevitable, and it didn't help that the day was chilly and overcast, nor that the metro train drivers were on strike.

To tie in with TV schedules, the start time was late, 4.15, but in the event the race did not get properly under way until after six, following an appalling accident within seconds of the start.

Pironi paced the field around the formation lap, then took his place on the grid, but the backmarkers were dilatory, and there was quite a wait before they were given the signal to go. When the Ferrari's clutch began to drag, Pironi was obliged to dab his brake pedal; as he did so, the engine stalled, and at precisely that moment the green light flashed.

Up went Didier's arm, but it was too late for that: they were on their way. Directly behind, Prost somehow jinked left, a lead followed by the rest, and until Boesel arrived all seemed well, but he glanced the Ferrari's left rear wheel. Immediately behind him was the Osella of rookie Riccardo Paletti, who, from his grid slot at the back, could not possibly have seen Pironi's raised arm.

Only six seconds elapsed between green light and impact.

Afterwards it was found that the Osella was in third gear, its rev counter reading 10,500, equating to about 120mph.

Safety personnel were on the spot, of course, and Professor Watkins at once took in the gravity of the situation, but matters went from bad to worse when the car erupted into flame. Given that it was carrying a full fuel load (over 40 gallons), the marshals did well to bring the fire under control within a minute, and the unconscious driver did not suffer any burns.

Paletti's injuries, though, were terrible, and the most difficult part of the rescue operation – releasing him from a dreadfully deformed cockpit – took nearly half an hour. Taken by helicopter to hospital, he died soon after arrival.

Pironi, shattered by this new tragedy, thought hard about restarting before deciding to do so. The spare Ferrari, without the revised suspension, was much less competitive, but he briefly led until slowed by a misfire. Into the pits, then again. And again. Finally the problem was fixed, and we saw Didier's true measure. Three laps down on the leading Piquet, he went by, left him behind, and right at the end set a new lap record, less than a second from his pole time.

As eight o'clock approached, and grey, frigid, evening came to the Ile Notre Dame, I watched the Ferrari running alone, tremendously fast and controlled, and it seemed that Pironi was driving something from his system, running at the limit for the sake of it. If anyone else wins this championship, I thought, it will be a surprise.

* * *

Others, better qualified to judge than I, thought the same. 'When Gilles was alive,' said Forghieri, 'maybe we underestimated Didier, simply because he was getting beaten by a man with the same car.' Alan Jones, assessing his rivals the year before, had been of the same opinion.

Following Villeneuve's death, Ferrari had made representations to FISA, asking that number 27 be dropped – at least for the balance of the 1982 season – but the request was turned down, and when Patrick Tambay appeared in a second

Ferrari at Zandvoort, his car bore the number on its nose and flanks.

This was not what Tambay himself wanted, either, for Villeneuve had been his closest friend in racing, and accepting Ferrari's offer had been no easy decision. In the end, though, he was persuaded that this was what Gilles would have wanted, and he was to do the job with some distinction.

The Dutch Grand Prix had not been on the original calendar, but when financial problems brought about the cancellation of the Spanish race (scheduled for 27 June), Bernie Ecclestone hurriedly arranged a replacement for the weekend after. Most unusually, it was run on Saturday, with an early start of 12.30, for there were TV clashes with both the World Cup and the Wimbledon finals.

These things being so, and the day arriving cool and cloudy, attendance was low, as in Canada, but those who were there witnessed a commanding performance by Pironi, who took the lead from Prost on lap five, and departed into a race of his own.

In Holland there was another massive accident – they were becoming a matter of routine – when Arnoux's front suspension broke under braking for the Tarzan hairpin, the Renault skating over the minimal run-off area, and into a tyre barrier, on top of which it came finally to rest. As Arnoux, bruised but otherwise intact, hobbled back to the pits, the feeling of relief was almost tangible.

At Brands Hatch, which suited his acrobatic style, Rosberg took a fantastic pole position (apart from de Cesaris's at Long Beach, the only one for a non-turbo driver in the entire season), but his engine refused to fire before the formation lap, and that meant starting from the back. He quickly worked through to sixth place, but hurt his tyres in the process – and tyre changes, as we have said, were not part of the plan back then.

Except, that is, for Brabham. Gordon Murray had thought about the circumstances of Prost's victory in the opening race, at Kyalami, and had acted upon it. The BT50s came to the British Grand Prix equipped with built-in air jacks and quick-release fuel fillers, and the plan was to start on soft tyres and half-tanks.

Judgement of its efficacy had to wait, though, for Patrese stalled at the start, and was hit by Arnoux, while Piquet, after leading easily enough, retired with injection problems on lap 10. That left Lauda in front, and he proceeded comfortably to his second win of the season, followed by Pironi and Tambay.

By the standards of 1982, the Brands weekend was unremarkable, but for Pironi it was a landmark, for his six points put him in the lead of the World Championship for the first time in his career, and it was in a confident frame of mind that he went, the following weekend, to Paul Ricard.

A very confident frame of mind. Harvey Postlethwaite, then Ferrari's Technical Director, put it more trenchantly than that. 'Something very odd came over Didier at that time,' he said. 'He went very … strange. He had big personal problems, but they didn't seem to concern him too much. It was more that he became incredibly arrogant and over-confident about everything – including the fact that he was going to be World Champion.'

Big personal problems he certainly had. For one thing, his marriage, just three months old, was effectively over, for he had become involved with an actress, whom he had met during a horse-riding photo shoot for a French magazine.

An hour or so before the start of the French Grand Prix, a Ferrari team member, clearly rattled, asked me if I had seen Pironi. It seemed a novel question at that stage of the proceedings, but I said no, and left him to his search. It transpired that Didier was closeted in his own motorhome. He was not, as they say, 'discussing race tactics'.

The episode seemed to blow one of racing's eternal clichés out of the water, for although Pironi was unable to run with the Renaults on this occasion, still he finished third, and extended his points lead over Watson.

For once, appropriately at home, Arnoux and Prost had no reliability problems, but on the podium Alain's expression told you all was not well, and it emerged that René had been asked, in the interests of his team-mate's title aspirations, to finish behind him. He had agreed, too, only to suffer an attack of amnesia once the race was under way. Well, French driver, French car, French Grand Prix…

*En route to victory in the 1957 Monaco Grand Prix, Fangio slides the Maserati 250F right out to the wall at the exit of Tabac. Below: Juan Manuel's day of days. As the 1957 German Grand Prix goes into its final stages, he has taken his Maserati past the Ferrari of Peter Collins, and is preparing to separate Mike Hawthorn from the lead. (LAT)*

*Heroic to the end. Nothing could live with the Vanwalls at Monza in 1957, but Maserati gave it their best shot. After Behra had retired, Fangio fought a lone battle against Moss, Brooks, and Lewis-Evans. (LAT)*

*Was ever there a more distinctive racing car than this? World Champion Phil Hill in the Ferrari 156 'sharknose' at Aintree in 1962. (Author)*

*Dan Gurney's beautiful Eagle-Weslake won only one Grand Prix, but fittingly it came at Spa-Francorchamps, where the brilliant Gurney always shone. (LAT)*

*Monza pit scene, 1967. Jimmy Clark chats, and Jabby Crombac, legendary journalist and close friend, sits. In the race Clark produced perhaps the greatest drive of his life. (LAT)*

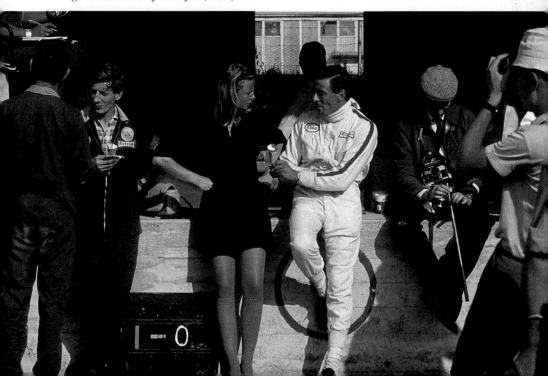

**Top** *Kyalami 1968, and the end of an era. Clark's last Grand Prix win, in the 49, was also the last for a Lotus in green with yellow stripe. (LAT)*

**Above** *Silverstone 1969. Jochen Rindt (Lotus 49) and Jackie Stewart (Matra MS80) scrapped like this for well over an hour, before Rindt hit trouble, and left JYS to cruise in. (LAT)*

**Left** *Jochen as we remember him, balancing the 49 on the throttle through Stowe. (LAT)*

**Right** *Another one that got away. At Montjuich Park, Amon's Ferrari was leading the 1969 Spanish Grand Prix by a clear minute when its engine failed. (LAT)*

**Below** *The serious end of the grid at Hockenheim in 1970. Rindt's Lotus 72 and Ickx's Ferrari 312B are on the front row. (LAT)*

**Bottom** *Four drivers – Rindt, Ickx, Clay Regazzoni (Ferrari) and Chris Amon (March) – broke clear of the rest, and ran as closely as this for a very long time. It was to be Jochen's last Grand Prix win. (LAT)*

**Above** *The first Grand Prix victory for a Tyrrell, at Barcelona's daunting Montjuich Park in 1971, was also the author's first race as a journalist. Pole man Ickx leads Stewart, but JYS was soon to dispense with the Ferrari. (LAT)*

**Below** *Running at the edge. Francois Cevert's Tyrrell nicely out of line through the Curva Grande during the 1971 Italian Grand Prix. (LAT)*

**Right** *Paddock vignette from another time. Ferrari mechanics work on Clay Regazzoni's B2 at the Österreichring in 1972. (LAT)*

*Above* The way it was – and the way it should have stayed. Gilles Villeneuve leads Didier Pironi in the closing laps at Imola in 1982. (LAT)

*Below* On the podium Pironi celebrates, and Villeneuve's expression says everything. A couple of weeks later, Gilles was killed in final qualifying at Zolder. (LAT)

*Right* Final qualifying at Monza in 1982. In the closing minutes, Mario Andretti, with Mauro Forghieri and the whole of Italy willing him on, prepares to go out for the pole. (LAT)

**Left** *In the monsoon conditions of Monaco in 1984, Nigel Mansell got the Lotus-Renault into the lead, but the car was to get away from the driver on the slippery climb from Ste Devote.* (LAT)

**Below** *Third man Elio de Angelis, winner Keke Rosberg and runner-up Rene Arnoux at the end of the chaotic Dallas Grand Prix. Sue-Ellen Ewing looks on ...* (LAT)

**Right** *The turbocharged Williams-Hondas of Nelson Piquet (nearest camera) and Nigel Mansell were clearly the fastest cars of 1986, Mansell leading Piquet home in the last British Grand Prix at Brands Hatch. Neither man, though, was to win the World Championship.* (LAT)

*Adelaide 1986. After a World Championshp decider which see-sawed this way and that, Alain Prost sweeps on to an emotional, last ditch, victory in the McLaren-TAG Porsche. (LAT)*

*All smiles in 1988. For McLaren 'team-mates' Alain Prost and Ayrton Senna, the problems really got started in '89 ... (Jeff Hutchinson)*

*Senna and Ecclestone were good friends – indeed Ayrton signed his first Formula 1 contract with Brabham, but never drove for Bernie's team. (LAT)*

*Above* Prelude to a weekend of catastrophe. Ayrton Senna's Williams-Renault leads Roland Ratzenberger's Simtek during Friday practice at Imola in 1994. (LAT)

*Below* Feet of clay. At Jerez in 1997, as Jacques Villeneuve's Williams goes by him on the inside, Michael Schumacher attempts to clinch the World Championship by running his rival off the road. (LAT)

*Right* The Prof. (LAT)

**Above** *The winning of a first World Championship. Mika Hakkinen locks up in celebration as he takes the flag at Suzuka in 1998. (LAT)*

**Below left** *Hakkinen and Ron Dennis at Monte Carlo in 1999. No driver and team owner are on closer terms. (LAT)*

**Below right** *Lord of all he surveys. And that includes passes. (LAT)*

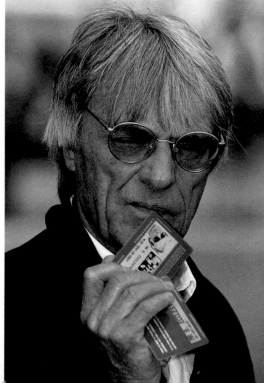

Of rather greater moment than a team's internal spat, though, was an accident between Jochen Mass and Mauro Baldi, whose cars touched at the flat-out Signes right-hander, with potentially catastrophic consequences. While Baldi's Arrows spun off harmlessly, Mass's March became airborne, clearing the catch-fencing altogether, hitting a tyre barrier, then bouncing into a spectator area debris fence, and briefly catching fire. A dozen or so people were injured, one of them burned, but somehow no lives were lost.

Jackie Stewart recalled that, in his time as a driver, you backed off a hundred yards before Signes, brushed the brake pedal, then feathered the throttle as you went through. Now, nine years on, it was flat, and for everyone.

Stewart knew he would be accused of scaremongering, but said he had never been so concerned for the future of the sport. Cornering speeds *had* to be reduced, and the governing body needed to take action, for if changes were left to the constructors, nothing would be done.

'Any risk of involving spectators in an accident cannot be tolerated, and you really can't put all the onus on the circuit owners. Things will only have to go really wrong just once, and everything will change. Only when there is tragedy does anything get done. That's the history of the sport.

'I don't believe most people in Formula 1 have any idea how threatened their business is. They need to recognise what a major shunt – a *major* shunt – would do to them. If sponsors decide to pull out, the decision will come from the Board of Directors, and it will be cold-blooded. There's no racing passion there.

'My major fear has never been for the drivers,' Stewart said, 'even when I was racing myself. I always reckoned that drivers go in knowing it is a calculated risk, but with things the way they are, I believe we shall be extremely fortunate to get through this year without another driver being killed.'

A week or so later, on the Saturday morning at Hockenheim, I arrived in the press car park a little late, and practice was already under way. The weather, baking the day before, was now murky, and there was heavy rain; as I buttoned up against the elements I chanced to look across to the end of the straight leading into the stadium.

There was a car – a Ferrari – in the air, 20 feet or so from the ground, its nose pointing skyward. It came down tail first, then began somersaulting, coming to rest finally at the trackside.

The rescue scene was from Hades. Pironi had suffered the appalling lower leg injuries so common in an era when drivers sat virtually between the front wheels, and his bloodied face was a mask of agony as the doctors worked on him. Finally he was released, and taken to hospital in Heidelberg, where, against all likely odds, his right foot was saved from amputation. Before being 'put under', still in the cockpit, he had asked Professor Watkins to ensure that his legs would be saved, and Sid had given his word.

As Didier recovered, over the months, so he began to speak of returning to Formula 1, and Enzo Ferrari said that, as and when, there would be a car for him. But no one took either man too seriously. Pironi's chaotic 1982 season had ended terribly, and it would be his last.

Simple lack of visibility had caused the accident. Prost, on the left-hand side of the track, was not at full speed, for he was coming in at the end of the lap, and Derek Daly went to pass him on the right. Pironi, moving considerably faster than both, assumed that Daly was moving over for him, and went left of the Williams – into the wall of spray which concealed Prost's car. The Ferrari hit the back of the Renault, flew clear over the top of it. Alain's hardline aversion to dead reckoning conditions dates back to that day.

Pole position was left vacant on Sunday, and not merely in tribute, either, for the rain had continued through final qualifying, and Pironi's Friday time therefore remained unapproached.

Tambay faced a big test. To win at Hockenheim in a turbocharged car was not in itself the most taxing of labours, but the circumstances in which his victory was achieved said much about his composure. Following the Pironi disaster, the Ferrari team was almost pleadingly dependent on him, and he didn't let them down.

The lead came his way on lap 19, when certain victory for Piquet – who had led from the start in the half-tanked, soft-tyred, Brabham – was squandered to impatience. Way in front, Nelson had time and to spare in picking his way through the backmarkers, but stupidly went to pass Eliseo Salazar's ATS into the *Ostkurve* chicane. Both cars were out on the spot.

There was something of the crazed marionette about Piquet as he struggled to get out of the cockpit, and more of the same as he remonstrated with Salazar, slapping and kicking at him like the petulant child he could sometimes be. Eliseo just shrugged. These superstars…

Twelve races in, it was unlikely that Pironi would keep his points lead, but the way this season was going none would lightly have bet against it. He had 39 points, and was followed by Watson (30), Rosberg (27), Prost (25), Lauda (24) and Arnoux and Patrese (19). With four races to go, it was still possible – mathematically, anyway – for 17 drivers to win the title.

To the Österreichring, then, for what used to be everyone's favourite Grand Prix. On paper, this was going to be a stroll for the turbos, and Piquet's Brabham-BMW duly took pole position, with a lap at 151.705mph. Rosberg, sixth, headed the non-turbo drivers, and if his speed – 147.189 – looked paltry by comparison with Piquet's, still it was a sensational lap, 1.3 seconds faster than the next normally-aspirated car, this the Lotus of de Angelis.

The Brabhams – Patrese ahead of Piquet – ran away in the early laps, chased only by the Renaults, for Tambay's Ferrari picked up a puncture on the second lap, and had to crawl an entire lap before getting new tyres. Stone last, he drove a strong race back to fourth.

It was in Austria that Brabham finally got to try out their planned pit stops, and they worked well enough, although Piquet took his mechanics by surprise, stopping earlier than expected, having blistered a tyre. Patrese came in shortly before half-distance, and the crew changed wheels and put in 100 litres of fuel in under 14 seconds. Seemed pretty quick at the time.

Engine failure eventually accounted for both Brabhams, however, and with Arnoux already gone (turbo), Prost looked on a canter for his first win since March. Five laps from the end, though, the Renault's injection system developed a mind of its own, and flames shot from the exhausts as the engine died. Alain's body language was untypically eloquent as he climbed out.

Now de Angelis led, chased by Rosberg, and as they emerged from the Rindtkurve for the last time, it looked as though Keke had timed his slipstreaming run to a nicety. Down to the flag he went right of the Lotus, but de Angelis was confident enough to give a victory wave, and won by a couple of feet. Not for four years had Colin Chapman been able to pitch his cap into the air.

Rosberg was disappointed, of course, to lose so nearly, but consoled by the knowledge that his six points took him to second place in the championship, half a dozen behind the stricken Pironi. And it couldn't be long, surely, before Keke, like Elio, joined the band of new Grand Prix winners.

It happened at Dijon two weeks later, in the quaintly named Swiss Grand Prix. Qualifying was dominated by the Renaults, Arnoux fighting strenuously for the pole, and no longer making any pretence of aiding Prost's quest for the World Championship; already it was known that he was off to Ferrari for 1983.

In the end, however, René was squarely beaten by Alain, and although he got ahead at the start, it was only for a lap. Prost motored away, and Piquet moved up to second, ahead of Arnoux, Rosberg and Lauda. They ran like this for a long time.

Towards the end, the picture began to change. Tyre problems had delayed Piquet, and Prost, although still in front, was troubled with worsening understeer, one of the Renault's skirts breaking up. As Arnoux looked set to take the lead, his injection system went haywire, just as Prost's had done in Austria, so that accounted for him.

As in Austria, too, Rosberg began a late charge after the leader, and his closing rate made victory look like a formality.

212

Then he came up to lap de Cesaris, who shamefully declined to let him by; in three laps Keke lost 10 seconds to Prost.

'I learned a very good lesson that day,' he said, 'because I actually lost my temper, and I was ashamed of myself – I could have caused an accident. I went berserk, which is a very dangerous thing to do in a race car, but de Cesaris was going to make me *lose that race*! He had more power, and it reached a point where I was banging my front wheel against the sidepod of his car – at 170mph at the end of the straight!'

Once by de Cesaris, Rosberg got hard after Prost once more, and by lap 78 – with two to go – he was right with him. Now it was nip and tuck to the flag, with the Renault hobbled through the corners, but much quicker in a straight line.

As the end of the lap approached, the man with the chequered flag was overcome by … confusion, let's say, and got into position to wave the thing. Williams team manager Peter Collins was fortunately alert to the situation, and restrained the fellow, so that his arms – and the flag – were pinned to his sides as the cars went over the line…

Collins's presence of mind saved the day for his team, for at that stage Prost still narrowly led, but on lap 79 Rosberg found a way past, and pulled away, a Grand Prix winner at last.

In scoring nine points, Keke also took the lead of the Championship, and was now the clear favourite to take it, for – Pironi apart – his nearest rival, Prost, was nine behind, and there were only two races to run.

One of them, though, was Monza, an inevitable gift for the turbos, one of which surely had to last. Rosberg could only hope that it wouldn't be Prost's Renault, for while four drivers – Watson and Lauda were the others – retained the possibility of becoming World Champion, only Alain had a turbo.

At stake, too, was the Constructors' Cup. Given the circumstances of the season, it was perhaps remarkable that Ferrari (64) narrowly led, from McLaren (60), Williams (55) and Renault (50), but as the Italian Grand Prix approached Enzo Ferrari had problems. Championships apart, it was obviously vital that the team should show well at Monza, but the *Ingegnere* found himself in a situation even he had never faced before: no drivers for his cars.

At Dijon the lone Ferrari had been withdrawn on race morning. All season long the drivers had suffered the jarring consequences of sitting in cars effectively without suspension, and in Tambay this resulted in a pinched nerve. Although he qualified for the Swiss Grand Prix, the pains in his neck and back and right arm were such that changing gear was excruciating.

Although Patrick immediately began a course of intensive treatment, there was no certainty he would be fit to race at Monza, so Enzo Ferrari thought for a minute or two, then put a call through to Nazareth, Pennsylvania.

Next day so did I. 'Did I accept?' Mario Andretti was incredulous at my question. 'Jeez, what do *you* think? This is a Ferrari – at *Monza*! Cream for the cat...'

Cream, too, for the race organisers, who had been getting panicky about their ticket sales, for admission prices had been steeply increased, and there was no Gilles Villeneuve to make the *tifosi* dig deeper.

The news that the cavalry – Italian, in their minds, rather than American – was on its way rather buried Bernie Ecclestone's facile contention, expressed vividly during the Kyalami strike, that 'no one comes to see drivers'. Immediately there was a rush for Monza tickets.

Typically, Andretti's arrival in Italy was a *tour de force*. The TV cameras were on the Alitalia jet even before it landed, and when the door finally opened, Mario came out alone, then stopped halfway down the steps, and held up both arms. He was wearing a Ferrari cap – blessed touch of theatre – and when they saw that they went nuts.

A press conference at Linate, and then Andretti went for lunch with the Old Man. Late in the afternoon he asked if it would be possible to run just a few laps that day. Enzo clicked his fingers, and it was done.

By the time he came to Monza, Mario had tested substantially, and was getting to know the car. On Saturday 70,000 turned up for final qualifying, in which Tambay –

somewhat recovered – fought Piquet for the pole. Their qualifying runs completed, Nelson had the edge, but then, with five minutes remaining, Andretti's Ferrari burbled out of the pit lane.

One warm-up lap, one flyer, and the commentator – close to apoplexy – screamed the news that Mario was quickest, that a Ferrari was on pole position! In all my years of going to Monza, I have never known the fans react as they did that day. They had lost Gilles, they no longer had Pironi, but now, as this season of tumult neared its end, Andretti had given them a moment of absolute joy.

'Mario and Patrick – win for Gilles' they daubed on the track overnight, but unfortunately it wasn't to be, for Arnoux took the lead on the first lap, and was never headed. Although Tambay gave gallant chase all the way, Ferrari's tyre choice had been too conservative, and Andretti was also troubled by a sticky throttle.

Still, he finished third, and if the fans wished for a home victory, they got the next best thing, for both Ferrari drivers made the podium, and the man who beat them was coming to Maranello at season's end. As well as that, the points scored by Patrick and Mario were to prove sufficient to clinch the Constructors' Cup.

For championship leader Rosberg Monza was disappointing – he finished eighth after an eventful race, in which his car at one point shed its rear wing – but for his nearest rival, Prost, it was disastrous, for once more injection trouble had put him out, and now, 11 points behind Rosberg, the title was beyond his reach.

Only the McLaren drivers could beat Keke. Watson had finished fourth in Italy, scoring points, astonishingly, for the first time since Montreal, back in June. He was under no illusions: to become World Champion, he had to win the final race, with Rosberg failing to score. That would put them equal, on 42 points, with Watson getting the decision by virtue of more wins.

Lauda's chances were even more flimsy, for to be in the picture at all he needed an FIA Tribunal to uphold McLaren's appeal against his disqualification from third place at Zolder (five months earlier!), where his car had been minimally under the weight limit. It was unlikely the appeal would succeed, but still the possibility existed, and Niki had to think in those terms.

So, after the romance of Monza, away we went to the cold heart of Las Vegas, from a place passionate about motor racing to one which couldn't have cared less.

'What's this deal they're fighting for?' a man asked, as I waited to check in at my hotel. 'The World Championship,' I said. 'Jesus,' the man said, 'I hate race cars – I wouldn't even care if it was the *American* Championship…' Said it all, really.

In qualifying, Rosberg was relieved to find McLaren in Michelin trouble again, with Watson ninth and Lauda 13th. Keke himself lined up sixth, with the Renaults on the front row, and – most unusually – Alboreto's Tyrrell and Cheever's Ligier behind them.

Tambay had a recurrence of his pinched nerve problem, and again had to pull out, so it was just as well that Andretti had persuaded his IndyCar team owner to let him race a Ferrari one last time – this despite a clashing CART race weekend. 'No problem,' Mario smiled. 'This race is Saturday, so I can run Michigan on Sunday.'

Which is what he did, and to good effect. While the Ferrari did not give him a happy Formula 1 finale, breaking its rear suspension early on, at Michigan – starting from the back, having missed qualifying – he brought his Wildcat through to second, behind Bobby Rahal. All in a weekend's work.

By then, of course, the World Championship was done. Lauda took pressure off the FIA by retiring with overheating, and although Watson drove a marvellous race to second, first was what he had needed. It was academic, in fact, for Rosberg kept out of trouble, and cruised in for two more points.

As so often, Prost led most of the way, then fell back with Renault trouble, on this occasion a vibration which made the car almost undrivable in the late laps. As Alain lost pace, so he was reeled in by Alboreto, who took the flag, accepted the trophy from Diana Ross, and became the 11th driver to win a Grand Prix in 1982.

On the podium, too, Rosberg celebrated his World Championship, and dealt deftly with an over-effusive interviewer.

'Kay-kay, did you find the track different at all this year?'

'Yes, sure, I thought it was much better than last time.'

'Oh, really? Why is that, Kay-kay?'

'Well, since last year we've been to Detroit...'

There were those who claimed that a man who had won but a single Grand Prix was not a worthy World Champion, but they sold Keke short. No one, after all, had won more than two, and certainly no one, race to race, had shown greater commitment and raw speed than this little fellow who, a year earlier, had been out of work. It was all very well to suggest that the title would have been Villeneuve's, should have been Pironi's, might have been Prost's; the cards didn't fall that way.

Next day, as we gathered at the airport, it was with a sense of huge relief, and not only because we were leaving Las Vegas. The most anarchic, the most emotional, Formula 1 season on record was finally at an end, and everyone wanted to go home, forget about racing for a while.

'To be honest, I've hated every second of this season,' said Derek Ongaro, then the FISA's circuit inspector. 'There's something very wrong when the chequered flag comes down, and all you feel is relief that another race weekend is out of the way without someone getting killed.'

That was the thought in many a mind. Surely it was untenable to contemplate another season with cars whose very specification militated against safety. Everyone, save perhaps one or two designers, was therefore inclined to celebrate when Jean-Marie Balestre later announced that ground effect cars were banned forthwith.

In the tail of 1982, however, there remained one last sting, and a devastating one it was. A few days before Christmas Colin Chapman died, following a massive heart attack. Given the way the year had been, it was somehow less of a shock than it should have been.

# DALLAS, 1984

# Keeping a cool head

A BIZARRE WEEKEND in the history of Formula 1. No one quite
believed Bernie Ecclestone when in 1984 he announced plans
for a Grand Prix in Dallas, but the FIA gave it a date, and the
promoters toured European capitals, holding press lunches,
speaking confidently of their intentions. Little by little, we
began to take it seriously. Maybe it was kosher, after all.

So it was. The timing, everyone agreed, was unsatisfactory,
for July is one of the months when Texans get out of Texas if
they can. The heat and humidity, we were warned, would be
crippling. And, as the third race in four weekends, it meant an
unusually lengthy North American tour.

It had been hot as hell at the two Grands Prix in Vegas, but
that had been an arid desert heat; summer in Dallas meant
crippling humidity, but suggestions were ignored that the race
should be scheduled later in the year. Keeping the cars that side
of the water, following the Montreal and Detroit races, made
sense financially, so that was that.

Undoubtedly there was an element of novelty here. The hit
TV series, *Dallas*, was at the height of its worldwide
popularity, and Benetton, then sponsoring Alfa Romeo, laid on
a lavish press party at Southfork Ranch, where much of the
show was shot. And the leading characters, including JR and

218

Sue-Ellen, would be present at the race, presumably at vast expense.

The track, went the word, was unusually quick for one through the streets, but in fact it wasn't through the streets at all, at least not in the 'downtown' sense. Situated a little way south of the city, it wound through a park, and a pretty tatty one at that.

Everyone arrived on the Wednesday, took a look at the 2.42-mile circuit, and immediately it was clear there would be problems; the drivers weren't taken with it.

Bumpy, they said, and dangerous. Where were the cranes to shift damaged cars? At a press conference they made their feelings clear, but only Nigel Mansell and Patrick Tambay seemed aware that the purpose of the get-together was to give a new town some kind of favourable impression of this strange 'furrin' world of Formula 1. The rest whinged, said they shouldn't be racing in a place like this. The *Dallas Times Herald* came forth with an appropriate headline the next morning: 'Not only the engines whine'.

Derek Warwick, not invited to the conference, was one of few drivers to approach the race in a positive frame of mind. 'I don't understand half the people in Formula 1,' he said. 'You look at the Indy and NASCAR people, and you see they still understand where their bread and butter's coming from – the public. Without the public, we've had it.'

This was not your standard Grand Prix venue. Alboreto found that out on Thursday morning, when he toured the circuit in a borrowed Ferrari 308. 'Hold it there, boy!' a large Texas State Trooper yelled, and Michele looked up in astonishment. 'You wuz goin' 30 at least,' the man said, and Alboreto allowed as how that was possible, but so what? 'Well, there's a limit of 20 here...'

Not all condemned the track, though. 'Actually, I don't think the bumps are as bad as at Detroit,' said Keke Rosberg. 'Driving here is not a pleasure, but I'm not too worried about the safety aspect.' And Warwick was quite upbeat: 'It's bloody dangerous, but as a track not bad – quite challenging, in fact.' Mansell, too, took a positive attitude: 'It's the toughest place

I've ever been to, but we've got to make the best of it, haven't we?'

People change, don't they? Those many years ago here was Mansell looking on the bright side, and débutant Ayrton Senna by no means the perfectionist we were later to know. In one practice session, Ayrton went out in his Toleman-Hart, put the brakes on at the first turn – and found he couldn't see anything, for his helmet had slipped over his eyes. In his eagerness to get going, he had forgotten to tighten the strap.

The track was quite quick, the drivers agreed, but the run-off areas were scarcely in the Texan tradition of 'biggest and best'. On Thursday afternoon there was an exploratory one-hour session, in which Warwick's Renault set the best time. Already, though, there were concerns about the track surface.

The FIA rule book stipulated that no circuit new to Formula 1 may stage a Grand Prix without first holding a race of lesser consequence – a trial run, if you wish. But street tracks were exempt from this rule, and in Dallas the folly of that was clear to all. By Friday afternoon the temperature was 107, and the surface was breaking up, badly.

Was there anything Alain Prost liked about the circuit? 'Yes,' he said. 'Suddenly, Detroit isn't so bad, after all.

'This isn't racing,' he went on. 'It's gambling. For a quick lap you have to be out at the right time – and the right time is when there aren't any wrecks on the track. Which isn't often. You have to miss all the walls, of course, and you have to stay exactly on a line avoiding where the surface is breaking up. I'm going into the debriefing session now, and I don't know what to tell them…'

None of the usual rules applied. The men of Goodyear, Michelin and Pirelli packed away their qualifying tyres before the first timed session, already knowing them to be useless in this place. 'Qualifiers?' Tambay laughed. 'Forget it. Four corners, maybe five, finished.'

Oh, Lordy, this was a weird Grand Prix weekend.

Brundle crashed badly that afternoon. Having finished second to Nelson Piquet in Detroit a couple of weeks earlier, he admitted that maybe he came to Dallas a little over-confident.

The Tyrrell hit a concrete wall, and Martin sustained serious fractures to both feet. They pain him to this day.

At the end of the first timed session the Lotuses of Mansell and Elio de Angelis were on top, followed by René Arnoux's Ferrari, and already the fastest conditions were gone. On Saturday there was further track deterioration, and this time it was Warwick who set the pace, almost equalling the Lotus times of the day before. Nearly two seconds quicker than anyone else on the worsening surface, Derek had therefore to be considered favourite. But in these conditions who knew?

Late on Saturday afternoon a 50-lap Can-Am race was scheduled, and in the circumstances the organisers' best plan would have been to cancel it. Tedious in itself, it also served to chew up what little remained of the racing surface. Heavy 5-litre cars are unkind to tarmac at the best of times; by the time they'd finished with Dallas Fair Park, it looked like a dirt track.

In deference to the heat, a start time of 11 o'clock had been chosen for the Grand Prix, which meant a warm-up session at seven. Jacques Laffite raised a laugh by arriving in his pyjamas, but there wasn't much else in the way of levity that morning. The warm-up, it was decided, should be scrapped to save further damage to the circuit.

'It's unbelievable,' commented Renault team manager Jean Sage, after a tour of inspection. 'There are places where you can lift the asphalt with your fingers...' An over-night bodge job with epoxy concrete compound proved ineffective: in the furnace heat it needed too long to cure properly. There arose rumours that the race would be postponed by a day – maybe even cancelled altogether. This last option had the support of Lauda, Prost and Piquet.

And all the while the stands were filling up. Whatever shortcomings may have been exposed in the track, the organisers had done a fine job in selling their race to the rich and socially aware in Dallas. By late morning there were 90,000 folk on hand, a figure never approached in Detroit or Phoenix or Vegas. The real high-rollers shelled out $20,000 apiece for hospitality suites – plus another five grand for air-conditioning, which was about as optional as black coffee at a

Gordon Brown press conference. The place was like a furnace.

Most of the drivers stood around and moaned, bucking up only when the TV stars toured the pits. But Warwick and Mansell, at least, were cheerful, and so also, in a world-weary kind of way, was Rosberg.

Just as Stirling Moss used to rub his hands at the onset of rain before a race, so Keke was in the Dallas heat. While the rest sought water and ice and umbrellas, he sat there on the pit wall, apparently soaking up the sun, as if at his villa in Ibiza.

And he chuckled at the politics and ranting around him. 'You can stop a race after two laps, you know, and award half-points. So maybe they'll stop it after three. Can you imagine those three laps? Everyone on qualifiers, with full boost...'

Was there a feeling among the drivers, asked a local journalist with a keen grasp of the situation, that they didn't want to race?

'We don't want to break bones,' replied Rosberg, always to the point. 'Everyone worries about pain. It's crazy to race, but what are you going to do? There's a huge crowd out there, and a lot of countries waiting for TV. There's no point in blaming anyone here in Dallas – this is the FIA's fault for not insisting on new circuits having a try-out race before a Grand Prix. And where are the FIA people? Not here, because it's too bloody hot for them.

'This sort of situation degrades Grand Prix racing, right? But we'll just have to bite the bullet. In the end, we're all whores – if the money's right, we'll do our stuff for anyone. *Of course* there'll be a race.'

And there was. Once the decision had been taken, the drivers asked for 10 laps' acclimatisation, in lieu of the cancelled warm-up, but were told that TV schedules were too tight for more than three. Thus, they ran those, then came to the grid, and gave us far and away the most exciting race of the 1984 season.

'Look at them,' grinned a spectating John Watson, as Mansell, de Angelis, Warwick, Senna and the rest stampeded by. 'Show them a green light, and they can't help themselves.'

Senna's Toleman was probably the best-handling car in the

race, but he blew his chances by spinning on the second lap, which meant a stop for new tyres. On lap nine he did the same again, and with the same result.

Much later Ayrton retired with a broken driveshaft, after which it transpired he had driven most of the way without belts. 'They were so tight,' he said, 'that my legs were going numb. I preferred to unfasten the belts, take a chance.' It was indeed a chance on this, a day when accidents were so much on the cards.

Mansell led for a long way, his main opposition initially coming from Warwick, who spun into the wall while trying to take the lead, and Rosberg. A dejected Derek walked in to face the wrath of the Renault personnel, but they made him feel even worse by saying nothing! 'Then my wife arrived,' he smiled, 'and she had things to say, all right…'

Rosberg, too, chiefly about Mansell's driving tactics. The Lotus driver, he felt, was blocking to an outrageous degree, and later he made his feelings publicly clear. Not until lap 36 did he get by, after which Mansell went in for new tyres, having clobbered a wall.

So Rosberg now led, in atrocious conditions, and in the most unwieldy car in Texas. This was the Williams FW09, Patrick Head's least distinguished creation, and it was powered by Honda's early F2-based turbo V6, whose power delivery, Keke said, was like a light switch: on or off. If ever a car were destined for the wall, it was this one.

Rosberg, though, was the great improviser, the freehand artist, the man who adapted perhaps better than anyone. He made no mistakes worth the name, but he couldn't long resist the stealthy advances of A. Prost and the McLaren-TAG. Alain went by on lap 49, and began to pull away until, incredibly, he stuck it in the fence. He was sad-faced as he walked back to the pits; at season's end he would be sadder still. Nine points that day – *any* points that day – would have given him the World Championship. Five minutes later Lauda, running third, also crashed. So did 11 others.

Not Rosberg though, who now found himself with a comfortable lead. But if the race had another star it was surely

Arnoux. He had qualified fourth, but at the start of the parade lap the Ferrari refused to fire up, obliging René to start from the back. He passed six cars on the opening lap, drove flat out on this chaotic afternoon, never so much as clipped a wall, and finished an amazing second.

The closing laps were quiet, metaphorically and also literally, for hardly any cars remained on the circuit. Piercarlo Ghinzani's ancient Osella was to finish fifth. The fastest lap, set by Lauda, was more than eight seconds away from the pole time, slower even than the fastest lap in the Can-Am race.

A theatrical finale was provided by – who else? – Mansell, whose gearless Lotus expired near the end of the lap. Nigel, already completely spent, climbed out and began to push. Just short of the line he collapsed by the side of the car, classified sixth. All that for a single point.

Rosberg looked remarkably fresh as he kissed Sue-Ellen, accepted his trophy. How so, Keke? 'Well, I had a cool hat under my helmet…' It was a skullcap (through which chilled liquid circulated) of a type used routinely by the NASCAR drivers, who race all summer long in the Southern states, but only Williams had given thought to them for the Dallas Grand Prix.

On the Monday morning, the man from the *Dallas Times Herald* recanted somewhat. 'All complaints aside,' he wrote, 'when these chaps climb into the cockpit, they flat go racing. There's no pouting there…'

Cool in the wranglings of the morning, cool when it mattered, in the race, Rosberg put in what was probably the greatest drive of his life. He won the first Dallas Grand Prix, and the only one, too, for later it was discovered that someone had gone AWOL with the takings. Formula 1, sadly, never went back to Texas.

# ADELAIDE, 1986

# The great race

THE WEATHER WAS FILTHY as we flew into Adelaide for the World Championship decider in October of 1986. Below us, the tarmac glistened with early morning rain, but a bigger surprise, when later we emerged from the airport, was that the day was actually cold. A year earlier, at the first Australian Grand Prix, temperatures had been high throughout, and this we had assumed to be the norm.

Alain Prost looked gloomily at the skies. 'I really hope,' he said, 'that we get a normal, dry, race, because in the rain anything can happen.' Then he brightened up a little. 'It's a long way down here, isn't it? So many hours of flying. I must say I'm glad to be coming here with some chance of winning the title, even if it is a small chance…'

He had that small chance primarily because he had driven a quite brilliant race in Mexico two weeks earlier. Through the year his McLaren-TAG had been considerably outpowered by the Williams-Hondas of Nelson Piquet and Nigel Mansell, and although there had been convincing demonstrations of his driving superiority – notably at Monte Carlo, where he simply left everyone behind – in the normal course of events he was hard pressed to stay with Piquet and Mansell. If he were in contention for the title, it was because he got the absolute maximum from his car every time out, because his racecraft and guile were without equal, and because he made fewer mistakes than anyone else. By far.

'In Mexico, Alain drove a really incredible race,' Ron Dennis said. 'He had quite a few problems with the car, and really had to fight to overcome them. Throughout 1986, even in normal circumstances, he had a lot less power than the Williams-Hondas, but, to make it worse, this time he was only on five cylinders for half the race, and simply didn't dare to make a second tyre stop, for fear of losing the engine. Therefore he had to make two sets of tyres last the whole race, on a track with a very abrasive surface; Mansell, on the other hand, needed three, and Piquet four. Alain finished second, ahead of both of them.'

Prost's other surpassing skill, in that era of turbocharged engines, was juggling speed and fuel consumption. In 1986, each car was restricted to 195 litres of fuel for a race, so that if a driver got his balancing act absolutely right, he ran out of gas immediately after taking the flag.

It took a lot of will to keep your boost down, hold yourself in check, in the early part of a race, while some of your less disciplined rivals charged away into the distance. 'Apart from anything else,' growled Keke Rosberg, Prost's McLaren team-mate, 'you felt such a bloody idiot in those circumstances. You wanted to scream out to the grandstands, "Hey, I'm not a wanker, you know! I could go a lot faster than this..."'

Not for nothing was Prost known as 'The Professor', however. He may have hated the 'restricted fuel' rule as much as anyone, but he acknowledged, as Jimmy Durante used to say, that 'Dese are de conditions dat prevail'. Whatever it took to win, Alain would adapt.

Going into the final race, though, his title hopes looked flimsy. At the time, a driver's World Championship score was calculated on his best 11 results from the 16 races, and both Prost and Mansell had already needed to drop points, having scored in more than 11 events. The net situation was that Nigel had 70 points, Alain 64, and Nelson Piquet 63 – but if either Mansell or Prost should take further points in Adelaide, they would have to shed their lowest score once more, whereas

Piquet, having scored in only ten races, would not. Any of the three could become World Champion in Australia, but Nigel was the heavy favourite; third place would do it for him whatever happened to his rivals.

Prost wasn't fazed. 'Actually, I like this situation. In a way, it's like driving for your life – you *have* to win. For Nigel, it's more difficult, because he has choices he can make. Of course he has to be the favourite, but I will fight to the end.'

It was not often (in those days when Grand Prix racing was first a sport, second a TV show) that the World Championship went down to the wire, to the final race of the season, and it was rarer still for more than two drivers to be in contention. If the weather – cool, grey, unfriendly – decided not to honour the occasion, it did not detract from an extraordinary atmosphere at the track through the qualifying days. Given his power deficit, Prost had acknowledged that he would not be a contender for pole position, and concentrated, as always, on arriving at a perfect set-up for race day.

The fight for the pole was exclusively between the two Williams-Hondas, with Ayrton Senna's Lotus-Renault predictably lurking close by. Ultimately, Mansell sealed the issue with a lap three-tenths faster than Piquet, with Senna third, and Prost fourth, albeit more than a second from Mansell.

'Hmmm,' Alain grinned when he saw the times. 'Three people ahead of me – Mansell, Piquet, Senna – and they all hate each other!'

For Nigel, the first hurdle was cleared, but the tension surrounding him was palpable, for he, more nearly than anyone, was touching the hem of the World Championship. 'To be honest,' his wife Rosanne murmured, 'I don't really care what happens. I just want it to be over.'

In the McLaren pit, meanwhile, Rosberg was insisting that Prost was going to win the race, if not the championship. This was to be Keke's last Grand Prix, and although his final season, with McLaren, had not lived up to expectations, he was resolved to go out on a high note. 'I have never,' he said, 'managed to adapt my style of driving to suit the McLaren – or vice versa. But what I've come to realise – to know – this

227

season is that Alain is the greatest driver I've ever seen. No question about it. For me, it would be a joke for anyone else to be World Champion, and I'm going to do everything possible to help him.'

No one doubted Rosberg's sincerity, but few believed he would be able materially to aid Prost's quest. They were wrong. The man who would lead the bulk of the Australian Grand Prix was Keke, who had won the year before.

On race day the weather was as before, dull and cheerless, but at least there was no forecast of rain. Senna set the fastest time in the morning warm-up, but Prost was right behind him, and ahead of Mansell and Piquet. 'Remember what I said,' Rosberg reminded us. 'Alain's going to win this…'

The first lap was as intense as anyone could remember, with Mansell leading away from pole position, then – keen not to get involved in any early wheel-banging battle – moving over to let Senna and Piquet by. At the end of the long Dequetteville straight, Nelson outbraked Ayrton, and thus the race already had its third leader in the space of two miles!

The man really on the move in the early stages, though, was Rosberg, who had qualified only seventh, but was up to third by the end of the opening lap, behind Piquet and Senna. On lap two, Keke passed Ayrton, and moved up to menace Nelson. By lap seven, he was through into the lead, and going away. 'I'll never understand it,' he sighed later, 'but that day the car was perfect for me, without its usual understeer. I hadn't liked it in practice at all, but on race day it transformed itself! I was enjoying myself so much I began to wish I hadn't decided to retire.'

At the same time Prost began to move. Typically, he had begun quietly, sitting in fifth place, waiting for the initial dust to settle. Now he moved past Senna for fourth, and on lap 11 went ahead of Mansell, too.

Patrick Head remembers the day vividly. 'I always think it's nice to see drivers' characters come through in their driving. Alan Jones was very much that way – when he got his head down, you knew it was Alan, from the way he was going. Rosberg was the same. As for Prost, very often we'd be way ahead of him at first, and think, "Where the hell's Alain?" He'd qualify third or fourth, make a slow start, and you'd think, "Great, he's ninth or whatever, that's him out of the way." Then you'd see that he was sixth, fifth, fourth, third, and you'd think, "Ooooh, shit!" That was very much him, wasn't it? This inexorable quality. It was just like that in Adelaide.'

By lap 23, with Rosberg gone into the middle distance, Prost passed Piquet for second place, after which Nelson immediately spun. He kept the Williams-Honda alive, and got on his way again, but was now back in fourth place. For McLaren, now running 1–2, everything was looking good, for if it came to it, Keke, despite an understandable desire to win his last race, would undoubtedly let Alain through in the late stages.

Mansell, though, continued to run a solid third, right where he needed to be. If he could simply hold station until the end, he would be World Champion, and on lap 32 his prospects vaulted, for Prost was slowing, his right front tyre punctured.

'Three laps before, I'd had a small touch with Berger, when I lapped him at the hairpin,' said Alain, 'but I don't think that caused the problem. It was just a normal puncture.'

Tyre changes were far from an automatic feature of Grand Prix races in the mid-1980s, and none of the front runners had been planning to stop. Therefore, as Prost slowly made his way to the pit lane, he seemed to be eliminating himself from the championship battle. After a 17-second stop – it was difficult to get a jack under the McLaren in its lowered state – he rejoined, now fourth, a long way back. Immediately a whole series of record laps began.

'People probably won't believe me when I say this,' Prost told me later, 'but I was *always* going to change tyres in that race. Even the lap for the stop was agreed.

'To be absolutely honest, though, before the race I almost took the decision not to stop: after all, if they were not stopping, maybe I should do the same. But I came back to logic. I had worked a lot with the car and tyres during practice, and I knew it would be marginal to go all the way without changing. I also knew that my car was easier on tyres than a Williams.'

He might have added that he, Prost, was easier on tyres than Mansell and, particularly, Piquet, but self-conceit was never Alain's way. 'What lost me the time,' he said, 'was the slow lap back to the pits with my flat tyre. After that, all I could do was push as hard as possible. There was nothing to lose. Even second place was no use to me.'

In the pits, Goodyear technicians examined the tyres discarded by Prost, and commented that the wear rate was less than they had expected. All being well, they concluded, no one would need to make a stop.

Patrick Head grimaces at the memory. 'Trouble was, we had quite a big horsepower advantage at that time – and therefore we were also able to run more downforce than anyone else. Honda couldn't tell us how much power we had, actually, because they didn't know themselves! Their dyno only registered up to 1,000 horsepower – which they were reaching at 9,300rpm. We were revving them to 13,500 or so...

'I've no doubts that it was because we were able to run so much wing that we encountered tyre problems, and I was a bit annoyed after the race when one of the Goodyear engineers told the press that Williams had been advised to make a tyre stop. That was absolutely not the case. We would never go against the advice of Goodyear engineers, basically because they know their product, and we don't.'

At this stage of the race, though, Williams had no cause for worry. For close to 30 laps there was virtual stalemate at the front of the field, Rosberg still leading convincingly from Piquet, a serene Mansell, and a charging Prost.

Then, on lap 63, with 19 to the flag, the full drama of the day began to unravel. Rosberg, having led for well over an hour, suddenly heard unwelcome noises from the back of his McLaren, and abruptly parked the car, initially convinced that the engine had run its bearings.

In fact, it was no such thing. When Rosberg got out, he swiftly realised that what he had heard was a delaminating tyre flapping against the bodywork. His right rear Goodyear was in tatters. 'In fact, I was lucky,' he commented, 'because one of my brake discs was about to come apart, and I wouldn't have wanted to find that out at the end of Dequetteville or somewhere.' It was a sad end to his last Grand Prix, but still he could take pleasure from what had been a stirring finale.

As Rosberg retired, so Prost, running at the limit, passed Mansell for second place, but still Nigel had a lock on the four points he needed.

'In fact,' said Head, 'at that stage he was in a position where he could have stopped for tyres, and still gone on to get the championship, because there was no one close behind him. I told a Goodyear engineer that we had the time to do that, but he said we should have no problem: from the tyre wear that they had measured, it seemed to be perfectly OK.'

Only a lap later the outcome of the World Championship was settled. Mansell, flat out down Dequetteville, and in the process of lapping Philippe Alliot's Ligier, suddenly had his left rear tyre disintegrate. From something approaching 190mph, he somehow fought the bucking, wayward, Williams to a halt, parking in the escape road, then stumbling back to the pits. 'To be honest, I'm glad simply to be in one piece,' he mumbled. It was beyond cruel.

'At no time did we consider we were taking any sort of gamble,' Head said. 'After all, we were in a position where we had to play things safe and conservatively. I don't blame Goodyear for the fact that it happened, but they gave us absolutely no reason to consider we needed to change tyres. And you've got to remember that it did not explode because it was worn out. The bits of tyre that were recovered indicated that the carcass had failed, by fatigue.'

Now it was simply Piquet against Prost, and each needed the nine points for victory to take them past Mansell's total – to become World Champion. It was absolutely a matter of winner take all, and Prost, still with the hammer down, was only two seconds behind.

The duel never materialised. 'After Nigel's tyre had failed, we were between a rock and a hard place with regard to Nelson,' said Head. 'If we'd left him out there, and he'd made it, we'd have looked like heroes, but if he'd had an accident, and hurt himself, we'd have looked idiots. There was no choice to be made, in fact: we called him in, and changed his tyres.'

Piquet stopped at the end of lap 65, and was still in second place when he went back out. 'It was the right decision, to stop,' he said afterwards. 'I knew I might be losing the championship, but I didn't care. I was alive.'

Now it was Nelson's turn to apply the pressure, to set the new fastest laps, but he made little impression on Prost until the last four laps, when Alain dramatically cut his pace. 'From the halfway point, my fuel computer read-out had been telling me I was five litres the wrong side – that I wouldn't make the finish unless I backed off. But of course I couldn't do that, because I was so far behind, after my puncture, so I just had to hope that, for once, the computer was wrong...'

For once, it was. Although Piquet set yet another record on the final lap, Prost's engine continued to run, and he crossed the line four seconds to the good, waving both arms in salute at the flag. At once, he pulled up, in front of the stands, climbed out, and literally jumped for joy.

For once, a championship decider had not only lived up to everyone's expectations, but actually exceeded them. Jackie Stewart best summed up the day: 'These days, you don't often see a guy win a Grand Prix in a slower car, do you? But this guy's won the World Championship in one! People are going to say Nigel lost it because of his tyre failure, and of course that's true – but you could also say he lost it in Mexico, where he started in third gear, dropped to the back, then began blistering tyres, and finished fifth. He could have clinched the championship that day, but instead he dropped four points to Prost. And he lost the title by two ... To my mind, there's no one near Alain.'

The 1986 Australian Grand Prix remains the most dramatic Formula 1 race I have ever seen. Who needed the sun?

# ENZO FERRARI

# His terrible
# joys

AT PRESS CONFERENCES, Michael Schumacher is not by any means a natural star. Usually his replies to questions are polite, if perfunctory, and the overall tone is detached, invariably dull. Once in a while, though, through arrogance or ignorance, or perhaps a combination of the two, he comes out with something that leaves you reeling.

For one who has spoken many times of his reasons for being with the team, of the holy task before him, the desire to restore pride to Italian motor racing, to win the World Championship in a Ferrari, he appears to know little of the heritage of Maranello. At the 1998 French Grand Prix, he and Eddie Irvine finished first and second. 'I don't know,' he said, 'if Ferrari have ever had a 1–2 before…'

Well, yes, Michael, as a matter of fact. Thirty-nine times, in fact, the first at Monza in 1951, when Alberto Ascari beat Froilan Gonzales, and the most recent – prior to Magny-Cours – at Jerez in 1990, when Alain Prost beat Nigel Mansell.

Schumacher's throwaway remark served to crystalise why I no longer feel about Ferrari the way I did. For so many years my heart beat a little faster for them. It helped that they were scarlet, of course, and had that uniquely rapturous scream, but there was also about the team an intangible quality which

233

preserved its segregation from the herd. Even when the cars weren't winning – which, in truth, was most of the time – they had a magic which plundered the emotions as no others ever could.

Undoubtedly some of that magic remains, but for me it has been progressively diluted over the last decade, to the point that now, rather sadly, I think of Ferrari as just another leading Formula 1 team, as multi-national and faceless as any other.

'It was a turning point when they started bringing PR people to the races, and dishing out press releases, like all the rest,' a colleague said. I knew what he meant.

In my mind, the ethos of Ferrari began to dissipate when Mauro Forghieri – that blend, as Niki Lauda put it, 'of genius and madman' – left at the end of 1984. So long as Mauro – noisy, emotional, good-humoured – was there, there never could be any doubt that this was, above all else, an *Italian* team, and everything that meant.

The mystique of Ferrari, of course, began with the enigma from whom the cars took their name. A man of contradictions, on occasion chillingly ruthless, yet capable of unexpected sentimentality. When Chris Amon, Enzo Ferrari's team leader in the late 1960s, picked up the mail on his 40th birthday, one of the cards bore a Maranello postmark. When Jean Behra was killed at Avus in 1959, a few weeks after parting acrimoniously from the team, there was not so much as a wreath from Ferrari at his funeral.

At Enzo's death, in 1988, I felt that now the last of my gods was gone. We had known for weeks that he was close to the end; he was 90 years old, and had lived what may indeed be termed a full life. Still, though, it seemed inconceivable he could disappear. Enzo Ferrari, surely, would be around for as long as cars were raced.

As it was, he slipped away on the morning of Sunday 14 August, and had been buried even before his death was formally announced. It seemed to me then that an era had gone with him to the grave, for this was the first, and also the last, of the great autocrats of motor racing. 'Red cars will continue to be built in the little town near Modena,' I wrote at the time, 'but other hands, perhaps susceptible to influences beyond a pure love of racing cars, will be in control.'

At the time Frank Williams suggested, only half in jest, that now he was truly worried about the threat from Ferrari. 'The Fiat men will move in,' he said, 'and it could be that the company will be really *managed* for the first time.'

Williams was right about the Fiat men, wrong about the effect they would have. Control of Ferrari indeed passed to executives from Turin, but most of them knew little of racing, and looked upon it chiefly as a marketing tool. Cynical, cunning, manipulative as he may have been, the Old Man had always raced from passion.

In an era when Ferrari's budget is regarded as fathomless, it is ironic now to recall that 30 and 40 years ago the company built and sold wildly expensive road cars simply to finance the racing programme. If Ferrari loathed that the majority were ordered by rich dilettantes, primarily attracted by the kudos of the name, still it was an evil necessary to pay for his obsession.

Until the Fiat money began to arrive in 1970, in point of fact, Ferrari was the relative pauper of Formula 1. Schumacher might now be making $25 million a year or more, but 30 years ago Amon got $25,000 – and that was for Formula 1, sports car racing, CanAm, the whole damn thing.

Even that was progress, though. Phil Hill says he can't remember exactly what he was paid. 'And even if I could,' the 1961 World Champion laughs, 'I'd probably be too embarrassed to tell you! The Old Man's line was very much that you drove for Ferrari for the honour of it. And he wasn't kidding.'

Since the arrival of Schumacher, Ferrari's entire racing operation has slavishly submitted to his every whim. Michael has gathered around him the personnel he feels he needs, even a team-mate who may not, under the terms of the contract, beat him. Such a scenario would have been inconceivable in Enzo's time. In 1986 he acknowledged that he had had talks with Ayrton Senna; they had been brief, he said.

'I felt it inappropriate to go to Marlboro (who pay our

drivers) with the … financial expectations advanced by the driver. They were, shall we say, *imaginativo*!'

Stirling Moss never thought that Ferrari cared too much about his drivers. 'I never drove for him, but I've no doubts that in my day he would allow different drivers to win by giving them better cars sometimes, thereby giving the impression that the driver didn't count for anything – that it was the *car* which had won.'

Beyond doubt is that competition between Ferrari drivers was always actively encouraged. The Old Man especially relished chargers, those, like Gilles Villeneuve, who were abnormally brave. Recrimination was always likely for a man who settled for second, never for one who had destroyed a car trying to be first.

'I remember watching the 1981 British Grand Prix on TV with Ferrari,' said Harvey Postlethwaite, then the team's design chief. 'That was the year of hydraulic suspension, when the cars were rock hard. Gilles clipped the kerb at the Woodcote chicane, and literally bounced into a spin, taking Jones and de Cesaris with him. There was no reaction from the Old Man during the shunt. Then, after a pause, he turned around to me. "Too narrow, that chicane," he says. Lovely…'

'At the end of each year,' Phil Hill remembered, 'he'd publish these annuals, you know. The Ferrari Yearbooks. And you could tell from the number of photos of you whether you were in favour or not. The only way you came out of it well was either to be on especially good terms with him – or to die. If you died, you got your picture in colour – with big ruby lips painted in! Terrible, huh?'

Ferrari called his autobiography *Le Mie Gioie Terribili – My Terrible Joys*. He chose it, he said, to illustrate the conflict he felt in constructing these exquisite machines in which young men often won, sometimes died.

Through more than 60 years in motor racing he was truly close to only a handful of his drivers: Tazio Nuvolari, Ascari, Peter Collins, Wolfgang von Trips, Villeneuve. 'He was an aggressive champion,' he said after Gilles's death in 1982, 'who gave and added much renown to the name of Ferrari. I loved him.' But when Didier Pironi crashed hideously at Hockenheim later the same year, his reaction to the news was, 'Addio Mondiale.' Goodbye, World Championship.

'I remember the day of Pironi's accident very clearly,' said Postlethwaite. 'Everyone was pretty depressed, as you can imagine, and Ferrari asked me to join him the following day, to watch the race on TV. Patrick Tambay, who had taken Villeneuve's place, won it, and the Old Man just sat there and cried. An incredible thing to witness. Then he went round and embraced everybody, and I understood just how emotionally involved with racing these people were.

'Villeneuve had been killed not long before, and that had a deep effect on Ferrari. In terms of talent, Gilles was on another level from the other drivers, but he was also the most unpolitical, disarmingly honest, person I've ever met. No hang-ups about anything. In front of the Old Man, he would say that his car was a shitbox, that it had no downforce, and he was wasting his time. "I'll drive it," he'd say, "all day long. I'll spin it, put it in the fence, do whatever you like – because that's my job, and I love doing it. I'm just telling you we're not going to be competitive..."

'Just completely honest, you see, and the Old Man *loved* him for it. He was a warrior, in the Nuvolari mould, and therefore, in Ferrari's eyes, he could do no wrong.'

Ferrari's son Dino died young, in 1956, and those close to him maintained that this was the defining moment of his life, that he never truly emerged from the shadow of his grief. Thereafter he attended only one more race, the 1957 Modena Grand Prix, not because it was close at hand, but because it marked the début of the V6 engine on which Dino had worked, and which was later named for him.

If Ferrari invariably put machinery before men, so even the love of his cars was an abstract thing. For the actual machinery there was no sentiment whatever. Millionaires across the world might devote themselves to collecting Ferrari racing cars, but the Old Man hadn't a sliver of interest in what he saw as museum pieces. The future was the thing, and the cars were routinely broken up once their useful purpose had been served.

The classic 'shark-nose' cars dominated the 1961 season, for example, but not a single model survives. 'At Ferrari,' the founder would say, 'the most beautiful victory is always the next one.'

For a driver, the lure of Maranello was always very real. 'When I first went there,' Stefan Johansson said, 'and saw Mr Ferrari, I was as nervous as if I'd been meeting Royalty. "Even if I don't get the drive," I thought, "at least one of my dreams has been fulfilled."'

He had that effect on people, this immaculately dressed old man with the ever-present sunglasses. At Ferrari press conferences, we always felt like schoolboys again, waiting for Morning Assembly; like Fangio, he had a presence to make the roof of your mouth dry.

I met him only a couple of times. At Monza, one year in the early 1970s, he turned up for practice on the Friday, and Amon, no longer driving for Ferrari, but still on good terms, introduced me. Shaking hands with him felt like an electric shock.

Much later, before the 1984 season, I made a trip to Maranello in the depths of winter. Shortly before I left, Piero Lardi Ferrari presented me with a signed copy of *Piloti Che Genti* (*Racers – An Amazing Breed*), his father's latest book, the violet ink still wet on the page. A big moment, I remember.

The last time I saw him was a few days before the Italian Grand Prix of 1986, when he took the unusual step of inviting the *stampa Inglese* to Maranello. By now he was frail in body, but his voice was strong enough as he replied to our questions, and certainly there was little awry with his mind. General factotum Marco Piccinini was on hand to act as interpreter, but in reality his function was to give Ferrari time to think before answering; more than once, the Old Man began to speak before Piccinini had finished, suggesting that he understood rather more English than he had led us to believe...

It is good that he never knew what happened to his beloved company in the three years or so after 1988. Following his death, the logical move would have been to install as his successor Luca di Montezemolo, team manager in the mid-1970s and all-round Fiat whizzkid, but at the time di

Montezemolo was preoccupied with the organisation of Italia '90, and so a succession of faceless Fiat executives took up the reins, to catastrophic effect.

One of Ferrari's last decisions had been to hire John Barnard as technical director, and he amazed everyone by acceding to JB's stipulation that he work from England. Thus, GTO – Guildford Technical Office, in this quirky instance – was set up, and from it came a succession of competitive cars. The engine department, though, remained in Maranello, and thus it was impossible to prevent 'factions' from developing.

In the end, Barnard, frustrated beyond measure, severed his ties with the team, and the pity was that he did so immediately before Alain Prost, with whom he had enjoyed a fine relationship at McLaren, came aboard as number one driver.

Certainly, though, John had left Alain with something good to drive in 1990; five times that year Prost won with the 641 – a car so classically elegant that an example resides permanently in New York's Museum of Modern Art – and he ran Senna close for the World Championship.

The following year, however, there were no victories, and the organisation of the team fell into shambles. After the Japanese Grand Prix, Prost was moved to compare his car unfavourably with a truck, and the management of the day promptly fired him for daring to insult the sacred name. 'They've done it now,' a team insider said. 'They're in deep trouble, and they've sacked the one bloke who might have got them out of it.'

Tambay, by now retired, considered his former team sadly. 'I think the situation is out of control,' he said. 'No one's in charge any more. When the Old Man was alive, the buck stopped with him. Maybe he took some curious decisions in his time – but at least he took them. I'm not saying that Ferrari will never win again. They'll probably be able to paper over the cracks, to some extent, but the fabric of what Ferrari meant has gone. There are so many levels of management now, so many bosses reporting to bosses, until ultimately it gets to Gianni Agnelli.'

Niki Lauda and Jody Scheckter, Ferrari World Champions both, had strong feelings, too. 'When I was there,' Jody said, 'if you had a problem, you went to the Old Man, and talked it out with him. Maybe it wasn't always resolved as you hoped, but at least you got an answer.' And Niki echoed him: 'I feel sorry for Prost, surrounded by these Fiat people. Who does he go to when something needs to be changed? And when he chooses one of them, how many others does he upset?'

It was indeed a time of Machiavellian chaos. Although di Montezemolo soon afterwards arrived to take over, Ferrari were not to win again until August of 1994, when Gerhard Berger triumphed at Hockenheim. After that, there was a wait of almost a year before Jean Alesi was victorious in Canada.

By and by, though, it began to look as though recovery might be at hand. For one thing, di Montezemolo had hired Jean Todt as racing director, and over time his influence was to be profound. 'I was able to bring some links in the chain to Ferrari,' Berger observed, 'but it took Todt to join them together. He has made a huge difference.'

Indeed so. But the clearest evidence of Ferrari's intent came late in 1995, when it was announced that Schumacher had signed a contract for the following year. 'If we don't win with Michael,' Agnelli unequivocally said, 'it will be our fault, not his.'

Before breaking his leg at Silverstone, Schumacher had driven in 56 Grands Prix for Ferrari, and 16 of them he had won, so there is no doubting the effect he has had; without him, I suspect that the team would have continued along the lines of 1994 and 1995, winning the odd race here and there.

Barnard, who came back for a second spell in 1993, left once again early in 1997, after which Ferrari increasingly took on the aspect of Scuderia Benetton Rosso, for not only is Schumacher there, but also Ross Brawn and Rory Byrne, linchpins of his World Championship years.

What, 10 years and more on, would Enzo have made of the team which was his life? I think he would have accepted, albeit with regret, the need to abandon 12-cylinder engines in favour of the V10, but I doubt he would have gone for the gaudy 'Scuderia Ferrari Marlboro' signwriting on the transporters, or the loss of Italian Racing Red on his cars.

As for Schumacher, I think the *Ingegnere* – he hated to be called *Commendatore* – might have flinched at his financial requirements, to say nothing of his lack of interest in everything Ferrari has meant to motor racing. But if I have my doubts that the Old Man would have grown close to Michael, there are none at all that he would have savoured his commitment, his absolute speed and combativeness, just as with Nuvolari, with Villeneuve. Better a damaged car than a limp finish.

Before the 1999 season began, Max Mosley suggested that a contemporary Grand Prix be regarded as a chess match, a matter of strategy and calculation. Not, I think, an argument he would readily have sold to Enzo Ferrari.

# NIGEL MANSELL

# A problem for every solution

EIGHTEEN LAPS into the 1995 Spanish Grand Prix, Nigel
Mansell drove his McLaren-Mercedes into its pit, stepped from
the cockpit, and strode away without a word. 'Nigel chose not
to continue,' was how Ron Dennis put it afterwards.

Although McLaren's MP4/10 was by no means a truly
competitive proposition, Mansell had qualified within a tenth
of team-mate Mika Hakkinen, but if they lined up on the same
row, when the lights went out they quickly went their separate
ways. By the end of the first lap, Mika was running sixth, Nigel
14th.

The relationship with McLaren was ill-starred from the
beginning, because, on both sides, it was forged for the wrong
reasons. Perhaps, if the car had proved instantly a front runner,
Mansell and McLaren could have amounted to something, but
Dennis, never a fan, hired him with considerable misgivings,
and Mansell, in the words of Derek Warwick, 'seemed to be
thinking mainly of the pounds, shillings and pence'.

The season began with the fiasco of a cockpit into which
Nigel couldn't comfortably fit, and two missed races for him
while a more commodious car was built. After that there were a
couple of lacklustre appearances, in the second of which, in
Spain, he abandoned a healthy, if ill-handling, car. 'I think it's

over,' murmured a McLaren man after the race, and so, a week later, it was.

Denis Chevrier, the Renault engineer with whom Mansell worked in his later Williams years, always appreciated the sheer physical enthusiasm with which he drove, but pointed out that his was an all-or-nothing approach. 'To Nigel, a racing car is like a toy to a child – and when it doesn't work as it should, he behaves like a kid with a broken toy…'

When I look back now on Mansell's 15 years, in Formula 1 and IndyCar racing, it seems to me that he is one of the strangest people I have known in a sport where strange people are not hard to find. Wherever he was in the world, he had fresh problems flown in daily, and it was no wonder that the tabloids, which he assiduously courted, gave over so much ink to him: when it came to Mansell, there was somehow always a story. It might be that he had brilliantly won a race somewhere, or contrived to bang his head on a steel girder, or both. Almost inevitably, somewhere in there would be theatre, would be conflict.

As I walked through the paddock, at the end of the 1990 British Grand Prix, a friend of his called out to me. Could I get a few of my colleagues together? Nigel had something to say.

As ever at Silverstone, he had been at his best, taking pole position in the Ferrari with perhaps the greatest single lap of his life, then leading much of the race. After retiring, with gearbox problems, he set off back to the pits, and if he always relished the adoration of his British fans, this time he seemed especially to be savouring the moment, trying to make it last. As he tossed his gloves and balaclava over the fence, it was if he were saying goodbye.

He was. As a dozen or so of us sat cramped around a small table, he announced that he had decided to retire at the end of the season, adding, in time-honoured style, that the moment had come 'to spend more time with my family'.

It wasn't long, however, before rumours surfaced, and grew, that certain folk – notably Frank Williams – were trying to change his mind. Mansell may have firmly wanted out of a Ferrari team increasingly devoted to his more successful team-mate Alain Prost, but perhaps, behind the proclamation of retirement, was an element of playing hard to get. He would only consider – consider – going back on his decision, he said to Williams, if offered a deal tailored precisely to his requirements. When acquainted with the details of Mansell's demands, Williams initially blanched.

The 1990 season went on. At Hockenheim Mansell damaged a front wing endplate, and while this could have been swiftly changed, he judged the damage to be reason enough to drive straight into his pit, and retire. Ferrari were not impressed, but they were even less so at Spa a month later, when he abandoned an apparently otherwise healthy car because he didn't care for the way it was handling.

At Monza, I bumped into him on the first morning of qualifying. He was limping, but that was something one came almost to take for granted with Nigel, and it was out of politeness, rather than curiosity, that I asked what was the problem this time? 'I was just getting some socks out, and the drawer fell on my foot. You wouldn't believe the pain...'

This was one of many paradoxes to do with Mansell which I was never able to resolve in my own mind. In a racing car he was as brave as anyone would ever need to be, yet this man who would sit it out with Senna into a 170mph corner would moan endlessly about a bad cold. On one occasion, I recall, the crisis of the weekend was toothache, and after the offending molar had been removed, he kept producing it from his pocket, as if proof of the first extraction since records began.

Back to Monza. 'Could you get a few of the journalists to come to the Ferrari motorhome at 12 o'clock? I've got something to say.' This had a familiar ring, but I did as bidden. At noon, the British press corps duly assembled for the latest announcement. 'There's a lot of rumours doing the rounds,' Mansell said, 'but I'd just like to make it clear that, whatever else, I will *not* be in Formula 1 in 1991.' That sounded pretty unequivocal, and we all wrote our stories accordingly.

Ten days or so later, I had a call from the very angry sports editor of the Sunday paper for which I was working at the time.

'What the hell's going on? This morning's tabloids say Mansell's going back to Williams…'

And so he was. We had suspected as much for many weeks, but at Monza he had gathered us together expressly to stress that it was not so. Now we felt we had been duped, and no one cares for that. Some time later I tried to convey to him how we resented apparently being used, but it was evident he had genuinely not a clue what I was on about.

In racing, this is a not uncommon attitude to life. 'We make history,' Ron Dennis once portentously said to a group of hacks. 'You only write about it.' Very good, sir.

As they discussed the future, so Mansell and Williams already had a considerable past, having worked together for four seasons, from 1985 to 1988. Nigel had not been Frank's first choice to partner Keke Rosberg, but the deals were done, and before long the perception of Mansell the eternal loser was substantially to change. After 72 Grands Prix without a victory, he scored at Brands Hatch, and a torrent of success began; in both 1986 and 1987, Nigel won more races than anyone else.

At the end of 1988, though, an irresistible financial offer from Marlboro took him to Ferrari, and the parting with Williams was cool, despite a remarkable sequence of shared victories, and two close tilts at the World Championship.

On the face of it, a liaison between Mansell and Ferrari brought little promise of calm, but in 1989, his first season there, Nigel seemed more at peace with the world than at any other time in his Formula 1 career. The new driver at Ferrari is always the darling of the team, and Mansell, remarkably, won in Brazil, his first race in a red car. Even he conceded the victory owed more than a little something to luck, but that didn't matter. In Italy, they went nuts for him, christening him 'Il Leone'.

It was in a Ferrari, too, that he scored what I have always considered the greatest of his 31 Grand Prix victories. After qualifying only 12th in Hungary, he made a last-minute set-up change, and the car was transformed. In the late stages of the race, tracking Senna for the lead, he took advantage of a rare moment's hesitation by Ayrton, and stayed ahead to the flag.

When it was announced that Prost would be joining the team for 1990, Mansell was initially delighted: 'The difference between Prost and Senna is that everything Alain's won has been not only by talent, but also by sportsmanship.'

Patrick Head, a man who worked with both men, summarised them thus: 'The difference between Mansell and Prost is that Alain never ... let anger, or any of the more direct emotions, overpower the intellect. One of the reasons Mansell was always so quick at the British Grand Prix was that his adrenalin was pumped up by emotion. His overtaking manoeuvres involved enormous risks, I thought, but he seemed to get away with it, so you had to conclude that he was making good judgements, even if it didn't always look that way.

'Alain would sit with his race engineer for hours after qualifying, going through every item of the car, trying to understand everything that had happened on it, relative to this track, and, through an intellectual process, arrive at an optimum set-up for tomorrow. Nigel would do it on a more emotional basis, in that he'd just say, "I want this, this and this", and if you asked why, he wouldn't really be prepared to discuss it.'

In their season together at Ferrari, Mansell very soon changed his tune about Prost, hinting darkly that the Frenchman was 'very good at getting people in the team on his side. I'm a greater racer than he will ever be – he's more of a chauffeur, in that he prefers to let the car do the work.'

In response, Prost, somewhat puzzled, said that *of course* he preferred to let the car do the work: wasn't that the object of the exercise?

At all events, Mansell went back to Williams for 1991, his dream contract realised to the letter, for on this occasion he had the whip hand: Frank, then running Thierry Boutsen and Riccardo Patrese, had desperate need of a top-line driver, and no other was available. By the late summer of 1992, though, the picture had changed. Although Mansell, with a vastly superior car, had strolled to the World Championship, Prost, after a sabbatical season, was coming back for 1993 – with Williams-Renault. And Frank, while keen also to retain Nigel, didn't actually need him any more; already he had a superstar on board.

Thus he played hardball with Mansell, declining to meet his terms, and it seemed never to occur to Nigel that this was nothing personal, but merely business, that now Williams held most of the good cards, as he, Mansell, had done before.

On a daily basis, he raved to the tabloids about how unfair it all was, but received rather less sympathy from the English specialist press, whom he had thoroughly alienated in an interview with *L'Equipe*, in which he described us as 'corrupt' for our unwillingness to rank him with Senna or Prost. Given that Mansell's relationship with the subtleties of the English language was never an easy one, it may be that this was not the adjective he had intended to use; whatever, the damage was done.

'It's not breaking any new ground,' said Head, 'to say that the guy is hugely confrontational. That was part of what made him so good, in fact, but he wears his competitiveness on his sleeve – doesn't rein it in, in any way at all. It's there the whole time. He also has a very strong persecution complex, and thinks everyone is trying to shaft him at all times. So you had an environment of strain whenever Mansell was around, and on a day-to-day basis that became extremely wearing.

'However, that was his way of getting the job done, and that he undoubtedly did in 1992. But it was hard sometimes, particularly when he was sitting in front of Frank and myself, giving us a lecture about our shortcomings – we had a considerable number of those, and he never had a trace of embarrassment about doing it. He thought we were there, simply to hang on every pearly word, but one has to say that when a man surrounds himself with sycophants – people who just sit there, and say, "Yes, Nigel, no, Nigel, three bags full, Nigel" – eventually he begins to believe that everything he says is important. Just agree with everything Nigel says and does, and you'll get on famously with him.'

Frank Williams put it this way: 'Nigel was terrific in the car, but a tough bastard out of it. He knew what he wanted, and pushed to get it – and when he didn't get it, life could be deeply unpleasant. But he did the job, no question about that.'

One of many mysteries about Mansell was that, for all the successes, he never shed his insecurities. At press conferences, he would routinely reel off statistics about himself with a conceit so overwhelming that somehow it ceased ultimately to give offence. You just mentally switched off. And in the same way, he could never allow that any race – even one he had dominated – had been straightforward.

Following the 1991 British Grand Prix, which he ran away with, he claimed to have been struggling with gearchange problems. 'In fact, he had no problem at all with his clutch,' said Head. 'We knew that from the telemetry. It was pure bull, and of course it maddened the technical people here, but that's the way it is with him. As a driver, he's got massive good points, but you know the way he is: everything has to be difficult, and he – on his own – has overcome it.'

After declining Williams's offer to stay on for 1993, alongside Prost, Mansell renounced Formula 1 altogether, and signed to drive for the Newman/Haas Indycar team, and declared that his new life was in America. At first he appeared to revel in it, and even his most dedicated critics had to doff their hats as he came swiftly to terms with the daunting ovals, and drove a series of brilliant races to claim the CART Championship in his maiden season.

By any standards, it was a remarkable achievement, and Nigel declared that he had never been happier. 'Formula 1,' he said again, 'is history.'

In his second year in America, though, he had a less competitive Lola than in 1993, and his interest evaporated. 'He made up his mind,' said Carl Haas, 'that the Penskes were unbeatable, and that was that.'

After the death of Ayrton Senna, in May 1994, Renault cast around desperately for a superstar, and, despite the acrimonies of the past, signed Mansell to a four-race contract, as and when his Indycar schedule permitted. By the autumn, Nigel's Florida mansion was on the market, and his sights were set on coming home, to England, to Formula 1. In November, following the contretemps between his team-mate Damon Hill and Michael Schumacher, he took a worthy, if somewhat fortunate, win in the Australian Grand Prix, and hoped that Williams would sign him for 1995.

Perhaps, despite his well-documented differences with Nigel, Frank might have taken him back, had he believed him the same driver as had left in 1992, but he and Patrick now considered him past his best, and went instead for the youthful David Coulthard. Mansell was handsomely compensated, to the rumoured tune of $3 million, and that should have been the signal to announce, yet again, that he was retiring. However he failed to take the opportunity, and thus ended his Formula 1 career, not after a final victory, but in ignominious withdrawal.

Mansell's essential problem was that he never learned how to lose – or, for that matter, win – with grace, nor, more importantly, to laugh at himself. Had he been able to do that, his highly successful racing career might have been much less tortuous, not only for those who worked with him, but also for himself. Being the way he was, contentment could never be his friend.

# PROFESSOR SID WATKINS

# The Surgeon-General

HEROES, PERHAPS, ARE SOMETHING you grow out of; in youth there is no problem. I worshipped Jean Behra when I was a kid, because he personified what I felt a racing driver should be. There is more to it than ability in a car; it is also a matter of charisma, how the man carries himself.

It is not easy to have a hero younger than oneself, I find, and since the retirement from Formula 1 of Jacques Lafitte, back in 1986, all the Grand Prix drivers have been that. And perhaps there's another element, too. Nearly every true hero in my life has been someone I never met, so the elements of glamour and mystique were always intact. Very important, that. On the inside, you can see the seams.

There are exceptions, however. Although I consider him a friend, still Mario Andretti has never been less than a hero to me. I thought Mario had it all, a great driver, but also a man of real quality, one of those very few, like Fangio, like Senna, with a presence to stop you in your tracks. The season Andretti won the World Championship, 1978, we did a book together, and the better I came to know him, the more of a hero he became. Probably no man who ever lived had a greater love for motor racing.

That same year, my other racing hero appeared on the scene.

He was 50 years old, and not a driver. Oddly enough, it was Andretti who introduced us. At Monza, Mario was bidding for the World Championship against his Lotus team-mate Ronnie Peterson. The day before the race, as we chatted in the Lotus motorhome, in came a fellow with a genial face, cigar in mouth. 'Hi, Sid, how ya doin'?' Andretti beamed. Sid said he was fine, thanks.

Thus I met, for the first time, Professor Sidney Watkins, consultant neurosurgeon, and for these many years the President of the FIA Medical Commission. The Prof.

He is an easy man to like. Over time I came to discover that, while regarded as one of the world's leading brain surgeons, he was more down-to-earth than most GPs of my acquaintance.

First of all, Sid Watkins loves the sport, and always has. Born in Liverpool, the son of a motor trader, his ambition always lay in the direction of the medical profession, but as he trained for neurosurgery he did not neglect a passion for motor racing. When he worked in Oxford, he acted as a medical officer at Silverstone, and after moving to Syracuse, in upstate New York, he became involved with Watkins Glen, in those days the circuit that hosted the US Grand Prix.

It was here that Watkins came to know the Formula 1 fraternity, and when he moved back to England Bernie Ecclestone had the idea of inviting him to take charge of the medical aspects of the entire Grand Prix trail. He has never had a better one. In his new capacity, Watkins went to the Swedish Grand Prix in 1978, and has not since missed a race.

Back to Monza, that same year. Andretti and Watkins bantered for a few minutes, and then Peterson came in, worrying about some lost sunglasses, and then mentioning a tooth that had been aching for a day or two. The Prof produced a pain-killer of some kind, then went on his way.

Twenty-four hours later I was in the motorhome again, and now the circumstances were very different, everyone's emotions jumbled and confused. Andretti had clinched the Championship, but Peterson had suffered dreadful leg injuries in a multiple accident within seconds of the start. Mario kept fingering a magnum of champagne, wanting to celebrate his greatest day, yet somehow not able to.

At mid-evening he spoke to Watkins, who had gone to the hospital with Peterson, and when he came off the phone his mood had lightened perceptibly. 'The Professor says all Ronnie's vital signs are good, and he'll be fine. The legs are badly broken, and maybe he'll miss the first few races of next year – but he's going to be OK!' Now Andretti felt he could uncork the Moet, begin to savour his triumph at last.

In the night, though, during a long operation to reset Peterson's legs, complications set in. And when Andretti arrived to see his buddy, soon after breakfast, he was met by the news that Ronnie had just died: embolism. 'I was told,' Mario said, 'that this was what killed more soldiers in World War II than anything else – also that it was now almost unknown in the civilised world.'

Occurrences of this kind were hardly unknown way back when. A Formula 3 star of the 1960s once told me of an accident in an Italian street race, after which a driver was taken to hospital with a broken leg. 'They screwed up with the anaesthetic,' he said. 'Gave him too much – literally put him to sleep. In some places, quite seriously, we regarded the hospital as more dangerous than the bloody race track.'

It was to eliminate disasters of this kind that Watkins was given control of the medical side of Formula 1. 'The circuit facilities were pretty basic at that time,' he said. 'At some tracks there was no hospital, as such, just a tent. In effect, we were starting almost from scratch, and at first there was resentment towards me from the doctors in some countries. I didn't really blame them, actually, but it took time before some of them appreciated what I was trying to do.'

Watkins is known in the business as the only man with whom Bernie Ecclestone never argues. The two have always got along, and Ecclestone accepts the Prof's opinion without question.

'Sometimes you have to do things that make you unpopular,' Watkins said. 'For example, Nelson Piquet had a huge accident in qualifying at Imola in 1987 – went off at Tamburello, at

160mph or so. He survived all right, but he got a big bang on the head. There was nothing wrong with him, beyond concussion, but a couple of hours later he didn't even know he was a racing driver…

'As he began to feel better, he decided he wanted to race the following day, and he tried everything to persuade me to let him – pleading, threatening, the lot. I understood, of course, but there was no way I was signing any authorisation for him to drive. "Nelson, if you black out on the first lap," I said to him, "with 20-odd cars behind you, it's not going to be my responsibility, OK?" And then he began to see my point of view.'

During the practice sessions, the Professor is to be found, kitted in fireproof overalls, lounging in the back of the medical car, as often as not with a Havana in his mouth. His natural manner is easy and languid, but on one occasion, as I chatted to him, word of an accident came through. The cigar was jettisoned as the car's engine fired up, and Watkins prepared himself for what might be an emergency.

'We carry a fair amount of stuff in the car. It's not an ambulance, obviously, but a quick road car to get us to the accident scene fast. The primary requirement, of course, is equipment to stabilise an injured driver, to keep his blood pressure good, and his pain controlled as much as possible. So we carry equipment to measure blood pressure, and to keep the airways clear.

'As well as that, there's a ventilation machine with oxygen, a special mattress, for back injuries, which moulds to the shape of the injured man, and equipment for dealing with spinal damage.'

Whenever an accident brings a race or practice session to a halt, Watkins's car instantly gets on its way, without needing clearance from race control. Quite often, though, the first people at the driver's side are the marshals working close by. If he is essentially all right, and conscious, they have instructions to help him from the car. If not, they are to leave him be until the Professor arrives, 'Unless there's a question of fire, of course, in which case the priority is obviously to get him out, whatever else is wrong.'

On occasion, the Prof's considerable physical courage has been put to the test. At Montreal, in 1982, Riccardo Paletti had an appalling accident at the start, his Osella hitting the back of Didier Pironi's stalled Ferrari.

The medical car follows the pack around the opening lap of the race, so Watkins was swiftly on hand, within 10 seconds of the impact. The car's fuel tank had split, spewing its contents out on to the road. Watkins went straight to the cockpit, and quickly established that Paletti, while very badly injured, had a pulse. A few seconds later the car was ablaze.

The driver, mercifully, knew nothing of this, having lost consciousness from the moment of impact. Releasing him took a further 25 minutes; that done, Paletti was removed to hospital, where efforts to save him ultimately failed.

Like all doctors, Professor Watkins tries hard not to become 'emotionally involved', but within a relatively tight-knit world such as Formula 1, he admits, sometimes it isn't easy. The death of Gilles Villeneuve upset him deeply.

'I was very fond of Villeneuve – a good, honest bloke, as well as a genius of a driver. On one occasion, at Monaco in 1980, we were out on the circuit in the medical car, and the whole pack caught up with us at the hairpin. All the drivers gave us a wide berth – except Gilles, who seemed to use us as his apex! I started to give him a bollocking afterwards, about how he'd missed us by an inch or so, and he couldn't understand what I was talking about. "That's the whole point," he said. "I missed you!" And then I realised that, to him, an inch was like a yard to anyone else. He was that precise with a car, that good. A lovely lad. I was really very upset at Zolder when it was obvious immediately there was nothing I could do for him.'

Undoubtedly, though, it was the loss of Senna, a dozen years later, which had the profoundest effect on Watkins, for the two men were close friends, and there is little doubt that Ayrton had come to look upon the Prof almost as a father figure.

'Oh, that weekend at Imola... When they released the cars, after the startline shunt had been cleared up, Ayrton went by my medical car (parked at the chicane, before the pit straight) like a bat out of hell. I'm not given to premonitions, but I said to Mario Casoni, my driver, "I've got a feeling there's going to be a fucking awful accident." I'd never had it before, and I never have since. I'm normally useless at predicting anything. But when we got the message that the race had been red-flagged, somehow I just knew it was Senna.'

For years Watkins would suggest to Senna that, once in the lead, he should back off a touch, that there was no need to win by a minute or whatever, but it was always to no avail. 'He couldn't help himself – and that, in my opinion, was his main fault as a racing driver. I used to tell him that the clever driver is the one who wins while taking the least out of himself and the car. And he'd say, "Yes, I know you're right. Every time I go past your medical car, I remember what you said, and I feel guilty about it. But by the time I get to the next corner, I've forgotten..."'

Over time Senna had taken an increasingly active role in safety matters, involving himself to an unusual degree in other drivers' accidents. When Martin Donnelly had his terrible crash in the Lotus at Jerez in 1990, Ayrton was among the first drivers through, and he immediately stopped. At the time I wondered to myself if that was a wise course of action for a man facing similar perils; would it not have been better – for his own sake – to keep a certain distance from it?

'Yes, I thought that, too,' Watkins said. 'Occasionally I've wondered if it might be a good idea if I got all the drivers together, and taught them a little bit about what to do if and when they arrived at an accident, where another driver was involved. And in the end I've always decided against it, because I don't want to raise the nightmares in their minds.

'In the case of Donnelly, Ayrton was watching what went on, over my shoulder. I didn't know he was there. Then the next day he came to see me in the pit lane, and he said, "I watched what you did. Why did you do this, and why did you do that?" It was all very intellectual, actually.

'Then, of course, subsequently he arrived once or twice at an accident before anyone else did. It happened with Erik Comas at Spa, for example. By the time I got there, Senna was kneeling down, holding his neck – in the correct way, I might add. As we took over, Ayrton said, "I made sure his breathing was all right, and I've asked the marshal to keep the helmet, so you can examine it for damage." He was a great student. I found that anything I ever said to him was filed away in his mind for ever. Never forgot a thing.'

In only one respect did the Prof have a problem with Senna. 'He was like Gilles, terrifying in a road car. Because *they* were so confident, they didn't allow for ordinary mortals. With people at their level, the biggest chance of an accident was always what the other driver's reaction was going to be to what they were doing.

'Eventually I refused to have any further lifts with either of them! I remember telling Ayrton he was scaring me, and he couldn't understand why. Perhaps he and Gilles might have changed in that respect as they got older – but then neither of them got old enough, did they? They were still youngsters when they died.

'They were very alike in lots of ways, those two: both chargers on the track, but wonderfully gentle human beings. What distinguishes people like them from the rest is their flair, their total commitment, and their precision.'

The Professor has no idea why he and Senna became so close. 'Just one of those things. I hit it off with some of the other drivers, too, of course… Niki, Jody, Gilles, Gerhard. There was no bullshit about any of them, and that's a quality I've always appreciated.'

On one occasion Watkins asked Senna to attend a lunch, between the two practice sessions on Friday, with the doctors at Silverstone, and Ayrton at once agreed. 'He made a little speech, and thanked them for their efforts, and so on. A perfect ambassador, I thought. Someone said to him, "A lot of the drivers have a retinue around them – a physiotherapist, this, that and the other, and special diets and so on. What do you do?" And he said, "Well, I don't do anything – if I've got a problem, I ring up Sid!"

'I still think a great deal about Ayrton. I dream about him a lot. It's one of the problems of old age: you dream more. There are two or three people in my life who have affected me a lot – my father, the neurosurgeon at Oxford with whom I trained, and Senna – and I dream about them constantly. And I hate it, too, because they're alive and well, and then you wake up, and have to face it again that they're gone.'

They say that many a physical problem has psychological roots, and the Prof has the most reassuring presence imaginable. There is nothing remotely elitist about him: he may be at a circuit primarily to look after the drivers, but is always available to anyone in the paddock. And his manner is such that when he says nothing is seriously awry, you immediately begin to feel better.

Although my father was a doctor, and I thus grew up in a medical household, my subconscious expectation was always that eminent physicians should have names like 'Sir Lancelot Spratt' (as immortalised by James Robertson Justice in *Doctor In The House*), and at first 'Sid' seemed to me a somehow inappropriate handle for a professor of neurosurgery. In fact, it suits him to a tee, for I know of no one more unpretentious.

Nor more healthily irreverent. The Prof has an exceedingly fine sense of humour, sharpened by a loathing of pomposity. At Aida one year, lacking the necessary pass, he dared to venture into the Paddock Club for a pee, and – being merely important, rather than self-important – was asked to remove himself. 'Did you say anything to them?' I asked. 'Yes,' he replied, deadpan. 'Don't get ill.'

Never less than good company, Watkins sparkles especially when armed with a glass of red wine and a Romeo Y Julieta. His fireproof overalls must, I think, be unique in having one pocket marked 'Cigars' and another 'Emergency Cigars'.

Some of his remedies are unorthodox: 'Forget sleeping pills – what you need is a stiff Scotch, last thing…' And he accepts, unlike doctors of the 'give up smoking, and then come and see me again' school, that real people rarely lead sensible, blameless, lives. 'I've often joked,' he says, 'that if you drive Formula 1 cars for a living, the last thing you need is a brain surgeon…'

AYRTON SENNA

# I race, therefore
# I am

HOWEVER, I WONDER, DID WE COPE with long flights before
Sony invented the Walkman? Twenty-odd hours from England
to Australia take a lot of filling, particularly if you don't sleep
well on aeroplanes. By the time the first of the three legs, to
Dubai or wherever, has been completed, the magic of reheated
'food' has already lost much of its appeal. On the movie screen
is *Terminator Nine*. There are 17 hours to go.

How, then, to pass the time, to find something which can lull
you into dreams? The Walkman comes into its own here. Some
swear by the dreary repetitiveness of *Tubular Bells*, but far
more effective, I have found, are tapes of contemporary
Formula 1 press conferences.

These work tremendously well. As Keke Rosberg has
observed, the Grand Prix driver of today is a muzzled man,
paid a great deal to get the most out of his car, and almost as
much to say nothing about it.

'What was the problem with the car in the first session?'

'I'm not prepared to go into that. You'll have to ask the team.'

'OK, but do you feel that progress has been made since
Hockenheim?'

'Yes, we tested for four days, and we've definitely made "a
step".'

'All right, but in what *way* is the car better?'

'I'm not prepared to go into that,' etc, etc.

Given that it is not easy to keep awake even as the words are being uttered, it will be appreciated that their soporific effect is further enhanced by repetition. With the volume low, and a Scotch-and-soda or two behind you, Singapore to Melbourne can be gone in a trice.

It wasn't always so. On the flight from Nagoya to Sydney, in 1991, I listened more than once to a tape of Ayrton Senna's post-Suzuka press conference, and didn't sleep a second. To this day its effect is electrifying.

In the race, yards from the line, Senna had handed victory to Gerhard Berger, his McLaren team-mate and good buddy, secure in the knowledge that he had clinched his third World Championship. But when he reached the press room, the joy of the moment was nowhere in evidence; instead he wished to talk only of the Japanese races in 1989 and 1990.

On both occasions, Senna and Prost had had a World Championship to settle, and each time there was a coming-together between them. In 1989 Prost led from the start, and when, late in the race, Senna tried to force by into the chicane, he found the door closed, whereupon the two McLarens locked wheels, and skittered to a halt. Subsequently, Ayrton was push-started, got on his way again, and ultimately won the race, only to be disqualified. The title went to Prost, and Senna was convinced that Jean-Marie Balestre, then President of the governing body, had influenced events to his rival's benefit.

Senna condemned Prost for causing the accident, but not everyone saw it in quite such clear-cut terms. 'It doesn't matter whether or not Alain closed the door,' said Jackie Stewart. 'The fact remains that Ayrton was in the wrong because he allowed himself to be at someone else's mercy. Once he made his move, the matter was out of his hands: if Prost was prepared to lose the race, OK, he'd be through; but if he wasn't, then Senna was in trouble...'

Prost was the cleanest driver of his time, and my belief was that Senna assumed that he would make way for him, give him space, as previously he always had.

Mario Andretti saw it as just one of those things. 'If I would have been in Prost's shoes, I'd have done the same – and, let's face it, if the situation had been reversed, Senna would have done the same. Senna should have expected it, but I can't fault him for trying. That was the only place he was going to pass.'

Twelve months later, the circumstances were a little different, in that the two giants of the sport were no longer in the same team, Prost having moved to Ferrari. And on this occasion it was Senna who led on points, Prost who needed to make up ground – to *finish*, above all.

Pole position at Suzuka had always been on the right, this theoretically offering the benefit of the inside line for the first corner. As at Monte Carlo, though, in practice it was anything but an advantage, for 'the line' at that point was on the left-hand side of the track, and Senna, arguing that the man on pole should benefit from the better traction on offer there, requested that the grid be thus reconfigured.

Ultimately this was rejected, and Senna, fastest in qualifying, was beaten away by Prost. Into the first turn, at close to 150mph, Ayrton never lifted, instead hammering into the Ferrari, and resolving the World Championship right there.

It may have been the most reprehensible piece of driving in the history of Formula 1. As Prost and Senna headed into that corner, they had 24 other cars behind them, and in the impact the rear wing of the Ferrari was sheared off; it could have come down anywhere.

Afterwards Senna absolved himself of any blame, suggesting only that Prost had left a gap, that he had naturally gone for it. Not too many saw it that way, but Ayrton was immovable. In Adelaide, a couple of weeks later, he was shown a photograph of the shunt, taken from the inside of the corner, and casting doubt on his account of events. 'That's a lie!' he responded.

A year on, though, Senna felt able to speak a little more freely on the subject – not least because the hated Balestre had been replaced in the god seat by Max Mosley. Although Berger and Riccardo Patrese were also present, the Suzuka press conference in 1991 amounted to a monologue – ever more impassioned – by Ayrton. He didn't even need a question to get him started.

'Before you ask me … 1989 was a disgraceful year here. I still today struggle to cope with that when I think about it. You all know what took place: I won the race, and I was robbed of it. And that was not justice. What took place over that winter was really shit.

'Then, 1990 was … to prove a point, to show everyone that what you do here, here you pay. When we came to Suzuka, I was in the lead of the championship. Before practice, myself and Gerhard went to the officials, to change pole position, because it was in the wrong place. They said, "Yes, no problem".

'I got pole – and then what happened? Balestre gave an order, and the officials said, "Oh, no, no, we don't change the pole position." And we said, "But we agreed before that it should be on the left." "No, no, no, we don't think so…"

'It was an order from Balestre – and I know that from inside the system. I said to myself, "OK, you try to work clean, to do your job properly, and you get screwed by stupid people. If, at the start, because I'm in the wrong place, Prost beats me off the line, at the first corner I'm going for it – and he'd better not turn in ahead of me, because he's not going to make it.

'And it just happened like this. I really wish I'd had the start, because then we'd have had a clean fight. But in the end it just happened exactly as it had to happen. He got the jump on me at the start, and I went for it at the first corner. He turned in, and I hit him, and we were both off. It was a result of the wrong decision, and partiality from people that were on the inside then.

'So, we've got to have fair rules, we've got to have fair decisions from the people in power. I believe now we have this possibility, with the new management in the sporting authority, and we should try to work together, to make a better environment, a better image – and a better atmosphere for us to work in, because it's enough stress just to do it.

'At the drivers' briefing today, there was no theatre, when Max [Mosley] stood up, just to say a few words. He was sensible, he was intelligent, and he was fair. And I think everyone was happy, because there was no bullshit, no people saying stupid things…'

No one in the press room made a sound. We were quite literally transfixed. Then Berger took a stab at lightening the atmosphere. 'I think,' he said to Senna, 'you should hope Balestre doesn't come back next year...'

Ayrton was having nothing of that. 'I don't care!' he shouted. 'I don't care. I think for once we all must say what we feel is right, because that's how it should be. You're not allowed to speak your mind any more – if you do that, you get banned, you get penalties, you get disqualified, you lose your licence. Is that a fair rule? It is not...'

For once, at a press conference, Senna was out of control, gabbling out a stream of consciousness, rather than choosing his words with care. Was he admitting that he had caused the previous year's accident?

'I was determined to get first to that corner, and I was not prepared to let the guy turn into that corner in front of me – he just had to let me go through. He took a chance – and it didn't work, because I went for it. I didn't care if we crashed. I went for it, and we crashed. That was the result of what happened in 1989. It was unavoidable.

'Why did I cause the accident? Because ... if you get fucked by the system every single time you try to do your job cleanly and properly, what should you do? Stay behind all the time, and say, "Thank you"? No. No, you should fight for what you think is right. And I really felt I was doing that.

'I tell you again, if pole had been on the good side last year, nothing would have happened, because I would have got a better start, I would have led into the first corner without any problem. It was again a result of a bad decision, influenced by Balestre. It was not my responsibility – I contributed to it, yes, but it was not my responsibility...'

It was Alex Hawkridge, Senna's boss during his début Formula 1 season with Toleman, who first suggested that Ayrton worked to an agenda strictly his own. In the late summer of 1984, with two more years of his Toleman contract to run, he blithely signed a contract with Lotus, and was astonished when Hawkridge took umbrage, more than that when he was 'stood down' for the Italian Grand Prix.

'I'm quite sure Ayrton doesn't believe he's done anything wrong,' said Hawkridge. 'In fact, he doesn't believe himself *capable* of doing anything wrong...'

The comment was perspicacious, and ahead of its time. Years later, reflecting on his feud with Senna, perhaps the bitterest racing has known, Alain Prost put it this way: 'Ayrton had his rules, and he believed in them, and that was it. In his own mind, he was always right – on the track, and off it. He always felt he was correct.

'He would talk a lot about his religion, his upbringing, and so on, and I used to wonder how, then, he could do some of the things he did on the track. Now, looking back, I believe he really didn't know he was sometimes in the wrong. He played by his rules, and he wasn't interested in anything else.'

Any racing journalist of my generation has written more words by far about Ayrton Senna da Silva than any other driver. Like Schumacher, he was a genius; unlike Schumacher, he also had charisma to throw away. Ayrton was a *presence*, a special force, in a car and out. As with Gilles Villeneuve, you would go out on the circuit to watch him in qualifying, choose a particular corner, and wait.

In the turbo days, when qualifying boost gave some drivers close to 1,400 horsepower, and when each had but two sets of one-lap qualifying tyres, pole position was Senna's almost by right. He developed a freakish ability to time his runs so as to have a clear track all the way round, and when he did encounter traffic, the sight of him in the mirrors was usually enough to persuade other drivers it might be a sound plan to give him room.

If they did not, by reason of inattention or – less likely – bloody-mindedness, Ayrton simply took it, and times without number we sucked through our teeth as some backmarker's car was shaved by a blur of McLaren. 'He literally frightens them out of the way,' James Hunt said, and it was true, prompting Prost to murmur that maybe he should get himself a yellow helmet.

Early in the race at Montreal in 1985 Senna found his turbocharged Lotus-Renault down on boost, and lost five laps in the pits while the problem was fixed. At almost the same moment Keke Rosberg had a similar problem with his Williams-Honda, and it happened that he rejoined immediately in front of Senna. Both drove flat out all the way to the flag.

Afterwards I walked back to the paddock with Ayrton, and can still recall his exhilaration. 'Following Keke through the traffic … he was *unbelievable*! He'd see a gap – and immediately he'd be through it. Judgement perfect, no hesitating. Was a great lesson for me, today. I hope I can be like that…'

The boy learned, you could say that. He won 41 of his 161 Grands Prix, the majority of them consummately, and he started from pole position 65 times. There was something almost primeval about Senna on a qualifying lap, and that is how I chiefly remember him now.

In that situation, he would say, he did not even look at the rev counter – if he did, he would be a fraction less committed to his driving at that moment; therefore, he changed gear by sound.

'When I have finished a lap, I can recall it completely, and always there is somewhere you know you lost time. That's why your second run should always be faster than your first – you have more information to work with.'

On a qualifying lap, Senna maintained, he did not consciously think of the corner he was in, but of the one beyond. 'Preparing for a lap like that, I concentrate as deeply as I can. I isolate all outside interference, whether it's photographers, fans, people around me. And in that state I am somehow able to get to a level where I am ahead of myself – maybe a fifth of a second, who knows?

'When my car goes into a corner, I am already at the apex, and so on. It's the same whether I'm braking, changing gear, putting on the power, or whatever. In effect, I'm predicting what I'm going to face, so I can correct it before it actually happens.

'You need a lot of concentration for that, as well as instant reactions, so a lot of tension goes through the body – like electricity. In race conditions, though, you can't keep to that level. There's too much stress, both mental and physical, so you have to be content to come down a little bit.'

Then there were the press conferences. Many a time, given

that they were quantifiably the greatest drivers of their era, Senna and Prost were together on these occasions, and invariably the atmosphere crackled. There they would sit, inches apart, avoiding eye contact, answering questions as if the other were not present.

There were times, though, when Ayrton simply held us in thrall. When the mood took him, he could mesmerise an audience as readily with his voice as with his sublime driving, and one such occasion was after qualifying at Jerez in 1990.

Over time Senna evolved a technique for press conferences which worked supremely well. Rather than simply respond to a succession of random questions, he would come forth with the story of his weekend. This was efficient, as one would have expected of him, and often had a quality which was hypnotic. It was just so in Spain that day.

The first question set him going. How did he feel about this, his 50th pole position? He began by thanking all who had participated in his achievement, be they from Lotus or McLaren, Renault or Honda, since that first pole position, at Estoril in 1985. At one time Ayrton would then have awaited the next question; now he volunteered more.

'That pole position lap, in Portugal, was a really special one,' he said, and again you had that impression of a man who could recall, probably, virtually any lap he had ever driven, just as Bobby Fischer can pluck from his memory every move in every game of chess he has ever played.

'Since then, I had had some incredible pole positions, but something about today seems unbelievable...'

The day before, Martin Donnelly had suffered the accident which would end his Formula 1 career, front suspension failure pitching the Lotus into a guardrail at 160mph. Especially grotesque was that Donnelly was hurled from the shattered car, and lay in the middle of the track.

'I went to the place where Donnelly was on the ground,' Senna said, 'and when I saw the immediate consequences of the accident with my own eyes, it was ... very difficult to cope with it, to understand and absorb it, and to go forward from there.'

When he returned from the accident scene, Senna went to the

motorhome, where he asked to be left alone a while. 'I spent some minutes on my own, quiet, and I was able to go through very special moments there, deal with everything inside of me.'

We all have beliefs, in our own fashion, and Ayrton made no direct reference to his religion because there was no need; it was implicit in his words, his tone. He considered, he said, not going out again when the last minutes of the session were run, some little time later. Before the accident he had set third fastest time, behind Jean Alesi and Prost, and finally – after it – he took his last set of qualifiers.

'It was an amazing lap,' he said, 'and for me unbelievable in the circumstances. Nevertheless, as much as I can try to express my feelings, I don't think anybody will ever be able to understand what I felt yesterday. After the accident, through the moments before I went back to the car again, how I felt when I climbed back in, the way I drove, the way I approached it and experienced it, is something I cannot express. In any way.'

That lap on the Friday afternoon, more than a second inside his previous best, was almost enough to keep Senna on the pole through Saturday's final session. All along, though, he had the conviction his time would be beaten, that he would need to improve, and Prost proved him correct. Out he came, with 15 minutes left.

The TV cameras were on the McLaren all the way around, and we watched. It was typical Senna, without compromise, but there was a moment in the press room when, as one, we gasped. Out of a quick right-hander he found Nelson Piquet's Benetton and Olivier Grouillard's Osella proceeding slowly down the road. Side by side. At the last instant they fell into single file, and the McLaren was through, but it was an instant of horror for an audience still jumpy after the events of the day before.

'It was a very fast lap,' Ayrton related, 'but it wasn't my maximum. If you were looking at the monitors, you probably saw the two guys in front of me. What they were doing is totally unacceptable in a qualifying session in modern Formula l.

'I lost time there because by the time I saw them I was almost on them, and I had such a scary moment that I hesitated with the throttle – and it's full throttle there. It was still a good lap, of course, but not as good as it was possible to do.'

For all that, it was astounding, half a second faster than Prost, half a second faster than Senna himself had managed the day before.

'I don't think we'll ever completely eliminate the problem of slow cars on the circuit during qualifying,' he said, 'but people need to understand how dangerous it can be. If you're disturbed by someone who doesn't see you, or whatever, you have to control your feelings.

'All the time we see drivers whose quick lap has been spoiled, and they draw alongside the guy responsible, maybe try to push him off the road, or get ahead of him and hit the brakes. Maybe your instincts tell you to do that, but at the same time you're doing something stupid, because there could be somebody coming up behind at 120mph more than you. And in a blind corner that could be fatal.

'Situations like this are not acceptable. If you have a problem with someone, OK, you sort it out in the pits and not on the circuit in the way I saw today. Of course, not everybody responds the same way. Some acknowledge their mistake, and sometimes they really didn't see you – they didn't do it on purpose. And when you're not sure if it was deliberate, instead of reacting hot, with blood, it's much better if you think about it first, discuss it with them, and then find out if it was on purpose or not.

'On the circuit, we are under such stress all the time that the natural thing is to overreact. It doesn't matter if you're going for pole, or simply trying to qualify, the pressure is the same for all of us. The values may be different, but they are all as important as each other.

'It makes me sad, this kind of thing,' Ayrton went on. 'Yesterday we all saw what an accident can cost any of us. And the way it happened to me today, in a place where I was flat out … if I had hit one of those guys, I was just going to take off. It's crazy, and I can't accept it.'

No one could have taken issue with that, but at the same time some remembered that, at Jerez the previous year, he himself had ignored a major accident in qualifying. When Gregor

Foitek trashed his Rial, Senna was on a quick lap, and in the course of it went flat out past black flags displayed all round the circuit, waved yellows at the accident scene and – crucially – a red at the start/finish line.

On that occasion Ayrton was fined $20,000, less than stringent punishment for a man who had bet Ron Dennis five grand he couldn't eat a bowl of chillis. 'Well,' Rosberg murmured, 'now Senna can refine the process a bit further, can't he? In future he can turn up, pay 40 grand in advance, and buy himself a clear lap on each qualifying day...'

In the course of his ten years in Formula 1, Senna became a figure of mythical proportions, not only for his artistry in a car, but also for the intensity of his ambition. He had come to Europe in 1981, and dominated Formula Ford, but he and his young wife adapted poorly to life away from Brazil, and returned home before the end of the season.

It seems astonishing that, at that stage of his life, Ayrton was by no means committed to a career in racing, and instead contemplated working in the family businesses. When the offer came to return, to move up a class, he thought long before accepting – and the decision, once made, was absolute. If he were to be a professional racing driver, he was going all the way.

Now, when Senna flew into Heathrow, he was alone. 'If I was going to make it to Formula 1,' he said, 'I had to give it all my time and attention. I couldn't do that if I was married, so we parted.'

At the time it sounded chillingly hard-nosed, and indeed Senna's frankness never lost its power to disturb. Just as it was always said of Rocky Marciano, the gentlest of men outside a ring, that his killer instinct had its roots in sacrifice, so Ayrton's resolve was hardened by exile.

'What I really cared about was my career, and I gave up a lot of important things for it – my marriage, living in Brazil, being with my family and friends. To justify that to yourself isn't easy.'

He never did come fully to terms with life in Europe, but as his wealth grew he moved from a modest house in Esher to an apartment in Monte Carlo, and finally to Faro, where at least the language was Portuguese, and there was a semblance of home.

If few doubted that the bulk of Senna's towering motivation came from beating Prost, so few ever understood quite why. True, Alain was undoubtedly the best when Ayrton arrived, and therefore the man at whom to aim, but somehow it went beyond that.

Perhaps, in a different era, some resolution to their feud might have been found. Time was when drivers socialised, took the same commercial flights, had an opportunity to talk. Now, though, a driver's motorhome is his castle, from which he rarely emerges unless it is to work. On Sunday evenings, Senna, Prost and others would board their private jets, and problems unresolved would stay that way, festering until the next race.

'The first time I met Senna,' Prost said, 'was when the new Nürburgring opened, in 1984. There was a small celebrity race, and we all drove Mercedes 190s. I gave Ayrton a lift from the airport to the circuit, and on the way we chatted, and he was very pleasant. Then we got to the track, practised the cars, and I was on pole, with Ayrton second – and after that he didn't talk to me any more!

'In the race I took the lead – and he pushed me off the track after about half a lap! So that was a great start...

'I always felt that Senna didn't want to beat me – he wanted to *destroy* me. That was his motivation from the first day, racing the Mercedes. I could see then that he wasn't interested in beating Alan Jones or Keke Rosberg – it was me, just me, for some reason.

'Still, we never had any problems until we became team-mates, and it was clear immediately that he had exceptional ability. We have to remember that back then there were a lot more *very* good drivers than there are now, and even in that company he looked special right away. He was the best driver I ever raced against. By far.

'It's true that Ayrton was always very tough on the track, and I didn't like a lot of the things he did, but then, how many times was he sanctioned? Never. So, because he always got away with it, in a way I can't really blame him for doing it.

'Everything was always on his terms, that was the point. As I was coming to the end of my career, he won in Japan, and I was second. Between the podium and the press conference, I said to him, "This may be the last race where we are at a press conference together, and I think we should show the people something nice – maybe shake hands, or something." He didn't answer me, but he didn't say no, either, so I thought he agreed. We went to the press conference, and he ignored me completely – wouldn't look at me, the usual stuff.

'Then we went to Adelaide, my last race – and on the podium he puts his arm round me, shakes hands, and everything. Why? Because now it was his idea. OK, in any case, it was nice. But that was Ayrton. If it was his idea, it was OK; if not, forget it.

'As soon as I retired, he changed completely towards me, and in time it's not impossible that we could have become friends. I think we always had great respect for each other as drivers, and that was the most important thing. Neither of us worried too much about anyone else.

'Now I look back on those years, and wonder why we put ourselves through all that. Honestly, sometimes it seemed like a bad dream. Maybe because usually we were so much in front, it was inevitable that there would be problems between us, but why did it have to get so *venomous*? I used to say to people, "You're a fan of Ayrton Senna? Good, that's fine – but please don't hate me!"

'If we had to do it all again, I'd say to Ayrton, "Listen, we're the best, we can screw all the others!" The pressure was so high, but still, though, it was a fantastic story, wasn't it? I think, in a way, we're missing that a little bit today...'

More than a little bit. If you were close to either man, you feared for him often through those seasons of strife, but you were aware, too, that it was a privilege to be around Grand Prix racing at a time when two drivers of such majesty were competing. Men of character, too, imperfect perhaps, but of real stamp; men who never read from a script in their lives. Some tapes you never throw away.

# BERNIE ECCLESTONE

# Absolute power

AS AN AFTER-DINNER SPEAKER, Stuart Turner is without peer, in my experience, and that night at Gleneagles he had his audience almost weeping with laughter. It was January 1986, and we were present at the glorious hotel to take part in the inaugural Mechanics' Grand Prix Challenge, this a clay-pigeon shooting contest organised by Jackie Stewart, whose shooting school is based in the grounds.

Towards the end of his address, Turner thanked his host – 'The Ayatollah Hogmanay' – and then began his final tale. 'Imagine this,' he said. 'Ken Tyrrell, Frank Williams and Bernie Ecclestone are all in Heaven.

'"Mr Tyrrell?" God enquires, and Ken steps forward. "This will be your room." And in there is this awful hag. "Ken Tyrrell," God says, "for your sins on earth, you will stay in this room for eternity."

'"Mr Williams, please?" Same story. Another horrible room, another dreadful old crone. "Frank Williams, for your sins on earth, you will pass eternity in here."

'"Right, now, Mr Ecclestone… You will be in here." God opens another door – and there inside is Joan Collins, reclining on a sofa in a black negligée. And God says, "Joan Collins, for your sins on earth…"'

Bernie is always painted as the bad guy, the malign influence, and it is a fact that, for 30 years, he has ruthlessly adjusted the path of Grand Prix racing to fit his personal vision of it. If Formula 1 is now one of the major entertainment circuses on earth, it is primarily because Ecclestone has made it so. 'Big things,' Benjamin Disraeli observed, 'have always been done by little people.'

Professor Sidney Watkins – a neurosurgeon, remember, one who knows a thing or two about the human mind – reckons that Ecclestone's is the sharpest he has ever come across. 'He has this extraordinary ability to hold 10 or 12 ideas at a time in his head,' Watkins said, 'and to be able to go from one to another instantly.'

It was at the end of 1971 that Ecclestone became involved in Formula 1 on a full-time basis. One way and another, he had been around racing for most of his life, first as a competitor in 500cc Formula 3 in the early 1950s, then as a friend and sponsor of Stuart Lewis-Evans. After Lewis-Evans's death (following an accident in the 1958 Moroccan Grand Prix), Bernie disappeared from the scene for almost a decade, and by the time he reappeared, as Jochen Rindt's manager, he was very comfortably fixed.

In 1970 Rindt was killed during qualifying for the Italian Grand Prix, but this time Ecclestone did not loosen his ties with racing; by the end of the following year he had bought the Brabham team, and it wasn't long before his inimitable blend of nous and *chutzpah* had been brought to bear on the Formula 1 world.

They might rail against some of his excesses, and sometimes reasonably so, but there is not one Grand Prix team owner of the modern era who is other than in Bernie's debt. After taking over Brabham, he came swiftly to see that people like him, who provided the cars, put on the show, were not getting a fair financial shake from race organisers. When he drew this to the attention of his colleagues, they were only too happy to give him a free hand, to put his business brain to work for the benefit of all.

Were they allowing a Trojan horse into the paddock? Some

would have you believe so now, but none would willingly return to their days of relative penury. I have been to many a Formula 1 luminary's house over the years, and these people – even those whose cars have not so much as sniffed at a Grand Prix victory, let alone a World Championship – live well indeed. While I wouldn't suggest his motives were entirely altruistic, it is undeniable that Ecclestone has made a lot of money for a lot of people.

Grand Prix team owners tend to be conservative (both upper- and lower-case) folk, not naturally sympathetic to the concept of unions, but when Bernie suggested they form one of their own, not a hand was raised in protest. Thus F1CA (Formula 1 Constructors Association) came into being, this later amended to FOCA ('One' instead of '1'), when it was realised that in certain Latin countries the original spelling had quite another meaning.

In forming FOCA, and becoming its President, Ecclestone put down the footings of a power base which has mushroomed, not least because he, more than anyone, understood that Grand Prix racing's commercial future lay with TV: difficult as it may be to appreciate nowadays, in the 1970s there was very little Formula 1 coverage on the box, and even for a man who could sell you the sleeves of a waistcoat it took a long time to turn the situation around.

The deal has always been the thing. He made his original fortune from secondhand cars, his next from property. 'If you're a runner or a skier or a driver, you go for the last hundredth of a second, don't you? Well, I'm a business athlete, in the sense that it's the last penny that makes all the difference – not in terms of cash, but satisfaction.'

In his early days as a team owner, Ecclestone found a natural ally in Max Mosley, one of the founders of March Engineering, then in its fledgling period. It was a 'good cop, bad cop' arrangement, with Bernie the straight talker who ruffled feathers, Max the urbane barrister who stroked them into place again; it was to serve both men well in a variety of different situations.

Through the 1970s Ecclestone's ascendancy was essentially unchecked, for many in charge at the CSI (then the sporting arm of the FIA) were weak and inept. I have never forgotten the behaviour of one of their number at the Spanish Grand Prix in 1975.

The race was to be run at Montjuich Park, a fantastic road circuit in the hills above Barcelona, but before practice began the drivers noted that, while guardrails ran the whole length of the track, many of them had not been actually bolted together.

Only six months before, the Austrian rookie Helmuth Koinigg had been decapitated at Watkins Glen, because the bottom layer of a section of guardrail had been insufficiently secured, allowing his Surtees to go under the top layer. The memory was very fresh and raw in the drivers' minds, and – with the exception of Jacky Ickx and Vittorio Brambilla – they declined to venture out.

The matter should, of course, have been sorted out between the three CSI men present and the race organisers. 'The CSI can't say it's unsafe, and stop it,' one of them commented, 'and we can't say it's safe, either. All we can say is that it's suitable, that it meets our rules. For my part,' he concluded, 'I have never seen a safe circuit...'

So that was helpful. Ultimately, the teams' mechanics weighed in, helping to assemble the Armco properly, and finally there was qualifying, and a race. At the start of lap 26 Rolf Stommelen, leading in one of Graham Hill's cars, lost control at the left-hander immediately beyond the start line when his rear wing centre-post broke.

At 150mph the car hit the left-hand guardrail, then bounced across the road, and vaulted over the one on the right, killing four bystanders in a marshals' post next to the spectator area. By supreme irony, it was the Hill mechanics who had secured the very guardails their car was to hit. Had they not done so, who knows how many would have died?

The CSI folk were not on hand to comment, having scarpered before the race. At a time when people like this were supposedly running the sport, it was hardly surprising that Ecclestone's influence grew.

By the end of the 1970s, though, a new man was in charge of the governing body, and one of a very different cut. By now the

CSI had been renamed the *Fédération Internationale du Sport Automobile* – FISA – and Jean-Marie Balestre was at its helm. A choleric fellow, this, and one not about to be pushed around.

From the very beginning of Balestre's reign – he considered it nothing less – it was evident that he and Ecclestone were on a collision course: Bernie's power, he declared repeatedly, was getting out of hand, and he needed to be reminded that the governing body was in charge. This last point, of course, was something of a break with recent tradition.

In the winter of 1980/81, matters came to a head in what became known as the FISA–FOCA War, a battle which, to this day, both sides claim to have won. There was much sabre-rattling, but ultimately there was peace, which was inevitable if Formula 1 were to survive in any worthwhile sense.

Talk of separate championships, one for the FOCA stalwarts (McLaren, Williams, Brabham, Lotus, etc) and one 'official' FIA World Championship for the grandee teams (Ferrari, Renault, Alfa Romeo *et al*), amounted to no more than that: talk. Two stumbling series would have done no one any good, as CART and the IRL have subsequently demonstrated so convincingly in the USA.

At the end of the day, both parties had cause to be content with the outcome: Balestre got what he wanted, in the form of acknowledgement that the FIA was the sole governing body of motorsport, and Ecclestone, aided by Mosley, was granted exclusive rights to enter into contract negotiations with the organisers of FIA World Championship events.

Ten years later the picture was complete. By 1991 Mosley had successfully challenged Balestre for the presidency of the FIA, and Ecclestone had become Vice-President (Marketing). The one-time poachers had taken over in the Place de la Concorde – and Bernie also retained his position as the President of FOCA. Heads I win, tails you lose, was how it looked to the outside world.

Was there not some possible clash of interests here? Mosley answered the question thus: 'As Lyndon Johnson said – if you'll excuse the vulgarity – "It's better to have him inside the tent pissing out than outside the tent pissing in…"'

For countless years, we in the press room have discussed the relationship between Ecclestone and Mosley: were they really at loggerheads over this issue, and that, or all the time hand-in-glove, a double act?

Bernie grins at the question. 'I think it's better left like that, don't you? You have to keep some secrets intact…'

According to the Formula 1 team owners, keeping secrets intact is something at which he has always been adept. Very adept. It was only right and proper, they acknowledged, that, as the man who did the deals, particularly those with TV companies across the world, he should be properly rewarded, but when, in the late 1990s, the degree of that remuneration became clear, some of them baulked. To say the least.

For one of his achievement, of his absolute power within his own fiefdom, Ecclestone has always been a man of remarkably little ego, in the sense that down the years he resolutely kept a low public profile, invariably, for example, declining invitations to appear on television. On one occasion, he participated in a round-table discussion about the commercial future of sport, and was content to let other, flashier, individuals dominate; when he spoke at all, he buried them.

Towards the end of the 1990s, though, Bernie had firmly entered the public consciousness; this can happen to you when the newspapers announce your annual income as just short of £29 million, the highest salary in the land. But what made Ecclestone front page lead material was the revelation that he had donated a million – almost a fortnight's earnings – to Tony Blair's election fighting fund; this, coming on the heels of the Government's surprising decision to grant Formula 1 some exemption from a forthcoming crackdown on tobacco advertising inevitably led some political pundits to suggest that the two facts may have been not unconnected.

At that time Bernie's dance card was indeed full. He deftly brushed off the Blair affair, for some months neglecting – with some style, as if it were a trifle – to cash the Labour Party's returned £1 million cheque, but on other fronts, notably the attempt effectively to 'float' Formula 1, he was rather less successful. And his dealings with the City were in no way aided by a temporary inability to present a united front: for a long time three teams, McLaren, Williams and Tyrrell, dissatisfied with the way the financial cake was being sliced, declined to put their names to a new Concorde Agreement.

You could say these were blips on a big screen, or perhaps, as some had it, signs that Ecclestone was beginning to lose his sure touch. Most observers inclined to the former view; very well, there had been a glitch or two, but Bernie's fundamental hold on Formula 1 remained – and would do so for as long as he chose.

'The most important thing for anyone in business,' he said, 'is to be able to make decisions quickly, and then stick by them. This means that the top job is a one-man job. If there are two top men, a lot of time is wasted just trying to agree.' If this comes across as a fair definition of dictatorship, Ecclestone wouldn't take issue. Political correctness, mercifully, has never been his thing; he cuts through cant like a scythe.

For all they may sometimes carp about issues involving Bernie, the team owners worry about the question of his successor, for there is a general belief that Grand Prix racing has grown to a point that, post-Ecclestone, the running of it will be beyond the wit of one man.

Bernie has always played up his 'instinctive' approach to management. 'Long-term planning is a nonsense,' he said. 'People who say they can predict what's going to happen in business are idiots. And liars.' So there.

Formula 1 has changed out of sight in the near-30 years of his influence, its progression from a sport to a business almost absolute, and while few would dispute that Ecclestone has brought to it an extraordinary amount that is good, so also the transformation has exacted its dues.

Not even he would deny it. By no means are all the folk in a contemporary paddock *racers*, in the true sense of the word, but I have never doubted Bernie in that regard. For all he has made from racing, he was around it 40 and 50 years ago, and does not forget.

'It seemed to me significant that he came to the Monaco historic race weekend in 1997,' said Stirling Moss. 'All right, it was just before the Grand Prix, and the track was in "modern" specification, with all the bloody guardrails, and so on, but the atmosphere was fantastic – very relaxed and informal, everyone having fun.

'I was in the pits, chatting to Bernie, and he said, "Isn't this great? Just like it used to be before I fucked it up!" I said, "Well, you said it, Bernie, not me!" In fact, I'm a great fan of his, and I think what he's achieved is incredible. But there's no doubt that he's fundamentally changed racing, to the point that now it's a completely different *activity* from what it was. Which was a sport...'

In the same way, Ecclestone admits to finding bland the drivers of today. 'There are no charismatic drivers left in Formula 1, are there? Maybe it's the pressure of money that's done that – and maybe that's my fault.'

Over time politics have come to play an ever greater role in Formula 1, to the point that many journalists now appear to savour the behind-the-scenes wranglings rather more than the seconds ticking away to two o'clock on Sunday afternoon. If there is a crisis in the paddock, there will Ecclestone be, at the centre, sorting it out.

Small he may be, but Bernie is never difficult to spot. Usually, he is ensconced in that large, rather sinister, grey motorhome, dealing with this problem or that, but out and about in the paddock he is a blur of waving arms. His uniform – white button-down shirt (with long sleeves, always down), razor-creased dark grey slacks, black loafers – is always the same. When off duty, as on a visit to the Long Beach CART race in 1998, the dress is rather more *dégagé*, in a jeans and bomber jacket sort of way.

Get Ecclestone talking *racing*, and any suspicions disappear that he may have lost sight of what originally captivated him. As Moss suggests, a part of Bernie misses some of what has been lost.

There are no frills in a conversation with Ecclestone; what you get is sharp, funny, unpolished. He likes to get to the point. 'The trouble with people in our business is that they will never face up to reality. They're all chasing bloody dreams and myths. There ain't nothing special about our business. Nothing at all. It's all facts. There they are, and that's the end of it.'

After more than 25 years of controlling Formula 1, he claims he is trying not to drive himself as hard as at one time, but while there is little evidence of that, on occasion he admits to a certain yearning for a simpler time, when he owned a team, and just went racing.

'There's a different sort of satisfaction between running a team and what I do now. When I come away from a race, and it's been successful, you could say, yes, that's job satisfaction. But it's not the same sort of satisfaction as having a team, and your car winning the race.

'People might not believe it, but I'm still a racer, and if I had the time, I would still have a race team. But it's impossible to do both jobs properly, which was why I started to neglect Brabham. You're competing against people who think of nothing else for 24 hours a day, seven days a week; you can't pop in on a part-time basis against that.'

By the early 1980s, Bernie was already regretting that Formula 1 was not 'the big happy family it used to be'. By the late 1990s, it had moved on apace.

'It's much worse than that now. For one thing, it's probably difficult for team owners to get close to their drivers these days, because there's so much competition – they always think their drivers are trying to screw them, and leave them if there's more money somewhere else, and at the same time they don't want to get too friendly with him, in case they have to chuck him out. It's a lot more cut-throat these days.'

Today's Formula 1 constructors, he insists, are not the same sort of people as were running teams when he first became involved, and a man he singles out is Colin Chapman, with whom he spent time socially as well as professionally.

'"Chunky" was my man. I really liked him. He was good company, one of the boys. He was a good businessman, he was probably the best designer there's ever been, and he was as quick as half the guys who ever drove for him. He was different from all the others, just a special guy. Come to that, I miss Mr Ferrari, too. He was good for the sport. Yes, of course he looked after himself, but he was fair. Any agreements I made with him always stuck.'

It might sound strange, coming from one who has devoted himself so absolutely to Formula 1, and for so long, but Ecclestone believes many of the folk involved in it today have its importance spectacularly out of proportion.

'They're so much into what they're doing that they believe that, if Formula 1 stops, the world comes to an end – there's nothing else, that's it. And perhaps for some of them that really is the case. If it is, you've got to feel sorry for them.'

When all is said and done, though, the fact remains, as Moss says, that the sport has fundamentally changed, not least because of the demands of the Great God Television. Time was when appalling weather might lead to a delayed start time, for example, but not any more.

Ecclestone accepts that racing had a laid-back quality now long gone, fondly remembers games of gin rummy with Rindt during official practice sessions. 'Chapman would go berserk at that, but Jochen would say, "He can wait!" Now that couldn't happen today. It used to be a matter of, "Is everybody ready to start practice? OK, then, we'll start – no, no, hang about a bit, so-and-so's not arrived yet, because he was out late last night..."

'You couldn't run like that today, because of TV. At that time TV didn't make any difference, because there wasn't any. Now it's different. We've got a show to put on: at two o'clock they turn their sets on, and we'd better be there. Back then, though, if the race started at two or three – so what?'

For me, and others in the press room, it is a conundrum that through the second half of the 1990s, an era of Formula 1 bland compared with some gone by, the business has boomed as never before. Media coverage has mushroomed, and Ecclestone admits that he has been surprised by the consistent rise in TV viewing figures.

'It might sound like a terrible thing to say, but if you think about it, this sudden surge has happened since we lost Senna. When that happened, suddenly the whole world was exposed to Formula 1.

'After poor Ayrton got killed, everyone said, "That's it,

Formula 1's finished, forget it. Brazil," they said, "don't even have a race in Brazil." Well, the following year we had the biggest crowd ever in Brazil. The TV ratings have continued to grow, and so have the crowds at the circuits.

'The world's changed, that's the point. At one time we used to lose drivers quite often, and although we obviously weren't happy with that situation, it was something that was accepted. I remember François Cevert's accident at Watkins Glen in 1973: I was sitting on a crate with Carlos Reutemann, my Brabham team leader, and the conversation was, sort of, "What happened?" "Oh, he went under the guardrail, and was almost cut in half." "Christ, why did he go off?" 'Well, he just lost it." "Oh. What gear ratios are we using this afternoon?"

'Nowadays, people would say that was callous, perhaps because they can't appreciate how different it used to be. It wasn't an everyday thing for someone to get killed, but it wasn't a surprise, either. By 1994, though, when Senna and Roland Ratzenberger died, it had been 12 years since the last death at a Grand Prix, and we had a new breed of journalist, spectator, television commentator – even *driver* – who'd never known anything like that.

'Largely through the efforts of Sid Watkins, racing is incredibly safe these days, but in an environment as competitive as racing cars or bicycles, climbing, hang-gliding, whatever, and taking things to the edge, people are going to get killed. So don't be surprised when it happens.'

Bernie is right on all counts, of course. Time was when a fatal accident was *not* a surprise; a shock, yes, always a shock, but not a surprise.

More than anything, he cannot abide hypocrisy, and much of what occurred in the aftermath of Senna's death appalled him. There were TV stations, for example, who took financial advantage of the situation, multiplying their normal rates for the supply of footage of the accident. 'In some cases, they were the same people that slaughtered Formula 1 later that same evening, saying this was a killer sport, that only money mattered. That made me sick.'

In the days and weeks following the loss of Senna,

Ecclestone was widely portrayed as a man without a heart, who cared only for profit, and nothing for people. The Brazilian press ran endless stories on that theme, widely quoting Ayrton's brother, Leonardo, who made it plain that he did not want to see Ecclestone at the funeral. Bernie acceded to the family's wishes, leaving his wife to go into the church alone, but the experience deeply distressed him.

There was indeed more than a touch of hysteria in the quotes from members of the family and entourage, suggestions that Ayrton was dead at the trackside, that Ecclestone knew it, but didn't want the race to be called off, because then the spectators would demand their money back.

That was manifestly untrue. Gerhard Berger told me that he had seen Senna in the hospital at six o'clock in the evening, and that he was alive, albeit on a life-support machine.

'In the first place,' Ecclestone said, 'stopping the race or not had absolutely nothing to do with me. And, anyway, why should the race have been stopped? It wasn't going to bring the guy back. We don't stop flying every time there's a plane crash, do we?

'I think most people react selfishly to a death. It's not so much that they're thinking about the person who's dead; they're thinking how it affects *them*.'

By no means does Ecclestone feel affection for all racing drivers, but to some – Lewis-Evans, Rindt, Carlos Pace, Riccardo Patrese, Nelson Piquet – he has been genuinely close, and plainly he was fond of Senna. 'I signed him, for Brabham, before anyone else; I've still got the contract. Nelson was very upset when he found out – I knew that because he spoke to a sponsor for the first time in his life! He told Parmalat it would be stupid to have two Brazilians, that they'd never get on. I said to Parmalat, "Listen, Senna's quicker than Nelson, and that's why Nelson doesn't want him..."'

Ecclestone's hold over Formula 1 is absolute, and one wonders how, for a man edging towards his 70s, he has the energy, let alone the time, to do all he does. He is involved in everything, it seems, and not only on the level of dealing with TV contracts or discussing new Grand Prix venues; at any given time he has a clear idea of what he wants to see in Formula 1, and has never been known for reticence when it comes to using his influence.

In 1995 he began talking up Jacques Villeneuve, Indianapolis 500 winner and star of the CART series, and you knew that Villeneuve would shortly be in Formula 1; knew, moreover, that he would drive for a top team. Frank Williams later allowed that, yes, Bernie had conveyed to him how much he would like to see Jacques in a Williams.

Similarly, when Michael Schumacher, one race into his Grand Prix career, became ensnared in a contracts wrangle between Jordan and Benetton, Ecclestone it was who … brokered the accommodation reached between the two parties. 'It was the night before first practice at Monza in 1991. Flavio Briatore was running Benetton, and he was new to the business, didn't know much about it, and no progress was being made. Schumacher himself didn't seem to know what to do. In the end I told him to shut up and go to bed. I said, "When you wake up in the morning, you'll be a Benetton driver, all right?"' And, lo, it was done.

Ecclestone also worked hard to get Nigel Mansell back into Formula 1, but acknowledged that the partnership with McLaren was doomed before it started. 'Again, it's simple. There are no mysteries in this business, as I always say. The guy had won a lot of races, and a World Championship. Why did he need to charge round, to prove he could be fifth? No mileage in that. Might as well be ninth – in fact, it's better to be ninth, because if you're fifth, people say you've gone off, and if you're ninth, they say the car's rubbish. Simple.'

For a long time Bernie has felt that some drivers are absurdly overpaid, and always resolutely refused to submit to what he felt were unreasonable demands. Fond as he was of Piquet, and central as Nelson was to Brabham, he had no interest in trying to match a Williams-Honda offer for 1986. 'I said, "Well, you'd better start polishing your Japanese, hadn't you?"'

'None of the drivers are worth the sort of money they're talking about. Mind you, I don't blame them; if a driver is offered 15 or 20 or 30 million dollars, you can't really expect him to say, "No, no, I really couldn't take that – it's much too much, it's an indecent amount." It's the constructors who should be certified, for offering it in the first place.

'Sometimes they get together, and try to cap driver retainers, but in the end it falls apart because they say, "We're here to win, and we've got to have the best of everything." At the moment, Schumacher is probably worth half a second a lap over anyone else – but if you've got him and a shitty car, that's no good. There's absolutely no point in shelling out for him unless everything else is right. If you've got one bit missing, you're wasting him – and the money you've spent on him.'

No nonsense, you see. No hedging. And no doubts, either, about his continuing grip on Formula 1. Over the years many a team owner has bridled bitterly to me and my press colleagues over something Ecclestone has done, or is about to do, but almost never do they dare voice criticism of him 'on the record'.

Trying to argue a point with Bernie, I have found, is like reading a paper in a high wind. No one thinks better on his feet, comes quicker with a riposte. When the mood takes him, he can be funnier than anyone I know.

In 1998 I skipped the Brazilian Grand Prix, as usual, and wrote in a magazine column my intention so to do. At a race soon afterwards, I arrived at the paddock entrance, slid my FIA 'credit card' press pass through the slot at the turnstile, and found that access was denied.

I looked closely at the little window, where normally the word is, 'OK'. The computer had been programmed with a new message for me. 'No Interlagos...' it read, and I could hear Bernie saying it. I stormed off to the grey bus, livid, which of course was precisely the response for which he had been hoping. 'I've been thinking,' said the proprietor, deadpan, 'of starting a new rule – if you don't go to all the races, you can't come in.'

The next time I tried to swipe my card, it worked fine, and there was a new message for me: 'OK – you're forgiven'. I told one of the team owners about it, and he smirked. 'We get things like that all the time,' he said. 'Little reminders of who's in charge.'

# New Age champion

A FEW DAYS BEFORE the Belgian Grand Prix of 1991, a colleague, who covers sports car racing, called me. 'I'll bet you,' he said, 'that Schumacher qualifies in the top 10.' I very nearly accepted the wager, but by mid-morning on Friday rejoiced that I had not.

The previous year I had watched on TV the World Championship sports car race in Mexico, and while it is not a category of racing which has much interested me for many years, I did recall being highly impressed by Michael's confidence and precision as he threaded the Mercedes-Benz through traffic in the torrential rain.

Now, at 22, he was to make his Formula 1 début with Jordan, at Spa of all places, and establishing his credentials took him no time at all. Just once in a while you get a feeling about a newcomer, an impression that this is the start of a major career. It was there with (Gilles) Villeneuve, with Prost, with Senna; undoubtedly, too, it was there with Schumacher.

This quality is more easily discernible, of course, when the novice gets his Formula 1 start in a car worth driving. Gilles, Alain and Ayrton were perhaps fortunate in that respect, but each had laid claim to the opportunity with his performances elsewhere. The same was true of Michael.

It is always fascinating to observe a new driver's manner out of the car. Some are jumpy, some unnaturally calm, and some have it just right. Schumacher at Spa reminded me of Mika Hakkinen at Phoenix earlier the same year, looking immediately as if he belonged in the Formula 1 pit lane. Once in the car he was calm, smooth, devastatingly quick. All weekend he had no complaints for his team. They liked that.

Michael's countrymen had waited a long time for a driver like this. Before the Second World War, there were on the scene such as Rudolf Caracciola, Bernd Rosemeyer and Hermann Lang, each of whom won the European Championship, as it then was. But Germany had a thin time of it thereafter. During the great Mercedes-Benz years of 1954 and 1955, the company's outstanding drivers were Stirling Moss and, above all, Juan Manuel Fangio, with Karl Kling and Hans Herrmann playing strictly supporting roles.

Wolfgang von Trips, the elegant count, won brilliantly for Ferrari at Zandvoort and Aintree in 1961, but lost his life at Monza, when the World Championship was at hand. He knew nothing of cars, save how to drive them, but that he knew well. Later, Hans-Joachim Stuck had his moments, but in reality Germany had to wait more until the mid-1980s for a new Grand Prix star to emerge.

Stefan Bellof came into Formula 1 with Tyrrell, in 1984, and what we should remember of him is that, in a year which also saw the début of Senna, he was not overshadowed. Everyone recalls that Ayrton was catching Prost for the lead of the Monaco Grand Prix when it was prematurely stopped, but how many remember that, at the same time, Bellof was catching Senna?

He was the great lost talent of his generation, one who never had his days in the sun. On the point of signing for Ferrari, he was killed in the 1985 Spa 1000 Km, when his Porsche 956 crashed at Eau Rouge, and it seemed, for his countrymen, that German motor racing had died with him.

At the same circuit, six years on, it was born again. Schumacher's Belgian Grand Prix lasted less than a lap, but it hardly mattered. Already we had seen enough. And a year later, now with Benetton, he won the race, the first of very many.

Hakkinen had a much longer wait before him. Here was a man who, on his very first appearance in a McLaren, out-qualified Senna, his team-mate, yet it would not be until the final race of 1997, at Jerez, that Mika finally took the highest step on the podium.

How so? It was Hakkinen's ill luck that he joined McLaren just as the team hit a fallow period unknown for a dozen seasons. Everyone knew that Mika should have been winning Grands Prix years before he did, and it must have been maddening that others, with only a sliver of his talent, were wracking up the victories while he was not.

'I was never one to look over the fence, and think that the grass was greener somewhere else. I believed in my own talent and speed, and I believed absolutely in McLaren. If other drivers were winning, and I was not, bad luck for me. That's the way it happens sometimes, but it didn't matter. I knew I was going to be winning one day; it was just a question of when...'

It is not by whim that Ron Dennis holds Hakkinen in such regard. 'When I wake up on a Monday morning,' Dennis has said, 'and I take in again that we didn't win the day before, I feel pain – genuine *pain*.' That being so, he must have worked his way through a lot of paracetamol in the mid-1990s, and for his number one driver the anguish can hardly have been less. Ron, after all, had at least known towering success; for Mika it was still to come.

He reckoned the Finnish mentality helped him. 'You don't want to give up; you want to do it right. And, of course, the salary helped to keep you smiling.'

The foundations of their close relationship lie in that period of shared discomfort. In successive seasons, McLaren went from Honda engines to Ford to Peugeot to Mercedes-Benz, which was hardly a gift to the team's designers, but while Hakkinen laboured away through a time of Williams (and, to a lesser extent, Benetton) domination, he never lost that sense of optimism, maintaining that McLaren was, after all, the best team. Dennis, himself a man fiercely loyal to those who work with him, appreciates the quality in others above all else.

Then there was the accident. During qualifying at Adelaide in

1995, Hakkinen's McLaren went out of control in a fast right-hander, spinning several times, then hitting a retaining wall, which was inadequately cushioned by a single-layer tyre barrier.

It was only by wonderful work by the doctors on hand – notably a desperately urgent tracheotomy – that Mika was alive as he was lifted from the cockpit, but he had suffered a massive blow to the head, and for some hours his life hung in the balance. On recovering consciousness, he wanted first to know why he had gone off – in other words, had it been his fault? Dennis was able to reassure him to the contrary, and that, Hakkinen said, was a very big moment.

'If my accident had been due to a mistake of mine, I don't think I'd have come back to Formula 1. When I woke up, at dawn the next day, it was terribly important to know that. If it had been my fault, I think I'd have said, "Well, thanks a lot, I'll go and do something else."'

Hakkinen crashed on 10 November. After three weeks in the Royal Adelaide Hospital, he was well enough to be flown back to Europe, there to begin a lengthy convalescence. He had lost a lot of weight – a stone and a half – from an already spare frame, and knew that his strength would return only with time.

A few days before Christmas the phone rang. 'Hi!' the caller said. 'How are you? What've you been up to in the last few weeks?'

The voice was perky, and momentarily I tried to place it. 'What have *I* been up to, Mika? Well, rather less than you, I'd say, all in all…'

Not surprisingly, he had only fleeting memories of the accident itself; not surprisingly, too, he had been thinking a lot about it, because he needed to sort out in his mind exactly what had happened. 'I was running at the maximum, of course, because it was a qualifying lap. Before the corner where I went off there is a long straight, and I remember shifting from second, third, fourth, fifth, sixth – I was flat out.

'I remember going down to fifth for the corner, turning in – and when I did that, I immediately knew there was a problem. I tried to keep the car on the track, not to lose the back end, because I knew if that happened, I was going off at a very quick place. Unfortunately, though, it was impossible at that speed to keep the car in the right direction.

'Several other drivers got punctures that day, and it was odd because there were no debris on the track, so maybe it was a kerb that was causing the problem. I was all right on the straight, going very fast, because the tyre maintains its pressure like that. Obviously, if I'd felt there was a problem, I'd have lifted, but I didn't feel anything until I turned in.'

Hakkinen had not seen the on-car camera footage of his accident, but knew from photographs that the McLaren bounced and flew over the kerbs for quite some way before hitting the wall. He recalled losing control of the car, but nothing of the impact. The next memory was of sitting in the car, and not being able to see.

'I was feeling pain, and I couldn't move, but I understood what was going on. I remember telling myself to relax, just to let the medical people do their job – I understood I was hurt quite badly. I felt them lifting me, and then it was difficult to breathe, and getting more difficult. Then I felt this massive pain in my throat, which I guess was when they put the tube in, and at that point I lost consciousness. After that, I remember nothing until being in the hospital, and looking up at Sid Watkins…'

The injuries were caused when his helmet struck the steering wheel, which is remarkable when you consider that a driver is strapped so tightly into his cockpit that, in normal circumstances, he can barely move. As in Alex Zanardi's accident at Spa in 1993, however, even aircraft-spec belts stretch considerably in a really colossal impact.

Hakkinen said he would never forget that moment he came to, and saw 'The Prof'. 'He asked if I could understand him, and I said yes, sure. Then he asked me to touch my fingers, and so on, and I did everything he asked. Lisa Dennis was there, holding my hand all the time, and Ron was there, too. It was the first moment I began to feel strong.

'Sid said, "Mika, you've been very fortunate, because you're not going to need any brain surgery." At first, I was a little bit shocked – what brain surgery? Then I just felt relief, as I began to understand I was lucky to have survived. I could see the emotion in people's faces, and it made me realise that this was something bad I'd been through.'

Gerhard Berger once told me that, immediately after his accident at Imola in 1989, he had decided never to go near a racing car again. The feeling had lasted about an hour, he said, after which he could think of nothing but coming back as soon as possible.

Mika understood that. 'I had no feeling of being scared of speed, or anything like that, but when your body isn't well, your mind says you can't do anything – you can't do what you love, which is racing. When I was lying in the hospital bed in Adelaide, the first 10 days ... to be honest, I can remember hardly anything of that.

'Then, slowly, your memory begins to come back, and you remember little things. You have problems with your body, so you don't know if you're going to be able to drive again, but you believe these problems are going to go away. And when you start getting stronger, you forget the pain, and you think of the next thing in your life. I tell you, I have this spark inside me at the moment, this excitement, you know, and I can't stop it. It's racing...

'I was very fortunate to have the right people on hand, and the right hospital. For me, it's good to know that Sid Watkins always comes to the races. He's just the ideal doctor, a tough guy when he has to be, and always making sure we get the best treatment.'

At the time of this, our first conversation following his accident, Hakkinen did not know when he would be in a racing car again. Already he was driving his Mercedes around Monte Carlo, but for now what mattered most was exercising, gently at first, getting a lot of rest, building himself up once more.

Dennis, of course, put no pressure on him: it would happen when it would happen. He was given time to prepare himself for coming back, and when the day came, it was organised with precision. Hakkinen had Paul Ricard to himself; no other teams were present, and journalists – quite understandably – were not allowed in. 'No rush, no panic, no pressure,' as Mika put it.

It was 5 February, about a month before the opening race of the 1996 season. 'I remember that day like yesterday. I was open-minded about it: was I going to like it or not? If I did, then the racing would continue, but it wasn't black and white.

'Everyone was so quiet when I got in the car. And then when I went out of the pits, the car felt smooth, the engine felt smooth – everything felt too good to be true. You think of driving a Formula 1 car, and you think of jumping and sliding all over the place, the seat uncomfortable, nothing right – and that was all gone. Suddenly, it all felt nice, the gearbox, the steering response, everything. I thought, "Jesus, what have I been complaining about?"

'Best of all, everything was automatic. I didn't have to think about anything, and I felt more ready than ever. But then, when I started driving really fast, I began to look around me, thinking, "Jesus, if I go off there…" I suppose that was natural. But it didn't slow me down.

'Everything that day – everything in life, really – is a matter of fighting against your emotions, isn't it? Something tells you inside, "Don't go faster", but you do. I drove about 60 laps, set quick times, and then I said, "OK, that's enough, let's go home."'

Set quick times indeed. Hakkinen's fastest lap in the McLaren-Mercedes was 1m 07.09s; the day before, Schumacher's best in the Ferrari had been 1m 07.60s.

Alain Prost was there at Ricard, and he told me how moving an experience it had been. 'I was very lucky in my career. During my first season in Formula 1, I broke my wrist at Kyalami, but otherwise I never hurt myself.

'Now here was this guy getting back in a racing car, three months after almost dying in one. And, you know, once he was out on the circuit, immediately it was as if he had never been away. It was something fantastic, almost unbelievable, and at first I worried that he was going too fast too soon. But he wasn't; he knew exactly what he was doing.

'His speed was more than anyone could have expected, but much more important was that he found he still loved driving a racing car. If that hadn't been there as strongly as before, even if he had been quick he wouldn't have had the right motivation. You can't forget a day like that.'

Confidence and arrogance may be easily confused in a racing

driver. Schumacher exudes both. 'Well,' he shrugged, after crashing out of the lead of the 1999 Canadian Grand Prix, 'I usually make one mistake a year...' It would never occur to Hakkinen – even if he believed it true of himself – to come out with something like that.

The irony is that Michael, so much the Ice Man in many ways, is actually far less cool under pressure than his rival. When the pair of them went to the grid at Suzuka in 1998, to settle the World Championship, it was Schumacher who wilted, who stalled before the off, then had to start from the back.

Rosberg, who manages Hakkinen, was in Japan to offer his boy moral support, but found that none was needed. 'I was no good to him at all! All week long I was nervous as hell, and on race morning I was a basket-case – *far* more so than before my own championship decider, in Las Vegas all those years before. In the end it was Mika calming *me* down! "Don't worry, Keke," he kept saying. "It'll be all right..."'

It was. And assuredly, given the points situation, together with Schumacher's less than pearly white record in previous title-deciding Grands Prix, it didn't hurt that Mika went to Suzuka in the knowledge that he didn't have to beat Michael this day, that Schumacher was the man who couldn't afford, let us say, a *contretemps* on the circuit. Even if the Ferrari won, second place would be enough.

This is not, however, to suggest that there was minimal pressure on Hakkinen. A beckoning World Championship makes for stress, whoever you are, and at the back of Mika's mind had to be the thought that a McLaren-Mercedes, while admirably reliable in 1998, was still not a match in that regard for a Ferrari. Six points would win him the title, but he had to be around at the end to collect them.

There was also Irvine to consider. No one in Formula 1 knew Suzuka like Eddie, who had many times raced there in the Japanese Formula 3000 Championship. A year earlier, he had helped Schumacher to victory at Suzuka, and would try to do so again this time, for that was his job description.

It has always been Bernie Ecclestone's contention, and I rather agree with him, that Schumacher will not warrant comparison with the all-time greats until he has the confidence, like Senna, like Prost, to allow another top-liner to be his team-mate – and to allow that driver, what's more, to race with him. In this respect, Michael's attitude to his work has always been decidedly feudal.

At McLaren, there are no such rules. Very well, once it became clear that only Hakkinen was in a position realistically to win the 1998 World Championship, David Coulthard was asked by Ron Dennis to subjugate his own ambitions to those of his team-mate, but up to that point Coulthard had been free to run his own business.

Healthy competition is how they look upon it. When Hakkinen first raced for McLaren, at Estoril in 1993, he out-qualified Senna, and team co-ordinator Jo Ramirez recalled the effect this had upon Ayrton. 'Until that race, Michael Andretti was in the other car, but he was never a threat to Senna. In Portugal, though, Mika was quicker – and, for the first time that year, suddenly Ayrton was taking a great interest in his team-mate's traces!'

Hakkinen maintains that he was not amazed to be quicker than Senna that day. 'You have to remember that for most of that year I was the test driver for McLaren. I did ten times more actual driving than Ayrton, even though I only raced towards the end of the season. I mean, I reversed more than he went forward!'

Fine, but still the fact remains that Senna was hardly ever out-qualified in equal cars.

Mika didn't think in those terms. 'We all drink water and eat bread, you know. It's just four wheels and steering at the end of the day. OK, there are millions of elements around it to make a complete package, but I was not amazed, no.

'What did surprise me in Portugal was Ayrton's speed in the race. He was *so* fast even at the beginning, when the cars were heavy with fuel – there was no refuelling then, of course. I was quick, too, but not quick enough. He wanted to put me in my place – and he did.'

'If maybe I woke Ayrton up that weekend, he woke me up, too, in many ways. I have to say that I never felt comfortable with him, in the sense of working together to make the team better. Before going to McLaren, I'd been at Lotus with Johnny

Herbert, who was always joking, always relaxed, but with Ayrton, it was a different world.'

After Prost had retired from racing, fourth World Championship won, he returned to McLaren for a time, working as a driver consultant, and also testing extensively. Hakkinen came almost to revere him.

'In my opinion, Alain was a man who worked with the team, and Ayrton was someone who felt he could do it all himself. In 1993 his attitude was, "I come to the race, and the car has to be good. At the next test, if we've got something unbelievably good to try, I'll be there. Otherwise, I'm not interested."

'Prost, on the other hand, worked and worked all the time. He was thinking, testing, thinking, testing, explaining to the engineers how the systems were working – and doing it in such an intelligent way that there was no question of "ifs" or "buts". A guy like Prost could really build something good in a team. Of course, when I was with Senna at McLaren, he had already decided he was leaving, so maybe that changed his attitude.

'Ayrton and Alain were so experienced in the way they worked. It was absolutely not a matter of wetting a finger, and holding it up to the wind. It was looking at the facts, studying the computers, working with realities. There was no guessing, no speculation, just pure logic. But still I never felt that Ayrton had Alain's will to work – and certainly not his willingness to share information.'

Looking back on those days, though, Hakkinen is inclined to understand Senna's coolness towards him rather more readily than he did. 'By McLaren standards, 1993 hadn't been a great season, mainly because our "customer" Ford engines didn't have enough power. Ayrton was a three-time World Champion, and if things weren't working, he got upset. Logically.

'As for me, I was a newcomer, the test driver who was now racing, feeling good mentally and physically, ready to beat everybody! I didn't go there to lose. My idea was to come into the team with Ayrton, and beat him, nothing else...'

It was precisely in that frame of mind, with regard to Prost, that Senna himself had arrived at McLaren, five years earlier. Maybe a chord was struck within him.

A month after the race in Estoril came Suzuka, and this time Senna out-qualified Hakkinen, albeit by hundredths. In the race Mika finished third – a good result, surely? 'Yes, up to a point – but Ayrton *won!*' These were indeed high standards the boy was setting himself.

The following season he came to appreciate that it was a matter of settling in for the long haul: of the 16 Grands Prix, eight went to Benetton, seven to Williams, and one to Ferrari. McLaren, now with weak and sometimes explosive engines from Peugeot, were nowhere, and there were times when Hakkinen distinctly over-drove, attempting to compensate for lack of horsepower.

'In 1994 the results were not there, so the pressure built up, and I was becoming desperate to win a race. All you ever heard was criticism – of the car, of the drivers – so you drove even harder, you got quite upset, quite tense.'

Hockenheim was a case in point. Following a last lap altercation with Rubens Barrichello at Silverstone, the previous race, Mika was racing in Germany under a suspended one-race ban, and this came into effect when he unsuccessfully attempted to squeeze past David Coulthard's Williams on the blast to the first corner. A multi-car accident ensued, and Mika was adjudged its instigator. Thus, he was obliged to sit out the Hungarian Grand Prix, where his place was fatuously taken, at the request of Peugeot, by Philippe Alliot.

The FIA was very heavily into punishing drivers in 1994. In Brazil, the Stewards of the Meeting held Eddie Irvine responsible for a four-car shunt, and banned him from the next race, at Aida. On his behalf, the Jordan team appealed against the decision, whereupon an FIA Court of Appeal promptly increased the ban to three races! Perhaps Irvine's renowned insouciance worked against him on this occasion, who knows, but the message seemed to be that probably it was best not to question the authority of the governing body.

Three years on, when Schumacher drove into Jacques Villeneuve in the course of their World Championship decider at Jerez, the punishments previously meted out to Irvine and Hakkinen seemed more than faintly ludicrous. If Eddie and Mika had caused accidents, it had certainly not been by intent, but no one – save the FIA Stewards – doubted that Michael had quite deliberately tried to take his rival out.

Subsequently the World Motor Sport Council reconsidered the affair, and a couple of weeks later its findings were announced by Max Mosley. People do not care to have their intelligence insulted, which is why no one there has ever forgotten that press conference. We had travelled in the expectation that Schumacher would be appropriately punished.

'The World Motor Sport Council,' Mosley began, 'has come to the conclusion that, although the act was apparently deliberate, it was instinctive and not premeditated.'

No one said a word, but everyone's expression spoke volumes. Later, Damon Hill, who had lost the 1994 title to Schumacher in circumstances not dissimilar, would point out that what you do instinctively is *avoid* an accident, not cause one.

On went Mosley. 'The WMSC has given careful consideration to banning Schumacher for 1998, but has concluded that to do so would be futile. It would not be a deterrent in any sense. The WMSC has therefore decided to exclude Michael Schumacher from the results of the 1997 World Championship. That is to say, his race results remain, but he will not feature in the 1997 championship.'

Fine – but what was his *punishment* to be?

'In addition,' Mosley said, 'the WMSC considered imposing a fine. It discussed, however, with Schumacher the possibility of his participating in a road safety campaign which the FIA is mounting, with the European Commission. He immediately agreed to take part. Accordingly, there will be no fine, there will be exclusion from the 1997 World Championship, and Schumacher has agreed to participate in our road safety campaign.'

A colleague broke the stunned silence. 'Excuse me,' he said. 'Is this April the first?'

After Mosley had spoken, Schumacher, doubtless barely able to keep a straight face, gave his reaction. 'For me personally it's quite a tough decision. On the other hand, I have to admit that I did make a mistake, and I accept the penalty.'

Next it was the turn of Jean Todt, Ferrari's Sporting Director. 'We feel that to lose second place in the championship is very tough for Michael. His human sensibility has been affected a lot these last days...'

'Poor baby,' someone murmured.

As we trooped out, there was much cynical talk of commercial expediency. Who knew, after all, how much the TV ratings might have suffered, had Schumacher been banned for the opening races of the following season? A bemused Italian colleague put it best. 'What time,' he murmured, 'does the Ferrari party start?'

In any meaningful sense, as Ken Tyrrell suggested, Schumacher had escaped punishment altogether – why, he even kept his 1997 results, as also did Ferrari, so all that was lost was a second place listing in the final Championship table. And was there ever a man, with the possible exception of Senna, who cared less about second place than Schumacher?

The irony was that, in recent years, the FIA had talked of little else but safety; quite how this squared with going easy on a driver who had deliberately tried to cause an accident was not immediately apparent. Three years earlier, after all, Michael had been banned for briefly ignoring a black flag at Silverstone; a very serious offence, certainly, but rather less of one than a cynical attempt to take out a rival.

'I don't think what Schumacher did is ethical at all, and I don't think the governing body can allow it,' Jackie Stewart had remarked a few days before the hearing. 'I think behaviour of that type has to be not just discouraged, but eliminated. This is Michael Schumacher, the most famous racing driver in the world: what kind of an example is he setting to all the kids in the junior formulae?'

Hakkinen, a resolutely apolitical soul in the paddock, was charitable on the subject. 'For me it's easy to say, "Of course I wouldn't have done what Schumacher did", and actually I really don't believe I would. But in that situation it's easy to lose control of yourself. All the emphasis is on the championship these days, isn't it?'

He paused, then picked his words with care. 'Sooner or later, though, something will happen, and perhaps one or two people will learn something. Success usually brings enormous confidence to a driver, and the more you have, the more you start to believe you can walk on the ceiling. You are something special. And in situations like that, you don't believe anything can happen. But the day will come when something will happen, will bite them back, and then they will learn – if it's not too late. Of course we must have close racing, but at the same time...'

Fortunately, Schumacher's tactic that day failed to work in his favour, for it was he who was eliminated, Villeneuve who continued to the finish, and thus became World Champion.

That same day, after coming so close so many times, Hakkinen won his first Grand Prix. My impression had always been that Mika was like a champagne cork bursting to get out of the bottle, that once he began winning, he would be unstoppable.

One didn't need to be a Rhodes Scholar to have reached this conclusion. If, in the post-Senna era, Schumacher had clearly emerged as the star of Formula 1, so there was little doubt, if you had eyes to see, that the raw talent of Hakkinen, too, was something quite out of the ordinary.

Stirling Moss, and others, contended that never in the history of Grand Prix racing had there been a period in which one man – Schumacher – was so superior to all his fellows, but to my mind that situation changed when Hakkinen got himself into a car that could win. In the second half of the 1990s, Hill and Villeneuve had their moments – and plenty of them – but neither man's talent, as a true challenge to Schumacher, was on the level of Hakkinen's.

When he came to Suzuka in November 1998, Mika had won seven of the 15 races run, and Michael six. Four points separated them, but the gap at one time had been far greater, for in the early part of the season nothing could get near a McLaren-Mercedes, and the MP4-13's advantage over Ferrari's F300 was amplified by its Bridgestone tyres, comfortably superior to Ferrari's Goodyears until mid-season.

Through the summer, though, Goodyear came on increasingly strong, and Ferrari closed the gap, not least by virtue of superior reliability. But just when Schumacher seemed to have gained the upper hand, at least psychologically, Hakkinen produced a stunning drive at the Nürburgring, beating the Ferrari fair and square, and dispelling any notion that he might be wilting under pressure.

Most satisfying of all for Mika was that he won the Luxembourg Grand Prix in precisely the manner which had become a Schumacher trademark, taking the lead by virtue of a string of electrifying laps at a crucial point in the race – after his rival's first pit stop, and before his own.

Thus, when he rejoined, he was in front, and there he comfortably stayed. At the post-race press conference, Schumacher was in something close to a state of shock. He had started from pole position, with Irvine next to him: how could Ferrari have lost?

In Japan, while Schumacher ultimately went out with a blown tyre, Hakkinen led from beginning to end, and thus became the third driver to thwart Michael's ambitions of winning a World Championship in a Ferrari.

Later Mika reflected on what it took to win a title in the contemporary era. 'These days natural talent is not enough. You have to understand data, too. Nothing wrong with that. I enjoy enormously working with the engineers: the data is so precise, and you can see so much, comparing your lap with the other driver's lap, or your own previous lap. You can go half a second quicker just by understanding one little thing.

'The thing is, though, you can take the data home with you, put it under your pillow – but at the end of the day you still have to do it.'

In 1999, to no one's great surprise, Hakkinen and Schumacher renewed their duel, and again the thing ebbed and flowed between McLaren and Ferrari. Essentially, it was the same story as before: Mika's car was a little better in the fast corners, and Michael's was rather more reliable. Both won races, and, somewhat unexpectedly, both crashed out of the lead.

At Silverstone, though, their battle ended for the season, for Schumacher crashed on the opening lap, breaking his right leg, and putting himself out for some months. Although not dangerously injured, as Hakkinen had been, still Michael had hurt himself in a racing car for the first time. It could happen to him, too. At 30, with a wife and children, together with financial security for several hundred years, he had something to think about.

Now Hakkinen looked a short-odds favourite to keep his title, but in Formula 1 nothing is sure, and although Mika was the dominant driver in Britain, Austria and Germany, he won none of those races – each time through no fault of his own. If it seemed that, operationally, McLaren were slipping a little, perhaps the most maddening loss of all was at the A1-Ring, where Coulthard, his own team-mate, inadvertently nudged him into a spin on the opening lap.

Instead of scoring 30 points from three races, therefore, Hakkinen's tally was just four, while Eddie Irvine – in Schumacher's absence, freed at last of the shackle of team orders – put 26 on the board. On straight pace, Irvine and a Ferrari were no match for Hakkinen and a McLaren, but to score points you need to be around at the end, and on reliability Ferrari were near bullet-proof. With six races to go, Eddie led Mika by eight points.

That came down to two at the Hungaroring, where Hakkinen had a trouble-free cruise to victory, with Irvine third. But although Mika regained the championship lead at Spa, the result was not what he would have wished.

McLaren, unlike the current regime at Ferrari, do not employ one star and one slave, for Ron Dennis does not care for team orders. He allows that this policy has its risks – championships have been lost in the past when two drivers in one team took points from each other, allowing a rival to sneak by – but he will not change it. In Belgium Coulthard beat Hakkinen to the first corner, and they finished the race in that order.

At Monza, though, Mika tossed 10 certain points away, spinning at a chicane after muffing a gearchange, thus multiplying the pressure on himself for the three last races. If he remained the logical favourite for the title, he was taking nothing for granted. 'This is Formula 1, and anything can happen. Ron is always looking for perfection but I've always felt very comfortable here, and I never worried about any question of number one or number two drivers. When we had 7 and 8 on the cars, I never cared which one I had. The only number that interests me is 1…'

That much never changes.

# Index